Table of Contents

Table of Contents...

Free Gift 16

Introduction 17

Instant Pot Breakfast Recipes 18

    Special French Toast... 18

    Vanilla Steel-cut Oats... 18

    Mushroom Oatmeal.. 19

    Delicious Pear Oatmeal 19

    Cinnamon Steel-cut Oats 20

    Breakfast Banana Cake 20

    Breakfast Cobbler 21

    Pomegranate Porridge 21

    Tomato and Spinach Breakfast 22

    Pumpkin Oats Granola... 22

    Scotch Eggs 23

    Poached Eggs 23

    Steamed Eggs 24

    Special Eggs Breakfast.. 24

    Breakfast Quiche 25

    Carrot Oatmeal 25

    Egg Muffins 26

    Breakfast Risotto 26

    Breakfast Rice Bowl.. 27

    Special Rice Pudding... 27

    Amazing Breakfast Quinoa 28

    Breakfast Quinoa Salad.. 28

    Breakfast Bread Pudding.. 29

    Millet Pudding 29

    Breakfast Millet Pilaf 30

    Breakfast Pudding 30

    Breakfast Chia Pudding 31

    Breakfast Hash.. 31

    Potato Hash 32

    Breakfast Burritos... 32

Breakfast Sandwiches 33

Breakfast Sausages and Peppers 33

Breakfast Tacos 34

Breakfast Jam 34

Lemon Marmalade 35

Blackberry Jam 35

Cheesy Grits 36

Tasty Breakfast 36

Chickpeas Spread 37

Chicken Liver Spread 37

Mushroom Pate 38

Ricotta Cheese Spread 38

Pecan Sweet Potatoes 39

Pumpkin Butter 39

Breakfast Salad 40

Breakfast Potatoes 40

Tofu Breakfast 41

Tofu Scramble 41

Barbecue Tofu 42

Potatoes and Tofu Breakfast 42

Instant Pot Side Dish Recipes 43

Wild Rice and Farro Pilaf 43

Quinoa Pilaf 43

Quinoa with Almonds 44

Pink Rice 44

Mushroom Risotto 45

Pumpkin Risotto 45

Vegetables and Rice 46

Flavored Mashed Sweet Potatoes 46

Tasty Saffron Risotto 47

Cherry Farro 47

Herbed Polenta 48

Mexican Rice 48

Cauliflower and Barley Risotto 49

Garlicky Potatoes 49

Lemon Parmesan and Peas Risotto 50

Spinach and Goat Cheese Risotto 50

Rice and Artichokes.. 51

Potatoes Au Gratin 51

Mashed Squash 52

Potato Casserole.. 52

French Fries.. 53

Green Beans and Mushrooms 53

Easy Refried Beans 54

Three Bean Medley... 54

Black Beans.. 55

Pineapple and Cauliflower Rice 55

Red Beans and Rice 56

Savory Stuffing.. 56

Parsnips and Onions 57

Cauliflower Mash... 57

Mashed Turnips 58

Sweet Carrot Puree 58

Butternut and Apple Mash.. 59

Glazed Carrots 59

Sweet Brussels Sprouts 60

Lemony Broccoli.. 60

Garlic and Parmesan Asparagus 61

Poached Fennel... 61

Drunken Peas 62

Artichokes.. 62

Harvest Vegetables 63

Eggplant.. 63

Calamari and Tomatoes... 64

Cauliflower, Broccoli, and Citrus... 64

Beets and Garlic.. 65

Fava Bean Sauté 65

Green Beans.. 66

Savory Bok Choy 66

Israeli Couscous... 67

Red Cabbage.. 67

Instant Pot Poultry Recipes 68

Lemongrass Chicken 68

Salsa Chicken 68

Chicken and Potatoes 69

Chicken Sandwiches 69

Moroccan Chicken..70

Cacciatore Chicken 70

Honey Barbecue Chicken Wings 71

Sweet and Tangy Chicken 71

Turkey Chili 72

Chicken Romano 72

Filipino Chicken...73

Chicken in Tomatillo Sauce 73

Braised Duck and Potatoes..74

Duck and Vegetables 74

Turkey Meatballs 75

Turkey Mix and Mashed Potatoes 76

Stuffed Chicken Breasts...77

Simple Chicken Salad 77

Chicken and Rice..78

Crispy Chicken...79

Braised Quail 80

Braised Turkey Wings..80

Roasted Chicken...81

Party Chicken Wings..81

Chicken Delight 82

Chicken Gumbo 83

Duck Chili 84

Coca-Cola Chicken 84

Chicken Curry 85

Coq au Vin..85

Italian Chicken...86

Teriyaki Chicken..86

Creamy Chicken...87

Buffalo Chicken 87

Colombian Chicken 88

Chicken and Lentils 88

Chicken Curry with Eggplant and Squash 89

Chicken and Chickpea Masala 90

Sesame Chicken 90

Chicken with Duck Sauce 91

Chicken and Dumplings 91

Chicken and Noodles 92

Chicken and Pomegranate 93

Goose with Cream 93

Goose with Chili Sauce 94

Chicken and Shrimp 94

Indian Butter Chicken 95

Chicken and Broccoli 96

Chicken with Corn 97

Chicken and Cabbage 97

Instant Pot Meat Recipes 98

Corned Beef 98

Beef Bourguignon 98

Beef Curry 99

Beef Stroganoff 99

Beef Chili 100

Chili Con Carne 100

Beef Pot Roast 101

Beef and Vegetables 101

Veal with Mushrooms 102

Beef and Pasta Casserole 103

Korean Beef 103

Beef and Broccoli 104

Beef and Cabbage 105

Lamb Shanks 105

Lamb Ribs 106

Mediterranean Lamb 106

Lamb Curry 107

Lamb Chops 108

Moroccan Lamb 109

Lamb Ragout 110

Lamb and Barley Dish 110

Lamb and White Beans 111

Mexican-style Lamb 111

Goat with Roasted Tomatoes 112

Goat and Potatoes 113

Apple Cider Pork 113

Pork Chops and Onion...114

Creamy Pork Chops...114

Pulled Pork 115

Pork Roast with Fennel 115

Chinese Barbecue Pork 116

Braised Pork 116

Pork Chops and Brown Rice 117

Pork Chops and Smashed Potatoes..117

Country-style Ribs 118

Ribs and Coleslaw 119

Asian Short Ribs 120

Short Ribs and Beer...120

Pork Carnitas 121

Pork with Orange and Honey 122

Pork Tamales...123

Pork Tostadas 124

Pork with Hominy...125

Kalua Pork 125

Sausage and Red Beans 126

Pork Sausages and Mashed Potatoes 126

Meatloaf..127

Beef Meatloaf 127

Meatball Delight 128

Meatballs and Tomato Sauce 128

Instant Pot Fish and Seafood Recipes 129

White Fish with Orange Sauce...129

Steamed Fish 129

Fish Curry 130

Mediterranean Fish 130

Cod and Peas 131

Poached Salmon 131

Crispy Salmon Fillet..132

Salmon and Rice 132

Salmon and Vegetables 133

Spicy Salmon 133

Salmon with Tomatoes 134

Salmon Burger 134

Creamy Fish Stew 135

Salmon and Raspberry Sauce 135

Fish Pudding.. 136

Jambalaya 136

Tuna and Noodle Casserole 137

Cheesy Tuna 137

Roasted Mackerel 138

Miso Mackerel 138

Mackerel with Lemon... 139

Steamed Mussels 139

Spicy Mussels 140

Mussels and Spicy Sauce....................................... 140

Mussels with Sausage 141

Cioppino 141

Clams and Chorizo 142

Parmesan Clams 142

King Crab Legs 143

Spicy Shrimp Delight 143

Shrimp Paella 144

Shrimp Boil.. 144

Spicy Shrimp Curry 145

Shrimp Curry 145

Shrimp and Dill Sauce 146

Shrimp and Potatoes... 146

Shrimp Creole.. 147

Shrimp Teriyaki 147

Spicy Shrimp and Rice 148

Shrimp Scampi 148

Fish and Shrimp 149

Shrimp with Risotto and Herbs 149

Octopus and Potatoes 150

Seafood Gumbo... 151

Octopus Stew...152

Greek Octopus...152

Stuffed Squid...153

Squid Masala..153

Braised Squid...154

Squid Roast..154

Instant Pot Vegetable Recipes..................................155

Artichokes with Lemon Sauce......................................155

Artichoke Hearts...155

Artichokes and Spinach Dip..156

Savory Artichoke Dip..156

Wrapped Asparagus Spears..157

Asparagus and Shrimp...157

Beet Salad..158

Beets with Blue Cheese...158

Beet and Orange Salad...159

Beet and Tomato Salad..159

Turkey-stuffed Bell Peppers..160

Stuffed Bell Peppers..160

Broccoli and Garlic..161

Brussels Sprouts with Pomegranate..............................161

Brussels Sprouts and Bacon..162

Brussels Sprouts with Parmesan Cheese........................162

Brussels Sprouts and Potatoes.......................................163

Savoy Cabbage and Cream..163

Cabbage with Bacon..164

Cabbage and Sausages..164

Sweet and Spicy Cabbage..165

Sweet Carrots..165

Maple-glazed Carrots...166

Carrots with Molasses..166

Cauliflower with Pasta...167

Collard Greens and Bacon...167

Savory Collard Greens...168

Classic Collard Greens...168

Braised Endive...169

Endive with Ham 169

Sautéed Endive 170

Endive Risotto 170

Eggplant Ratatouille 171

Eggplant Marinara 171

Babaganoush 172

Eggplant Surprise 172

Braised Fennel 173

Fennel Risotto 173

Kale with Garlic and Lemon 174

Braised Kale 174

Kale and Bacon 175

Okra Pilaf 175

Okra and Corn 176

Steamed Leeks 176

Crispy Potatoes 177

Roasted Potatoes 177

Zucchinis and Tomatoes 178

Turnips and Carrots 178

Spicy Turnips 179

Stuffed Tomatoes 179

Instant Pot Soups and Stews Recipes 180

Chicken Soup 180

Corn Soup 180

Butternut Squash Soup 181

Potato and Cheese Soup 182

Split Pea Soup 182

Beef and Rice Soup 183

Chicken Noodle Soup 183

Chicken and Wild Rice Soup 184

Creamy Tomato Soup 184

Zuppa Toscana 185

Minestrone Soup 185

Tomato Soup 186

Carrot Soup 187

Ham and White Bean Soup 187

Lentil Soup 188

Cabbage Soup..188

Cream of Asparagus 189

Artichoke Soup..189

Beet Soup 190

Cream of Broccoli 190

Celery Soup 191

Chestnut Soup 191

Fennel Soup 192

Cauliflower Soup 192

Turkey and Sweet Potato Soup 193

Chicken Meatball Soup...194

Vegetable Soup 195

Chicken Chili Soup 195

Broccoli and Bacon Soup 196

Chorizo, Chicken, and Kale Soup 196

Endive Soup 197

Chicken Enchilada Soup 197

Beef and Barley Soup 198

Beef Stew 198

Pork Stew...199

Chicken Stew..199

Simple Fish Chowder 200

Fast Bean Stew...200

Sweet Potato Stew 201

Spinach Stew..201

Cabbage Stew...202

Simple Turkey Stew..202

Mushroom and Beef Stew 203

Oxtail Stew 203

Lamb Stew 204

Drunken Lamb Stew 204

German Stew 205

Beef and Root Vegetables Stew 205

Italian Sausage Stew 206

Okra Stew 206

Instant Pot Beans and Grains Recipes.........................207

Barley and Mushroom Risotto 207

Barley with Vegetables 207

Barley Salad 208

Wheat Berry Salad 208

Cracked Wheat and Vegetables 209

Cracked Wheat Surprise 209

Bulgur Salad 210

Bulgur Pilaf 210

Buckwheat Porridge 211

Couscous with Chicken and Vegetables 211

Israeli Couscous 212

Millet with Vegetables 212

Creamy Millet 213

Oats and Vegetables 213

Quinoa and Vegetables 214

Mexican Cranberry Beans 214

Cranberry Beans and Pasta 215

Cranberry Beans Mixture 215

Cranberry Bean Chili 216

Lentil Tacos 216

Italian Lentils 217

Lentils and Tomato Sauce 217

Indian Lentils 218

Lentils Salad 218

Chickpeas Curry 219

Chickpeas and Dumplings 219

Chickpeas and Garlic 220

Chickpeas and Pesto 220

Kidney Beans Étouffée 221

Kidney Bean Curry 222

Kidney Beans and Ham 223

Black Beans and Chorizo 223

Black Beans 224

Black Beans in Sauce 224

Chili Lime Black Beans 225

Marrow Beans with Lemon 225

White Beans and Shrimp 226

Baked Beans 226

Creamy White Beans 227

Mung Beans 227

Indian-style Mung Beans 228

Navy Beans and Cabbage 228

Black-eyed Pea Curry 229

Fava Bean Dip 229

Fava Bean Puree 230

Full Mudammas 230

Butter Beans with Bacon 231

Split Pea Curry 231

Split Pea and Squash Curry 232

Pea and Pineapple Curry 233

Instant Pot Sauce Recipes 234

Simple Spaghetti Sauce 234

Marinara Sauce 234

Applesauce 235

Cranberry Sauce 235

Ancho Chili Sauce 236

Orange and Ginger Sauce 236

Barbecue Sauce 237

Gravy 237

Zucchini Pesto 238

Vegetarian Sauce 238

Cheese Sauce 239

Mushroom Sauce 239

Cauliflower Sauce 240

Mango Sauce 240

Hot Sauce 241

Strawberry Sauce 241

Tomato Chutney 242

Tomato Sauce 242

Green Tomato Sauce 243

Plum Sauce 243

Pineapple Sauce 244

Onion Sauce 244

Clementine Sauce 245

Orange Sauce 245

Bread Sauce 246

Chili Jam 246

Sriracha Sauce 247

Grape Sauce 247

Pomegranate Sauce 248

Apricot Sauce 248

Mustard Sauce 249

Eggplant Sauce 249

Broccoli Sauce 250

Carrot Sauce 250

Cherry Sauce 251

Date Sauce 251

Elderberry Sauce 252

Fennel Sauce 252

Pear Sauce 253

Guava Sauce 253

Melon Sauce 254

Peach Sauce 254

Peach and Whiskey Sauce 255

Leek Sauce 255

Parsley Sauce 256

Cilantro Sauce 256

Chestnut Sauce 257

Quince Sauce 257

Rhubarb Sauce 258

Corn Sauce 258

Instant Pot Dessert Recipes 259

Pumpkin Chocolate Cake 259

Chocolate Cheesecake 260

Apple Bread 261

Banana Bread 261

Chocolate Lava Cake 262

Apple Crisp 262

Candied Lemon Peel 263

Baked Apples 263

Chocolate Fondue 264

Holiday Pudding 264

Pumpkin Pie 265

Tapioca Pudding 265

Upside-down Apple Cake 266

Brownie Cake 266

Dulce De Leche 267

Pears with Wine Sauce 267

Crème Brûlée 268

Bread Pudding 268

Ruby Pears 269

Rice Pudding 269

Ricotta Cake 270

Pumpkin Rice Pudding 270

Lemon Marmalade 271

Orange Marmalade 272

Berry Jam 272

Tomato Jam 273

Pear Jam 273

Peach Jam 274

Raspberry Curd 274

Berry Compote 275

Key Lime Pie 275

Stuffed Peaches 276

Peach Compote 276

Fruit Cobbler 277

Simple Carrot Cake 277

Zucchini Nut Bread 278

Samoa Cheesecake 279

Pina Colada Pudding 280

Quick Flan 280

Chocolate Pudding 281

Sticky Pudding 281

Rhubarb Compote 282

Simple Chocolate Cake 282

Simple Carrot Pudding 283

Eggnog Cheesecake 284

Poached Figs 284

Lemon Crème Pots 285

Super Sweet Carrots 285

Pineapple and Ginger Risotto Dessert 286

Corn Pudding 286

Conclusion 287

Recipe Index 288

Free Gift

I'd like to thank you for purchasing this book and hope you will enjoy it.
In addition, I prepared a present for you:
Great Cookbook: 1000 Classic Recipes Collection
Please follow this link to get instant access to your Free Cookbook: http:/massbookbox.pro/

Introduction

Instant Pots are quite popular these days.They have managed to impress many consumers around the world, and they've become one of the most-appreciated tools in the kitchen.
If you don't have such a device, and you've made the decision to purchase one, there are some things you need to know about it.

First of all, you should know that it may take you awhile to get familiarized with this machine. It has many settings and buttons, and you should make sure you understand them before you start cooking in it. This wonderful cookbook that you are about to discover contains some simple and easy Instant Pot recipes specifically created for those of you who are using this machine for the first time.

For example, you will learn how to prepare simple recipes for beans, vegetable, ones, breakfast meals, and so on. Make sure you follow all of the additional directions as mentioned in the recipes, including all prep work outside of using the Instant pot. For example, be sure to cut ingredients in equal-size pieces, use enough liquid to cook your dishes, and use a variety of spices.

Another thing you should know is that the Instant Pot is probably one of the easiest kitchen appliances to clean. Also, it replaces many other kitchen devices like rice cookers, slow cookers, and even pressure cookers. The best thing is that, for much of the time, you won't even need to dirty any of your pans and pots. Many of the dishes you can make into the Instant Pot just require it and only it.

One of the most important aspects you need to know about your new Instant Pot is that it allows you to make delicious, healthy foods in a more effective way. Your dishes maintain all their flavors and textures, and they are cooked in one of the healthiest ways possible. With its simplicity, you won't have to consume all your energy in the kitchen, and you don't need special cooking skills to make memorable dishes.

From now on, you won't have to worry about your success in the kitchen because the Instant Pot will do the hard parts for you. We are sure we've convinced you that purchasing an Instant Pot is one of the best things you could do for yourself and your family.

Try your best to prepare all the special recipes we've provide for you as part of this cookbook. As you are about to discover, there are enough recipes to suit all tastes, even the most picky ones.

Don't wait any longer. Dive in and see what you can do with your new the Instant Pot?

Instant Pot Breakfast Recipes

Special French Toast

Preparation time: 10 minutes
Cooking time: 30 minutes
Servings: 6

Ingredients:
For the orange sauce:
- ¼ cup orange juice
- ½ cup sugar
- 2 cups cranberries
- A pinch of salt
- ¼ teaspoon cinnamon, ground

For the toast:
- 2 cups milk
- 3 eggs, whisked
- 4 tablespoons melted butter
- ½ cup sugar
- Zest from 1 orange, grated
- A pinch of salt
- 1 teaspoon vanilla extract
- 1 loaf bread, cubed
- 1 cup water

Directions:
Heat up a small pot over medium heat, add the cranberries, orange juice, ¼ teaspoon cinnamon, a pinch of salt, ½ cup sugar, stir well, and cook for 5 minutes. Pour this into a greased pan and set the dish aside. In a bowl, mix the butter with the milk, ½ cup sugar, eggs, vanilla extract, a pinch of salt, and orange zest and stir. Add the bread cubes and stir again. Pour this onto the cranberry mixture, place pan in the steamer basket of the Instant Pot, add the water on the bottom, cover, and cook on the Manual setting for 25 minutes. Release the pressure, take the pan out, divide the mix among plates, and serve.

Nutrition:
- Calories: 300
- Fat: 14
- Fiber: 2
- Carbs: 80
- Sugar: 12
- Protein: 14

Vanilla Steel-cut Oats

Preparation time: 10 minutes
Cooking time: 10 minutes
Servings: 4

Ingredients:
- 1 cup milk
- 1 cup steel-cut oats
- 2½ cups water
- 2 tablespoons sugar
- A pinch of salt
- 1 teaspoon espresso powder
- 2 teaspoons vanilla extract
- Whipped cream, for serving
- Grated chocolate, for serving

Directions:
In the Instant Pot, mix the oats with water, sugar, milk, salt, and espresso powder and stir. Cover the Instant Pot and cook on the Porridge setting for 10 minutes. Release the pressure for 10 minutes, take the lid off, add the vanilla extract, stir and let it rest for 5 minutes. Divide into bowls, and serve with whipped cream and grated chocolate.

Nutrition:
- Calories: 250
- Fat: 3.1
- Fiber: 5.4
- Carbs: 43
- Sugar: 4
- Protein: 5

Mushroom Oatmeal

Preparation time: 10 minutes
Cooking time: 15 minutes
Servings: 4

Ingredients:

- 1 small yellow onion, peeled chopped
- 1 cup steel-cut oats
- 2 garlic cloves, peeled and minced
- 2 tablespoons butter
- ½ cup water
- 14 ounces canned chicken stock
- 3 thyme sprigs, chopped
- 2 tablespoons extra virgin olive oil
- ½ cup Gouda, grated
- 8 ounces mushrooms, sliced
- Salt and ground black pepper, to taste

Directions:

Select the Sauté mode on the Instant Pot, add the butter and melt it. Add the onions, stir and cook for 3 minutes. Add the garlic, stir and cook for 1 minute. Add the oats, stir and cook for 1 minute. Add the water, salt, pepper, stock, and thyme, cover the Instant Pot and cook on the Manual setting for 10 minutes. Release the pressure and the Instant Pot, set the dish aside. Heat up a pan with the olive oil over medium heat, add the mushrooms and cook for 3 minutes. Add them to the Instant Pot with the cheese and more salt and pepper, stir and divide among plates.

Nutrition:

- Calories: 300
- Fat: 14
- Fiber: 6.7
- Carbs: 30.2
- Protein: 20.5

Delicious Pear Oatmeal

Preparation time: 5 minutes
Cooking time: 6 minutes
Servings: 4

Ingredients:

- 1 cup water
- 2 cups milk
- 1 tablespoon butter, softened
- A pinch of salt
- ¼ cups brown sugar
- ½ teaspoon ground cinnamon
- 1 cup rolled oats
- ½ cup walnuts, chopped
- 2 cups pears, peeled and chopped
- ½ cup raisins

Directions:

In a heatproof dish, mix the milk with sugar, butter, salt, oats, cinnamon, raisins, pears, and walnuts and stir. Place the dish in the steamer basket of the Instant Pot, add the water to the Instant Pot, cover, and cook on the Manual setting for 6 minutes. Release the pressure, divide the oatmeal into bowls,, and serve.

Nutrition:

- Calories: 250
- Fat: 10
- Fiber: 11.3
- Carbs: 14
- Protein: 7

Cinnamon Steel-cut Oats

Preparation time: 10 minutes
Cooking time: 13 minutes
Servings: 4

Ingredients:

- 1 cup steel-cut oats
- 3½ cups water
- A pinch of salt
- 1 tablespoon butter
- ¾ cup raisins
- 1 teaspoon ground cinnamon
- ¼ cup brown sugar
- 2 tablespoons white sugar
- 2 ounces cream cheese, softened
- 1 teaspoon milk

Directions:

Select the Sauté mode on the Instant Pot, add the butter and melt it. Add the oats, stir, and toast for 3 minutes. Add a pinch of salt and the water, cover the Instant Pot, and cook on the Manual setting for 10 minutes. Release the pressure naturally for 5 minutes and uncover the Instant Pot. Add the raisins, stir, and set the dish aside. In a bowl, mix the cinnamon with brown sugar and stir. In another bowl, mix the white sugar with the cream cheese and milk and stir well. Transfer the oats mixture to breakfast bowls and top each with the cinnamon mixture and cream cheese mixture.

Nutrition:

- Calories: 140
- Fat: 3
- Fiber: 3
- Carbs: 26
- Sugar: 4
- Protein: 4

Breakfast Banana Cake

Preparation time: 10 minutes
Cooking time: 55 minutes
Servings: 5

Ingredients:

- 1 cup water
- 1½ cups sugar
- 2 cups flour
- 3 bananas, peeled and mashed
- 2 eggs
- 1 stick butter, softened
- 2 teaspoons baking powder
- A pinch of salt
- 1 teaspoon ground cinnamon
- 1 teaspoon ground nutmeg

Directions:

In a bowl, mix the eggs with the butter and sugar and stir well. Add the salt, baking powder, cinnamon, and nutmeg and stir well again. Add the bananas and flour and stir again. Grease a springform pan with some butter, pour the batter into it and cover the pan with a paper towel and aluminum foil. Add the water to the Instant Pot, place the pan in the Instant Pot, cover and cook on the Manual setting for 55 minutes. Release the pressure, remove the pan, let the banana breakfast cake cool briefly, cut, and serve it.

Nutrition:

- Calories: 326
- Fat: 11
- Fiber: 1.1
- Carbs: 55
- Protein: 4.3

Breakfast Cobbler

Preparation time: 10 minutes
Cooking time: 15 minutes
Servings: 4

Ingredients:
- 1 plum, pitted and chopped
- 1 pear, chopped
- 1 apple chopped
- 2 tablespoons honey
- ½ teaspoon ground cinnamon
- 3 tablespoons coconut oil
- ¼ cup pecans, chopped
- ¼ cup coconut, shredded
- 2 tablespoons sunflower seeds

Directions:
Put all the fruits in a heatproof dish, add the coconut oil, cinnamon and honey and toss to coat. Place the dish in the steamer basket of the Instant Pot, cover and cook on the Manual setting for 10 minutes. Release the pressure naturally, take the dish out and transfer all the fruit to a bowl. In the same baking dish, mix the coconut with sunflower seeds and pecans and stir. Transfer these to the Instant Pot, set it on Sauté mode, and toast them for 5 minutes. Add these to the fruit in the bowl, toss to coat, and serve.

Nutrition:
- Calories: 150
- Fat: 7
- Fiber: 3
- Carbs: 12
- Sugar: 7
- Protein: 6

Pomegranate Porridge

Preparation time: 5 minutes
Cooking time: 2 minutes
Servings: 2

Ingredients:
- 1 cup rolled oats
- A pinch of salt
- 1 cup water
- ¾ cup pomegranate juice
- Seeds from 1 pomegranate

Directions:
Put the oats into the Instant Pot. Add the water, a pinch of salt, and pomegranate juice, stir, cover the Instant Pot and cook on the Porridge setting for 2 minutes. Release the pressure, add the pomegranate seeds, stir well, divide into bowls, and serve.

Nutrition:
- Calories: 200
- Fat: 2.8
- Fiber: 4.4
- Carbs: 40
- Protein: 7.3

Tomato and Spinach Breakfast

Preparation time: 10 minutes
Cooking time: 20 minutes
Servings: 6

Ingredients:
- ½ cup milk
- Salt and ground black pepper, to taste
- 12 eggs
- 3 cups baby spinach, chopped
- 3 green onions, sliced
- 1 cup tomato, diced
- 4 tomato sliced
- ¼ cup Parmesan cheese, grated
- 1½ cups water

Directions:

Put the water into the Instant Pot. In a bowl, mix the eggs with salt, pepper, and milk and stir well. Put the diced tomato, spinach and green onions in a baking dish and stir them. Pour the eggs mixture onto the vegetables, spread tomato slices on top, and sprinkle with the cheese at the end. Place this dish in the steamer basket of the Instant Pot, cover, and cook everything at Manual for 20 minutes. Release the pressure, open the Instant Pot and place the baking dish under a preheated broiler under a preheated broiler until the mixture is brown on top. Divide among plates and serve.

Nutrition:
- Calories: 200
- Fat: 10.1
- Fiber: 1.8
- Carbs: 16
- Sugar: 1
- Protein: 10

Pumpkin Oats Granola

Preparation time: 20 minutes
Cooking time: 15 minutes
Servings: 6

Ingredients:
- 3 cups water
- 1 tablespoon butter, softened
- 1 cup pumpkin puree
- 1 cup steel-cut oats
- ¼ cup maple syrup
- 2 teaspoons ground cinnamon
- 1 teaspoon pumpkin pie spice
- A pinch of salt

Directions:

Select Sauté mode on the Instant Pot, add the butter and melt it. Add the oats, stir, and cook for 3 minutes. Add the pumpkin puree, water, cinnamon, salt, maple syrup, and pumpkin spice, stir, cover the Instant Pot, and cook on the Manual setting for 10 minutes. Release the pressure naturally for 10 minutes, stir the granola, set it aside for 10 minutes, divide it, and serve.

Nutrition:
- Calories: 200
- Fat: 7
- Fiber: 3
- Carbs: 33
- Sugar: 14
- Protein: 5

Scotch Eggs

Preparation time: 10 minutes
Cooking time: 15 minutes
Servings: 4

Ingredients:
- 1 pound sausage, ground
- 1 tablespoon vegetable oil
- 4 eggs
- 2 cups water

Directions:

Put the eggs in the Instant Pot, add 1 cup water, cover the Instant Pot and cook on the Manual setting for 6 minutes. Release the pressure slowly, uncover the Instant Pot, remove the eggs, and put them in a bowl filled with ice water. Peel the eggs and place them on a working surface. Divide the sausage mix into 4 balls, flatten them, place 1 egg in the center of each sausage piece, wrap the meat around each egg, and put them all on a plate. Set the Instant Pot on Sauté mode, add the oil and heat it up. Add the scotch eggs, brown them on each side and transfer them to a plate. Add the rest of the water to the Instant Pot, arrange the eggs in the steamer basket of the Instant Pot, cover, and cook on the Manual setting for 6 minutes. Release the pressure, divide the eggs among plates, and serve.

Nutrition:
- Calories: 300
- Fat: 21
- Fiber: 0
- Carbs: 16
- Protein: 12

Poached Eggs

Preparation time: 10 minutes
Cooking time: 10 minutes
Servings: 2

Ingredients:
- 1 bunch arugula leaves
- 2 eggs
- 2 bell peppers, ends cut off
- 2 slices mozzarella cheese
- 2 slices whole wheat bread, toasted
- 1 cup water

For the sauce:
- 1½ teaspoons mustard
- ⅔ cup mayonnaise
- Salt, to taste
- 1 teaspoon turmeric
- 1 teaspoon lemon juice
- 3 tablespoons orange juice
- 1 tablespoon white wine vinegar

Directions:

In a bowl, mix the mayonnaise with the salt, turmeric, mustard, lemon juice, orange juice, and vinegar, stir well, cover the bowl, and keep in the refrigerator for now. Break an egg into each bell pepper, place them in the steamer basket of the Instant Pot, cover the basket with aluminum foil, add the water to the Instant Pot, and cook on Manual for 5 minutes. Release the pressure naturally and uncover the Instant Pot. Divide the toasted bread into 2 plates, add cheese on each, some arugula and top with pepper tops. Drizzle the sauce all over, and serve.

Nutrition:
- Calories: 129
- Fat: 8
- Fiber: 1
- Carbs: 9
- Protein: 12

Steamed Eggs

Preparation time: 10 minutes
Cooking time: 5 minutes
Servings: 2

Ingredients:

- 1⅓ cup water
- 2 eggs
- Salt and ground black pepper, to taste
- A pinch of garlic powder
- A pinch of sesame seeds
- 2 scallions, diced
- Hot rice, for serving

Directions:

In a bowl, mix the eggs with ⅓ cup water and whisk well. Strain this into a heatproof dish. Add the salt, pepper, sesame seeds, garlic powder, and scallions and whisk very well. Put the remaining water into the Instant Pot, place the dish in the steamer basket, cover the Instant Pot and cook on the Steam setting for 5 minutes. Release the pressure, uncover the Instant Pot, divide the rice among plates, and add eggs mixture on the side.

Nutrition:

- Calories: 230
- Fat: 13
- Fiber: 3
- Sugar: 1
- Protein: 21

Special Eggs Breakfast

Preparation time: 10 minutes
Cooking time: 20 minutes
Servings: 6

Ingredients:

- 1 yellow onion, peeled and diced
- 6 eggs
- 1 cup ham, cooked and diced
- 1 cup kale leaves, chopped
- ½ cup heavy cream
- Salt and ground black pepper, to taste
- 1 teaspoon herbs de Provence
- 1 cup cheddar cheese, grated
- 1 cup water

Directions:

In a bowl, mix the eggs with salt, pepper, heavy cream, onion, kale, cheese, and herbs, whisk well and pour into a heatproof dish. Put the water into the Instant Pot, place dish in the steamer basket, cover the Instant Pot and cook on the Manual setting for 20 minutes. Release the pressure, uncover the Instant Pot, remove the dish, divide the eggs between plates, and serve.

Nutrition:

- Calories: 189
- Fat: 12.3
- Fiber: 1
- Carbs: 1
- Protein: 20.3

Breakfast Quiche

Preparation time: 10 minutes
Cooking time: 30 minutes
Servings: 4

Ingredients:

- ½ cup milk
- 6 eggs, whisked
- Salt and ground black pepper, to taste
- 4 bacon slices, cooked and crumbled
- 1 cup ground sausage, cooked
- ½ cup ham, diced
- 1 cup cheddar cheese, shredded
- 2 green onions, chopped
- 1½ cups water

Directions:

Put the water into the Instant Pot and set it aside for now. In a bowl, mix the eggs with salt, pepper, milk, sausage, ham, bacon, onions, and cheese and stir everything well. Pour this into a baking dish, cover with some aluminum foil, place the dish in the steamer basket of the Instant Pot, cover and cook on the Manual setting for 30 minutes. Release the pressure for 10 minutes, uncover the Instant Pot, take the quiche out and set it aside for a few minutes to cool down. Cut the quiche, arrange it on plates, and serve.

Nutrition:

- Calories: 220
- Fat: 3.4
- Fiber: 1.1
- Carbs: 22
- Protein: 15.3

Carrot Oatmeal

Preparation time: 20 minutes
Cooking time: 13 minutes
Servings: 6

Ingredients:

- 1 cup steel-cut oats
- 4 cups water
- 1 tablespoon butter
- 3 tablespoons maple syrup
- A pinch of salt
- 2 teaspoons ground cinnamon
- 1 teaspoon pie spice
- 1 cup grated carrots
- ¼ cup chia seeds
- ¾ cup raisins

Directions:

Select the Sauté mode on the Instant Pot, add butter and melt it. Add the oats, stir and toast for 3 minutes. Add the carrots, water, maple syrup, cinnamon, spice, and a pinch of salt, stir, cover the Instant Pot and cook on the Manual setting for 10 minutes. Release the pressure naturally for 10 minutes, add the raisins and chia seeds, stir, leave the oatmeal aside for 10 minutes, divide it between bowls, and serve.

Nutrition:

- Calories: 145
- Fat: 3
- Fiber: 1.3
- Carbs: 25
- Protein: 3.5
- Sugar: 11

Egg Muffins

Preparation time: 10 minutes
Cooking time: 10 minutes
Servings: 4

Ingredients:
- 1½ cups water
- 1 green onion, chopped
- 4 bacon slices, cooked and crumbled
- 4 tablespoons cheddar cheese, shredded
- ¼ teaspoon lemon pepper
- 4 eggs
- A pinch of salt

Directions:

In a bowl, mix the eggs with a pinch of salt, and lemon pepper and whisk well. Divide the green onion, bacon and cheese into muffin cups. Add the eggs and stir a bit. Put the water into the Instant Pot, add the muffin cups to the steamer basket, cover the Instant Pot and cook on the Manual setting for 10 minutes. Release the pressure, divide the egg muffins among plates, and serve.

Nutrition:
- Calories: 70
- Fat: 2.4
- Fiber: 1
- Carbs: 1.5
- Protein: 4.6

Breakfast Risotto

Preparation time: 10 minutes
Cooking time: 12 minutes
Servings: 4

Ingredients:
- 1½ cups Arborio rice
- 1½ teaspoons ground cinnamon
- ⅓ cup brown sugar
- A pinch of salt
- 2 tablespoons butter
- 2 apples, cored and sliced
- 1 cup apple juice
- 3 cups milk
- ½ cup cherries, dried

Directions:

Set the Instant Pot on Sauté mode, add butter and melt it. Add the rice, stir and cook for 5 minutes. Add the sugar, apples, apple juice, milk, a pinch of salt and cinnamon, stir, cover, and cook on the Manual setting for 6 minutes. Release the pressure naturally for 6 minutes, uncover the Instant Pot, add the cherries, stir, cover, and set aside for 5 minutes. Divide into breakfast bowls and serve.

Nutrition:
- Calories: 160
- Fat: 16
- Fiber: 3
- Carbs: 30
- Sugar: 1
- Protein: 11

Breakfast Rice Bowl

Preparation time: 5 minutes
Cooking time: 7 minutes
Servings: 4

Ingredients:
- 1 cup brown rice
- ½ cup coconut chips
- 1 cup coconut milk
- 2 cups water
- ½ cup maple syrup
- ¼ cup raisins
- ¼ cup almonds
- A pinch of ground cinnamon
- A pinch of salt

Directions:
Put the rice in a pot, add the water, place on the stove over medium-high heat, cook according to instructions, drain, and transfer it to the Instant Pot. Add the milk, coconut chips, almonds, raisins, salt, cinnamon and maple syrup, stir well, cover the Instant Pot and cook on the Manual setting for 5 minutes. Release pressure, transfer the rice to breakfast bowls, and serve.

Nutrition:
- Calories: 240
- Fat: 7
- Fiber: 9.5
- Carbs: 45
- Sugar: 13
- Protein: 13

Special Rice Pudding

Preparation time: 10 minutes
Cooking time: 35 minutes
Servings: 4

Ingredients:
- 6½ cups water
- ¾ cup sugar
- 2 cups black rice, washed and rinsed
- 2 cinnamon sticks
- A pinch of salt
- 5 cardamom pods, crushed
- 3 cloves
- ½ cup coconut, grated
- Chopped mango, for serving

Directions:
Put the rice into the Instant Pot, add a pinch of salt and the water, and stir. In a cheesecloth bag, mix the cardamom with cinnamon and cloves and tie it. Place this in the Instant Pot with the rice, cover, and cook on Manual for 35 minutes. Release the pressure naturally, uncover the Instant Pot, stir the rice, add coconut, and set the Instant Pot to Sauté mode. Cook for 10 minutes, discard the spices bag, transfer to breakfast bowls, and serve with chopped mango on top.

Nutrition:
- Calories: 118
- Fat: 1
- Fiber: 1
- Carbs: 21
- Protein: 8

Amazing Breakfast Quinoa

Preparation time: 10 minutes
Cooking time: 10 minutes
Servings: 6

Ingredients:
- 2¼ cups water
- 1½ cups quinoa, rinsed
- 2 tablespoons maple syrup
- A pinch of salt
- ¼ teaspoon ground cinnamon
- ½ teaspoon vanilla extract
- Fresh berries, for serving
- Milk, for serving
- Almonds, sliced for serving

Directions:

In the Instant Pot, add the water, quinoa, vanilla, cinnamon, salt, and maple syrup. Stir, cover the Instant Pot, and cook on the Multigrain setting for 10 minutes. Release the pressure naturally, fluff the quinoa with a fork, divide it into breakfast bowls, add the milk and stir. Top with almonds and berries and serve.

Nutrition:
- Calories: 100
- Fat: 3
- Fiber: 1
- Carbs: 4
- Sugar: 3
- Protein: 2

Breakfast Quinoa Salad

Preparation time: 10 minutes
Cooking time: 15 minutes
Servings: 8

Ingredients:
- 2 garlic cloves, peeled and minced
- 2¼ cups water
- 1½ cups quinoa, rinsed
- A pinch of salt
- 2 tomatoes, cored and chopped
- 1 cucumber, chopped
- 1 jalapeño pepper, chopped
- 1 cup corn, already cooked
- ½ cup scallions, diced
- 1½ cups chickpeas, already cooked
- ⅔ cup fresh parsley leaves, diced
- ⅓ cup mint leaves, chopped
- 1 avocado, pitted, peeled and diced
- 3 tablespoons vegetable stock
- ¼ cup lime juice
- Ground black pepper, to taste
- ½ teaspoon chipotle pepper

Directions:

In the Instant Pot, mix the quinoa with 1 garlic clove, a pinch of salt, and the water, stir, cover and cook on the Sauté setting for 1 minute. Release the pressure, uncover the Instant Pot, fluff the quinoa with a fork, and let it cool briefly. Transfer the quinoa to a bowl, add the tomatoes, cucumber, jalapeño pepper, corn, scallions, chickpeas, parsley, mint, and avocado. In a bowl, mix the vegetable stock with the pepper, the remaining garlic clove, the lime juice, and chili pepper, and stir very well. Pour this onto the salad, toss to coat, and serve.

Nutrition:
- Calories: 239
- Fat: 6.4
- Fiber: 7.7
- Carbs: 39
- Protein: 9

Breakfast Bread Pudding

Preparation time: 10 minutes
Cooking time: 25 minutes
Servings: 6

Ingredients:

- 1 cup water
- Vegetable oil cooking spray
- 4 tablespoons butter
- 1 cup onions, peeled and sliced thin
- 1 cup mushrooms, sliced
- 1 cup ham, diced
- ¼ cup sugar
- 3 eggs, whisked
- 2 cups half and half
- ½ teaspoon dry mustard
- Salt and ground black pepper, to taste
- 1 cup Swiss cheese, grated
- ½ teaspoon thyme, dried
- 14 ounces loaf and bread, cubed

For the sauce:

- 1½ teaspoons rice wine vinegar
- ½ cup mustard
- 2 tablespoons maple syrup
- Salt and ground black pepper, to taste

Directions:

Heat up a pan over medium heat, add the butter and melt it. Add the onions, stir and cook for 2 minutes. Add the ham, stir again, cook for 2 minutes, take off the heat and set aside. Spray a pan with some cooking oil. In a bowl, mix eggs with sugar, half and half, thyme, half of the Swiss cheese, salt, pepper, bread cubes, mushroom, and ham and onions mixture, and stir well. Pour this into the greased pan, place it in the steamer basket of the Instant Pot, add the water in the Instant Pot, cover with aluminum foil, cover the Instant Pot, and cook on Manual for 25 minutes. Heat up a small pot over medium heat, add the dry mustard, salt, pepper, vinegar, and maple syrup, stir well, and cook for 2-3 minutes. Release the pressure from the Instant Pot, uncover, take the pan out, sprinkle the rest of the cheese, place under a preheated broiler and brown for a few minutes. Divide the bread pudding on plates, drizzle the sauce on top, and serve.

Nutrition:

- Calories: 270
- Fat: 12
- Fiber: 2
- Carbs: 14
- Protein: 10

Millet Pudding

Preparation time: 10 minutes
Cooking time: 10 minutes
Servings: 4

Ingredients:

- 14 ounces coconut milk
- 7 ounces water
- ⅔ cup millet
- A pinch of salt
- 4 dates, pitted
- Honey for serving

Directions:

Put the millet into the Instant Pot. Add the milk, dates and a pinch of salt and stir. Add the water, stir again, cover the Instant Pot and cook on the Manual setting for 10 minutes. Release the pressure naturally, uncover the Instant Pot, divide the pudding into bowls, top with honey, and serve.

Nutrition:

- Calories: 240
- Fat: 2
- Fiber: 2.6
- Carbs: 25
- Sugar: 33
- Protein: 8

Breakfast Millet Pilaf

Preparation time: 10 minutes
Cooking time: 10 minutes
Servings: 4

Ingredients:
- 1 tablespoon ghee
- 1 teaspoon cardamom, crushed
- 3 teaspoons cumin seeds
- 1 bay leaf
- 1 inch cinnamon stick
- 2 cups organic millet
- 1 white onion, chopped
- Salt, to taste
- 3 cups water

Directions:

Set the Instant Pot on sauté mode, add ghee and heat it up. Add cumin, cinnamon, cardamom and bay leaf, stir and cook for 1 minute. Add onion, stir and cook for 4 minutes. Add millet, salt and water, stir, cover the Instant Pot and cook on the Manual setting for 1 minute. Release the pressure naturally, fluff the mix with a fork, transfer to bowls, and serve.

Nutrition:
- Calories: 100
- Fat: 3.1
- Fiber: 1.3
- Carbs: 16
- Protein: 2.5

Breakfast Pudding

Preparation time: 5 minutes
Cooking time: 10 minutes
Servings: 4

Ingredients:
- 1½ cups water
- ⅓ cup tapioca pearls
- 1¼ cup whole milk
- Zest from ½ lemon
- ½ cup sugar

Directions:

Put 1 cup water into the Instant Pot. Put tapioca pearls in a heat proof bowl add milk, ½ cup water, lemon zest and sugar. Stir everything, place the bowl in the steamer basket of the Instant Pot, cover and cook on the Manual setting for 10 minutes. Release the pressure, transfer pudding to cups, and serve.

Nutrition:
- Calories: 122
- Fat: 2
- Fiber: 0
- Carbs: 21
- Sugar: 6
- Protein: 5

Breakfast Chia Pudding

Preparation time: 2 hours
Cooking time: 3 minutes
Servings: 4

Ingredients:

- ½ cup chia seeds
- 2 cups almond milk
- ¼ cup almonds
- ¼ cup coconut, shredded
- 4 teaspoons sugar

Directions:

Put chia seeds into the Instant Pot. Add milk, almonds and coconut flakes, stir, cover and cook on the Manual setting for 3 minutes. Release the pressure, divide the pudding between bowls, top each with a teaspoon of sugar, and serve.

Nutrition:

- Calories: 130
- Fat: 12
- Fiber: 22
- Carbs: 2
- Protein: 14

Breakfast Hash

Preparation time: 10 minutes
Cooking time: 7 minutes
Servings: 4

Ingredients:

- 8 ounces sausage, ground
- 1 package hash browns, frozen
- ⅓ cup water
- 1 yellow onion, chopped
- 1 green bell pepper, chopped
- 1 cup cheddar cheese, grated
- Salt and ground black pepper, to taste
- 4 eggs, whisked
- Salsa for serving

Directions:

Set the Instant Pot on Sauté mode, add sausage, stir and cook for 2 minutes. Drain excess fat, add bell pepper and onion, stir and cook for 2 more minutes. Add hash browns, water, eggs, salt and cheese, stir, cover and cook on Low for 4 minutes. Release the pressure, divide hash among plates, and serve with salsa.

Nutrition:

- Calories: 300
- Fat: 16
- Fiber: 4
- Carbs: 30
- Protein: 17

Potato Hash

Preparation time: 10 minutes
Cooking time: 8 minutes
Servings: 4

Ingredients:

- 1 cup cheddar cheese, shredded
- 6 eggs, whisked
- Salt and ground black pepper, to taste
- 6 potatoes, peeled and roughly chopped
- 1 cup ham, chopped
- A drizzle of olive oil
- ¼ cup water
- Toasted bread for serving

Directions:

Set the Instant Pot on Sauté, add the oil and heat it up. Add potatoes, stir and brown them for 3 minutes. Add ham, eggs, cheese, salt, pepper and the water, stir, cover the Instant Pot and cook on the Manual setting for 5 minutes. Release the pressure, transfer hash to plates, and serve with toasted bread.

Nutrition:

- Calories: 250
- Fat: 12
- Fiber: 2
- Carbs: 20
- Protein: 17

Breakfast Burritos

Preparation time: 15 minutes
Cooking time: 15 minutes
Servings: 6

Ingredients:

- 8 ounces pork meat, ground
- Salt and ground black pepper, to taste
- 1 teaspoon thyme, dry
- 1 teaspoon sage, dry
- 1 teaspoon fennel seed, crushed
- 1 teaspoon brown sugar
- A pinch of nutmeg
- ½ teaspoon red pepper flakes, crushed
- 1 tablespoon water
- 1½ cups water
- 6 tortilla shells
- 8 eggs
- A drizzle of olive oil
- ¼ cup milk
- Cheddar cheese, shredded for serving
- Salsa for serving

Directions:

In a bowl, mix pork with salt, pepper, thyme, sage, fennel, pepper flakes, nutmeg, sugar and 1 tablespoon water, stir very well, cover the bowl and keep it in the refrigerator for now. Brush tortilla shells with some olive oil, arrange them on a baking sheet, cover them with aluminum foil and seal edges. In a heat proof dish, mix eggs with salt, pepper, and milk and whisk well. Add meat mix, stir and cover the dish with some aluminum foil. Place dish in the steamer basket of the Instant Pot, add wrapped tortilla shells on top, add 1½ cups water to the Instant Pot, cover and cook on the Manual setting for 15 minutes. Release the pressure and take tortilla shells and eggs and meat mix out of the Instant Pot. Unwrap tortilla shells, fill them with eggs and meat mix and top with salsa and cheddar cheese. Arrange on plates, and serve.

Nutrition:

- Calories: 380
- Fat: 25
- Fiber: 11
- Carbs: 19
- Protein: 21

Breakfast Sandwiches

Preparation time: 10 minutes
Cooking time: 40 minutes
Servings: 8

Ingredients:

- 2 tablespoons brown sugar
- 4-pound beef roast, cut into small chunks
- Salt and ground black pepper, to taste
- 2 teaspoons paprika
- 2½ teaspoons garlic powder
- 2 teaspoons mustard powder
- 2 teaspoons onion flakes
- 3 cups beef stock
- 1 tablespoon balsamic vinegar
- 2 tablespoon Worcestershire sauce
- 4 tablespoons butter, soft
- 8 hoagie rolls
- 8 slices provolone cheese

Directions:

Put the meat into the Instant Pot. Add salt, pepper, paprika, 2 teaspoons garlic powder, mustard powder, onion flakes, stock, vinegar and Worcestershire sauce, stir well, cover the Instant Pot and cook on the Manual setting for 40 minutes. Release the pressure, transfer the meat to a cutting board, strain the liquid, and keep it in a bowl. Shred the meat and divide among rolls after you've buttered them. Add the provolone cheese on top, place the sandwiches under a preheated broiler and broil until the cheese melts. Dip the sandwiches in the sauce from the Instant Pot, and serve them.

Nutrition:

- Calories: 340
- Fat: 21
- Fiber: 2
- Carbs: 12
- Protein: 34

Breakfast Sausages and Peppers

Preparation time: 10 minutes
Cooking time: 25 minutes
Servings: 5

Ingredients:

- 15 ounces tomato sauce
- 28 ounces canned tomatoes, diced
- 10 Italian sausages
- 4 green bell peppers, cut into thin strips
- 1 cup water
- 4 garlic cloves, peeled and minced
- 1 tablespoon dried basil
- 1 tablespoon Italian seasoning

Directions:

Put the tomatoes, tomato sauce, basil, water, garlic, sausages, bell peppers, and Italian seasoning into the Instant Pot, and stir gently. Cover the Instant Pot and cook on the Manual setting for 25 minutes. Release the pressure, divide the mix between plates, and serve.

Nutrition:

- Calories: 400
- Fat: 31
- Fiber: 1
- Carbs: 8
- Protein: 23

Breakfast Tacos

Preparation time: 10 minutes
Cooking time: 5 minutes
Servings: 4

Ingredients:
- 1 pound turkey meat, ground
- 1 tablespoon Worcestershire sauce
- 1 tablespoon extra virgin olive oil
- 1¼ cups beef stock
- 2 teaspoons corn flour
- 1½ teaspoons cumin, ground
- 1 tablespoon chili powder
- ¼ teaspoon onion powder
- ¼ teaspoon garlic powder
- ¼ teaspoon dried onions
- ½ teaspoon paprika
- ¼ teaspoon dried oregano
- A pinch of cayenne pepper
- Salt and ground black pepper, to taste
- Tacos shells, for serving

Directions:
Set the Instant Pot on Sauté mode, add the oil, and heat it up. Add the meat½ cup stock, stir, and brown for a few minutes. Discard the excess fat, add the rest of the stock, Worcestershire sauce, flour, cumin, chili powder, garlic powder, onion powder, dried onions, paprika, oregano, salt, pepper, and cayenne pepper, stir, cover the Instant Pot and cook on the Manual setting for 5 minutes. Release the pressure naturally, uncover the Instant Pot, stir the meat mix and divide it in taco shells, and serve.

Nutrition:
- Calories: 240
- Fat: 11.5
- Fiber: 1
- Carbs: 3.4
- Protein: 31.1

Breakfast Jam

Preparation time: 20 minutes
Cooking time: 1 hour and 15 minutes
Servings: 12

Ingredients:
- 16 ounces cranberries
- 16 ounces strawberries, chopped
- Zest from 1 lemon
- 4 ounces raisins
- A pinch of salt
- 3 ounces water
- 2½ pounds sugar

Directions:
In the Instant Pot, mix the strawberries with the cranberries, lemon zest, and raisins. Add the sugar, stir and set aside to 1 hour. Add the water and a pinch of salt, cover the Instant Pot and cook on the Manual setting for 15 minutes. Release the pressure, let the jam rest for 5 minutes, stir, pour into small jars, and serve with toasted bread slices.

Nutrition:
- Calories: 60
- Fat: 0
- Fiber: 0
- Carbs: 12
- Protein: 1
- Sugar: 12

Lemon Marmalade

Preparation time: 10 minutes
Cooking time: 15 minutes
Servings: 8

Ingredients:
- 2 pounds lemons, washed, and sliced thin4 pounds sugar
- 1 tablespoon vinegar

Directions:

Put the lemon slices into the Instant Pot. Cover the Instant Pot and cook the marmalade at Manual for 10 minutes. Release the pressure, add the sugar, cover the Instant Pot again, and cook on the Manual setting for 4 more minutes. Release the pressure again, stir the marmalade, pour it into jars, and refrigerate until you serve it.

Nutrition:
- Calories: 60
- Fat: 1
- Fiber: 0
- Carbs: 12
- Sugar: 13

Blackberry Jam

Preparation time: 10 minutes
Cooking time: 20 minutes
Servings: 4

Ingredients:
- 4 pints blackberries
- Juice of 1 small lemon
- 5 cups sugar
- 3 tablespoons pectin powder

Directions:

Put the blackberries into the Instant Pot. Add the sugar, stir, select Sauté mode, and cook for 3 minutes. Transfer the jam to clean jars, close them, and place them in the steamer basket of the Instant Pot. Add the water to cover the jars halfway, select Steam mode on the Instant Pot, cover, and steam for 20 minutes. Remove the jars, allow them to cool down, and keep the jam in the refrigerator until you serve it with some toasted bread.

Nutrition:
- Calories: 63
- Fat: 6
- Fiber: 7.6
- Carbs: 12
- Protein: 2
- Sugar: 7

Cheesy Grits

Preparation time: 10 minutes
Cooking time: 10 minutes
Servings: 4

Ingredients:
- 2 tablespoons coconut oil
- 1¾ cup half and half
- 1 cup stone ground grits
- 3 cups water
- 2 teaspoons salt
- 3 tablespoons butter
- 4 ounces cheddar cheese, grated
- Butter, for serving

Directions:
Set the Instant Pot on Sauté mode, add the grits, stir, and toast them for 3 minutes. Add the oil, half and half, water, salt, butter, and cheese, stir, cover and cook on Manual mode for 10 minutes. Release the pressure naturally, set the cheesy grits aside for 15 minutes, transfer to bowls, add the butter on top, and serve.

Nutrition:
- Calories: 280
- Fat: 13
- Fiber: 1
- Carbs: 26
- Sugar: 2
- Protein: 13.2

Tasty Breakfast

Preparation time: 10 minutes
Cooking time: 25 minutes
Servings: 4

Ingredients:
- 3 cups green tea
- 1 tablespoon ground cinnamon
- 1 cup red lentils, soaked for 4 hours and drained
- 2 apples, diced
- 1 teaspoon ground cloves
- 1 teaspoon turmeric
- Maple syrup, for serving
- Coconut milk, for serving

Directions:
Put lentils into the Instant Pot, add the tea and stir, cover, and cook on the Manual setting for 15 minutes. Release the pressure, uncover the Instant Pot, add the cinnamon, apples, turmeric, and cloves, stir, cover and cook on the Manual setting for 15 minutes. Release pressure, divide lentils between bowls and add some maple syrup and coconut milk.

Nutrition:
- Calories: 140
- Fat: 1.2
- Fiber: 8.4
- Carbs: 35
- Sugar: 14
- Protein: 5

Chickpeas Spread

Preparation time: 5 minutes
Cooking time: 20 minutes
Servings: 8

Ingredients:

- 1 cup chickpeas, soaked and drained
- 6 cups water
- 1 bay leaf
- 4 garlic cloves, peeled and crushed
- 2 tablespoons tahini paste
- Juice of 1 lemon
- ¼ teaspoon cumin
- Salt, to taste
- ¼ cup fresh parsley, chopped
- A pinch of paprika
- Extra virgin olive oil

Directions:

Put the chickpeas and water into the Instant Pot. Add the bay leaf, 2 garlic cloves, cover the Instant Pot and cook on the Manual setting for 18 minutes. Release the pressure, discard the excess liquid and bay leaf and reserve some of the cooking liquid. Add the tahini paste, the cooking liquid you've reserved, lemon juice, cumin, the remainder of the garlic, and salt. Transfer everything to a food processor and pulse well. Transfer the chickpeas spread to a serving bowl, sprinkle with olive oil and paprika on top and serve.

Nutrition:

- Calories: 270
- Fat: 19
- Fiber: 5.1
- Carbs: 21.5
- Protein: 6.8

Chicken Liver Spread

Preparation time: 5 minutes
Cooking time: 15 minutes
Servings: 8

Ingredients:

- 1 teaspoon extra virgin olive oil
- ¾ pound chicken livers
- 1 yellow onion, peeled and chopped
- 1 bay leaf
- ¼ cup red wine
- 2 anchovies
- 1 tablespoons capers, drained and chopped
- 1 tablespoon butter
- Salt and ground black pepper, to taste

Directions:

Put the olive oil into the Instant Pot, add the onion, salt, pepper, chicken livers, bay leaf and wine. Stir, cover the Instant Pot, and cook on the Manual setting for 10 minutes. Release the pressure, add the anchovies, capers, and butter. Stir, transfer to a blender and pulse several times. Add the salt and pepper, blend again, transfer to a bowl, and serve with toasted bread slices.

Nutrition:

- Calories: 150
- Fat: 12
- Fiber: 0
- Carbs: 5
- Sugar: 2
- Protein: 4

Mushroom Pate

Preparation time: 6 minutes
Cooking time: 18 minutes
Servings: 6

Ingredients:
- 1-ounce dried porcini mushrooms
- 1 pound button mushrooms, sliced
- 1 cup boiled water
- 1 tablespoon butter
- 1 tablespoon extra virgin olive oil
- 1 shallot, peeled and diced
- ¼ cup white wine
- Salt and ground black pepper, to taste
- 1 bay leaf
- 1 tablespoon truffle oil
- 3 tablespoons Parmesan cheese, grated

Directions:

Put the porcini mushrooms in a bowl, add 1 cup boiling water over them, and set aside. Set the Instant Pot on Sauté mode, add the butter and olive oil and heat them. Add the shallots, stir and cook for 2 minutes. Add the porcini mushrooms and their liquid, button mushrooms, wine, salt, pepper, and bay leaf. Stir, cover the Instant Pot and cook on the Manual setting for 16 minutes. Release the pressure, remove the bay leaf and some of the liquid, transfer everything to a blender and pulse until smooth. Add the truffle oil and grated Parmesan cheese, blend again, transfer to a bowl, and serve.

Nutrition:
- Calories: 220
- Fat: 15
- Fiber: 0
- Carbs: 15
- Sugar: 3
- Protein: 5

Ricotta Cheese Spread

Preparation time: 10 minutes
Cooking time: 5 minutes
Servings: 4

Ingredients:
- 10 ounces canned diced tomatoes with green chilies
- 1¾ cups Italian sausage, ground
- 4 cups processed cheese, cut into chunks
- 4 tablespoons water

Directions:

In the Instant Pot, mix the tomatoes and chilies with the water, ground sausage, and cheese. Stir, cover and cook on the Manual setting for 5 minutes. Release the pressure naturally for 5 minutes, uncover the Instant Pot, stir the spread, transfer to a bowl, and serve.

Nutrition:
- Calories: 294
- Fat: 18
- Fiber: 1
- Carbs: 4
- Protein: 7

Pecan Sweet Potatoes

Preparation time: 10 minutes
Cooking time: 10 minutes
Servings: 8

Ingredients:

- 1 cup water
- 1 tablespoon lemon peel
- ½ cup brown sugar
- ¼ teaspoon salt
- 3 sweet potatoes, peeled and sliced
- ¼ cup butter
- ¼ cup maple syrup
- 1 cup pecans, chopped
- 1 tablespoon cornstarch
- Whole pecans, for garnish

Directions:

Put the water into the Instant Pot, add the lemon peel, brown sugar, and salt and stir. Add the potatoes, cover the Instant Pot and cook on the Manual setting for 15 minutes. Release the pressure and transfer the potatoes to a serving plate. Select Sauté mode on the Instant Pot, add the butter and melt it. Add the pecans, maple syrup, and cornstarch and stir well. Pour this over the potatoes, garnish with the whole pecans, and serve.

Nutrition:

- Calories: 230
- Fat: 13
- Fiber: 4
- Carbs: 15
- Protein: 6

Pumpkin Butter

Preparation time: 15 minutes
Cooking time: 10 minutes
Servings: 18

Ingredients:

- 30 ounces pumpkin puree
- 3 apples, peeled, cored and chopped
- 1 tablespoon pumpkin pie spice
- 1 cup sugar
- A pinch of salt
- 12 ounces apple cider
- ½ cup honey.

Directions:

In the Instant Pot, mix the pumpkin puree with the pumpkin pie spice, apple pieces, sugar, honey, cider and a pinch of salt. Stir well, cover the Instant Pot, and cook on the Manual setting for 10 minutes. Release the pressure naturally for 15 minutes, transfer the butter to small jars, and keep it in the refrigerator until serving.

Nutrition:

- Calories: 50
- Fat: 1
- Fiber: 0
- Carbs: 10
- Sugar: 9
- Protein: 1

Breakfast Salad

Preparation time: 10 minutes
Cooking time: 4 minutes
Servings: 4

Ingredients:

- 6 potatoes, peeled and cubed
- 4 eggs
- 1½ cups water
- 1 cup mayonnaise
- ¼ cup onion, peeled and diced
- 1 tablespoon dill pickle juice
- 2 tablespoons parsley, diced
- 1 tablespoon mustard
- Salt and ground black pepper, to taste

Directions:

Put the potatoes, eggs and the water into the steamer basket of the Instant Pot, cover, and cook on Manual mode for 4 minutes. Release the pressure, transfer the eggs to a bowl filled with ice water and set aside to cool. In a bowl, mix the mayonnaise with the pickle juice, onion, parsley, and mustard, and stir well. Add the potatoes and toss to coat. Peel the eggs, chop them, add them to salad, and toss again. Add salt and pepper, stir, and serve your salad with toasted bread slices.

Nutrition:

- Calories: 150
- Fat: 8
- Fiber: 1.3
- Carbs: 11
- Protein: 3

Breakfast Potatoes

Preparation time: 5 minutes
Cooking time: 7 minutes
Servings: 2

Ingredients:

- 4 Yukon gold potatoes, washed
- 2 teaspoons Italian seasoning
- 1 tablespoon bacon fat
- 1 cup chives, chopped, for serving
- Water
- Salt and ground black pepper, to taste

Directions:

Put the potatoes into the Instant Pot, add enough water to cover them, cover the Instant Pot and cook on the Manual setting for 10 minutes. Release the pressure naturally, transfer potatoes to a working surface, and set aside to cool. Peel the potatoes, transfer them to a bowl, and mash them with a fork. Set the Instant Pot on Sauté mode, add the bacon fat and heat. Add the potatoes, Italian seasoning, salt and pepper, stir, cover the Instant Pot and cook on the Manual setting for 1 minute. Release the pressure, stir the potatoes again, divide them between plates, and serve with chives sprinkled on top.

Nutrition:

- Calories: 90
- Fat: 3
- Fiber: 1
- Carbs: 11
- Protein: 1

Tofu Breakfast

Preparation time: 10 minutes
Cooking time: 7 minutes
Servings: 4

Ingredients:

- 1 bunch kale leaves, chopped
- 1 leek, cut into halves lengthwise and sliced thin
- 1 teaspoon paprika
- 1 tablespoon olive oil
- ½ cup water
- Salt, to taste
- Cayenne pepper
- 2 teaspoons sherry vinegar
- 3 ounces tofu, cubed and baked
- ¼ cup almonds, chopped

Directions:

Set the Instant Pot on Sauté mode, add the oil and heat it up. Add the leeks, stir and sauté them for 5 minutes. Add the paprika, stir and cook for 1 minute. Add the water, kale, salt, and cayenne, cover the Instant Pot and cook on the Manual setting for 2 minutes. Release the pressure, add the tofu and vinegar and more salt, if needed, stir, and transfer to plates. Sprinkle the almonds on top, and serve.

Nutrition:

- Calories: 170
- Fat: 12
- Fiber: 7
- Carbs: 18
- Protein: 16

Tofu Scramble

Preparation time: 10 minutes
Cooking time: 7 minutes
Servings: 4

Ingredients:

- 1 yellow onion, peeled and sliced thin
- 1 teaspoon walnut oil
- 3 garlic cloves, peeled and minced
- ¼ cup vegetable stock
- 1 cup carrot, peeled and chopped
- 1 block firm tofu, drained
- 12 ounces canned tomatoes, diced
- 1 teaspoon cumin
- 2 tablespoons red bell pepper, chopped
- 1 tablespoon Italian seasoning
- 1 teaspoon nutritional yeast
- Salt and ground black pepper, to taste

Directions:

Set the Instant Pot on Sauté mode, add the oil and heat it up. Add the onion, carrot, and garlic, stir, and cook for 3 minutes. Crumble the tofu, add it to pot, and stir. Add the stock, bell pepper, tomatoes, cumin, Italian seasoning, salt, and pepper, stir, cover the Instant Pot and cook on the Manual setting for 4 minutes. Release the pressure, transfer to bowls, and serve with nutritional yeast on top.

Nutrition:

- Calories: 144
- Fat: 5.7
- Fiber: 3.1
- Carbs: 11.8
- Protein: 13

Barbecue Tofu

Preparation time: 10 minutes
Cooking time: 10 minutes
Servings: 6

Ingredients:
- 28 ounces firm tofu, cubed
- 12 ounces barbecue sauce
- 2 tablespoons extra virgin olive oil
- 4 garlic cloves, peeled and minced
- 1 yellow onion, peeled and chopped
- 1 celery stalk, chopped
- 1 red bell pepper, chopped
- 1 green bell pepper, chopped
- Salt, to taste
- Curry powder

Directions:
Set the Instant Pot on Sauté mode, add the oil and heat it up. Add the bell peppers, garlic, onion and celery, and stir. Add the salt and curry powder, stir, and cook for 2 minutes. Add the tofu, stir, and cook 4 minutes. Add the barbecue sauce, stir, cover the Instant Pot and cook on the Manual setting for 5 minutes. Release the pressure, uncover the Instant Pot, transfer to plates, and serve.

Nutrition:
- Calories: 200
- Fat: 11
- Fiber: 3
- Carbs: 14.1
- Protein: 14.4

Potatoes and Tofu Breakfast

Preparation time: 10 minutes
Cooking time: 4 minutes
Servings: 4

Ingredients:
- 3 purple potatoes, cubed
- 1 yellow onion, peeled and chopped
- 2 garlic cloves, peeled and minced
- 1 carrot, peeled and chopped
- 1 ginger root, peeled and grated
- ½ pound firm tofu, cubed
- 3 tablespoons water
- 1 tablespoon tamari
- Mexican spice blend, to taste
- 1½ cups Brussels sprouts

Directions:
Set the Instant Pot on Sauté mode, add the onion and brown it for 1 minute. Add the potatoes, ginger, garlic, tofu, carrots, tamari, spices, Brussels sprouts, and water, cover, and cook on the Manual setting for 2 minutes. Release the pressure, uncover the Instant Pot, uncover the Instant Pot, transfer to plates, and serve.

Nutrition:
- Calories: 156
- Fat: 10
- Fiber: 3
- Carbs: 11.4
- Protein: 13

Instant Pot Side Dish Recipes

Wild Rice and Farro Pilaf

Preparation time: 10 minutes
Cooking time: 35 minutes
Servings: 12

Ingredients:

- 1 shallot, peeled and diced
- 1 teaspoon garlic, minced
- Extra virgin olive oil
- 1½ cups whole grain faro
- ¾ cup wild rice
- 6 cups chicken stock
- Salt and ground black pepper, to taste
- ½ tablespoons dried parsley, minced
- ½ tablespoons dried sage, minced
- ½ cup hazelnuts, toasted and chopped
- ¾ cup cherries, dried
- Minced chives, for serving

Directions:

Set the Instant Pot on Sauté mode, add a drizzle of olive oil and heat it up. Add the onion and garlic, stir, and cook for 2-3 minutes. Add the farro, rice, salt, pepper, stock, sage, and parsley, stir, cover the Instant Pot and cook on Multigrain mode for 25 minutes. Put the cherries in a pot, add enough hot water to cover, set aside for 10 minutes, and drain. Release the pressure from the Instant Pot for 5 minutes, drain the excess liquid, add the hazelnuts and cherries, stir gently, divide among plates, and garnish with chopped chives.

Nutrition:

- Calories: 120
- Fat: 1
- Fiber: 1.5
- Carbs: 21
- Protein: 4.5

Quinoa Pilaf

Preparation time: 10 minutes
Cooking time: 2 minutes
Servings: 4

Ingredients:

- 2 cups quinoa
- 2 garlic cloves, peeled and minced
- 2 tablespoons extra virgin olive oil
- Salt, to taste
- 2 teaspoons turmeric
- 3 cups water
- ½ cup fresh parsley, chopped
- 2 teaspoons cumin

Directions:

Set the Instant Pot on Sauté mode, add the oil and heat it up. Add the garlic, stir, and cook for 30 seconds. Add the water, quinoa, cumin, turmeric, and salt, stir, cover and cook on the Manual setting for 1 minute. Release the pressure naturally for 10 minutes, fluff the quinoa with a fork, transfer to plates, season with more salt, if needed, sprinkle the parsley on top, and serve.

Nutrition:

- Calories: 130
- Fat: 0.9
- Fiber: 3.2
- Carbs: 12
- Protein: 6.9

Quinoa with Almonds

Preparation time: 10 minutes
Cooking time: 11 minutes
Servings: 4

Ingredients:

- ½ cup yellow onion, peeled and diced
- 1 tablespoon butter
- 1 celery stalk, chopped
- 1½ cups quinoa, rinsed
- 14 ounces chicken stock
- Salt and ground black pepper, to taste
- ¼ cup water
- ½ cup almonds, toasted and sliced
- 2 tablespoons parsley, chopped

Directions:

Set the Instant Pot on Sauté mode, add the butter and melt it. Add the onion and celery, stir, and cook for 5 minutes. Add the quinoa, water, stock, salt, and pepper, stir, cover and cook on the Manual setting for 3 minutes. Release the pressure for 5 minutes, uncover, fluff with a fork, add the almonds and parsley, stir, divide among plates, and serve.

Nutrition:

- Calories: 140
- Fat: 3
- Fiber: 2
- Carbs: 12
- Protein: 12.4

Pink Rice

Preparation time: 10 minutes
Cooking time: 5 minutes
Servings: 8

Ingredients:

- 1 teaspoon salt
- 2½ cups water
- 2 cups pink rice

Directions:

Put the rice into the Instant Pot. Add the water and salt, stir, cover and cook on the Manual setting for 5 minutes. Release the pressure naturally for 10 minutes, uncover the Instant Pot, fluff rice with a fork, divide among plates, and serve.

Nutrition:

- Calories: 114
- Fat: 1
- Fiber: 2
- Carbs: 13
- Protein: 4

Mushroom Risotto

Preparation time: 10 minutes
Cooking time: 15 minutes
Servings: 4

Ingredients:

- 2 cups risotto rice
- 4 cups chicken stock
- 2 garlic cloves, peeled and crushed
- 2 ounces extra virgin olive oil
- 1 yellow onion, peeled and chopped
- 8 ounces mushrooms, sliced
- 4 ounces heavy cream
- 4 ounces sherry vinegar
- 2 tablespoons Parmesan cheese, grated
- 1 ounce fresh basil, minced

Directions:

Set the Instant Pot on Sauté mode, add the oil and heat it up. Add the onions, garlic, and mushrooms, stir and cook for 3 minutes. Add the rice, stock and vinegar, stir, cover the Instant Pot and cook on the Manual setting for 10 minutes. Release the pressure, uncover the Instant Pot, add the cream and Parmesan and stir. Divide among plates, sprinkle with the basil, and serve.

Nutrition:

- Calories: 340
- Fat: 1
- Fiber: 1
- Carbs: 15
- Protein: 4

Pumpkin Risotto

Preparation time: 5 minutes
Cooking time: 10 minutes
Servings: 4

Ingredients:

- 2 ounces extra virgin olive oil
- 1 small yellow onion, peeled and chopped
- 2 garlic cloves, peeled and minced
- 12 ounces Arborio rice
- 4 cups chicken stock
- 6 ounces pumpkin puree
- ½ teaspoon nutmeg
- 1 teaspoon fresh thyme, chopped
- ½ teaspoon ginger, grated
- ½ teaspoon ground cinnamon
- ½ teaspoon allspice
- 4 ounces heavy cream

Directions:

Set the Instant Pot on Sauté mode, add the oil and heat it up. Add the onion and garlic, stir and cook for 1-2 minutes. Add the rice, chicken stock, pumpkin puree, thyme, nutmeg, cinnamon, ginger and allspice, and stir. Cover the Instant Pot and cook on the Manual setting for 10 minutes. Release the pressure, add the cream, stir well, and serve.

Nutrition:

- Calories: 263
- Fat: 5
- Fiber: 2
- Carbs: 37
- Protein: 6

Vegetables and Rice

Preparation time: 6 minutes
Cooking time: 15 minutes
Servings: 4

Ingredients:

- 2 cups basmati rice
- 1 cup frozen mixed vegetables
- 2 cups water
- ½ teaspoon canned green chilies, minced
- ½ teaspoon ginger, grated
- 3 garlic cloves, peeled and minced
- 2 tablespoons butter
- 1 cinnamon stick
- 1 tablespoon cumin seeds
- 2 bay leaves
- 3 whole cloves
- 5 black peppercorns
- 2 whole cardamoms
- 1 tablespoon sugar
- Salt, to taste

Directions:

Put the water into the Instant Pot. Add the rice, vegetables, chilies, grated ginger, garlic, cinnamon, cloves, butter, cumin seeds, bay leaves, cardamoms, peppercorns, salt, and sugar. Stir, cover, and cook on the Rice setting for 15 minutes. Release the pressure, remove the cinnamon stick, bay leaves, peppercorns, cloves, and cardamoms, divide among plates, and serve.

Nutrition:

- Calories: 340
- Fat: 6
- Fiber: 5.5
- Carbs: 40
- Protein: 14.2

Flavored Mashed Sweet Potatoes

Preparation time: 10 minutes
Cooking time: 9 minutes
Servings: 8

Ingredients:

- 2 garlic cloves
- 3 pounds sweet potatoes, peeled and chopped
- Salt and ground black pepper, to taste
- ½ teaspoon dried parsley
- ¼ teaspoon dried sage
- ½ teaspoon dried rosemary
- ½ teaspoon dried thyme
- 1½ cups water
- ¼ cup milk
- ½ cup Parmesan cheese, grated
- 2 tablespoon butter

Directions:

Put the potatoes and garlic in the steamer basket of the Instant Pot, add 1½ cups water to the Instant Pot, cover, and cook on the Manual setting for 10 minutes. Release the pressure, drain water, transfer the potatoes and garlic to a bowl and mix them using kitchen hand mixer. Add the butter, cheese, milk, salt, pepper, parsley, sage, rosemary, and thyme and blend everything well. Divide among plates, and serve.

Nutrition:

- Calories: 240
- Fat: 1
- Fiber: 8.2
- Carbs: 34
- Protein: 4.5

Tasty Saffron Risotto

Preparation time: 10 minutes
Cooking time: 10 minutes
Servings: 10

Ingredients:
- 2 tablespoons extra virgin olive oil
- ½ teaspoon saffron threads, crushed
- ½ cup onion, peeled and chopped
- 2 tablespoons hot milk
- 1½ cups Arborio rice
- 3½ cups vegetable stock
- Salt, to taste
- 1 tablespoon honey
- 1 cinnamon stick
- ⅓ cup almonds, chopped
- ⅓ cup dried currants

Directions:

In a bowl, mix the milk with the saffron, stir and set aside. Set the Instant Pot on Sauté mode, add the oil and heat it up. Add the onions, stir and cook for 5 minutes. Add the rice, stock, saffron and milk, honey, salt, almonds, cinnamon stick, and currants. Stir, cover the Instant Pot and cook on the Rice setting for 5 minutes. Release the pressure, fluff the rice a bit, discard the cinnamon stick, divide it among plates, and serve.

Nutrition:
- Calories: 260
- Fat: 7
- Fiber: 2
- Carbs: 41
- Sugar: 1.5
- Protein: 3.9

Cherry Farro

Preparation time: 10 minutes
Cooking time: 40 minutes
Servings: 6

Ingredients:
- 1 tablespoon apple cider vinegar
- 1 cup whole grain farro
- 1 teaspoon lemon juice
- Salt, to taste
- 3 cups water
- 1 tablespoon extra virgin olive oil
- ½ cup cherries, dried and chopped
- ¼ cup green onions, chopped
- 10 mint leaves, chopped
- 2 cups cherries, pitted and cut into halves

Directions:

Put the water into the Instant Pot, add the rinsed farro, stir, cover and cook on the Multigrain setting for 40 minutes. Release the pressure, drain the farro, transfer to a bowl and mix with the salt, oil, lemon juice, vinegar, dried cherries, fresh cherries, green onions, and mint. Stir well, divide among plates, and serve.

Nutrition:
- Calories: 160
- Fat: 1
- Fiber: 2
- Carbs: 12
- Protein: 4

Herbed Polenta

Preparation time: 15 minutes
Cooking time: 6 minutes
Servings: 6

Ingredients:
- 4 cups vegetable stock
- 2 tablespoons extra virgin olive oil
- 2 teaspoons garlic, minced
- ½ cup yellow onion, peeled and chopped
- ⅓ cup sundried tomatoes, chopped
- Salt, to taste
- 1 cup polenta
- 1 bay leaf
- 2 teaspoons fresh oregano, diced
- 3 tablespoons fresh basil, diced
- 1 teaspoon fresh rosemary, diced
- 2 tablespoons fresh parsley, diced

Directions:
Set the Instant Pot on Sauté mode, add the oil and heat it up. Add the onion, stir and cook for 1 minute. Add the garlic, stir again and cook for 1 minute. Add the stock, salt, tomatoes, bay leaf, rosemary, oregano, half of the basil, half of the parsley, and polenta. Without stirring, cover the Instant Pot, cook on the Porridge setting for 5 minutes and release pressure naturally for 10 minutes. Uncover the Instant Pot, discard the bay leaf, stir the polenta gently, add the rest of the parsley, basil and more salt, stir, divide among plates, and serve.

Nutrition:
- Calories: 150
- Fat: 1.6
- Fiber: 3.6
- Carbs: 35
- Protein: 3.7

Mexican Rice

Preparation time: 10 minutes
Cooking time: 4 minutes
Servings: 8

Ingredients:
- 1 cup long grain rice
- 1¼ cups vegetable stock
- ½ cup fresh cilantro, chopped
- ½ avocado, pitted, peeled and chopped
- Salt and ground black pepper, to taste
- ¼ cup green hot sauce

Directions:
Put the rice into the Instant Pot, add the stock, stir, cover and cook on the Rice setting for 4 minutes. Release the pressure naturally for 10 minutes, uncover the Instant Pot, fluff it with a fork and transfer to a bowl. In a food processor, mix the avocado with the hot sauce and cilantro and puree until smooth. Pour this over the rice, stir well, add salt and pepper, stir again, divide among plates, and serve.

Nutrition:
- Calories: 100
- Fat: 2
- Fiber: 1
- Carbs: 18
- Protein: 2

Cauliflower and Barley Risotto

Preparation time: 10 minutes
Cooking time: 1 hour
Servings: 4

Ingredients:

- 4 tablespoons extra virgin olive oil
- Salt and ground black pepper, to taste
- 1 cauliflower head, separated into florets
- ½ cup Parmesan cheese, grated
- 2 garlic cloves, peeled and minced
- 1 cup pearled barley
- 1 yellow onion, peeled and chopped
- 3 cups chicken stock
- 2 thyme sprigs
- 2 tablespoons fresh parsley, chopped
- 1 tablespoon butter

Directions:

Spread the cauliflower florets on a lined baking dish, add 3 tablespoons oil, salt and pepper, toss to coat, introduce in the oven at 425 degrees Fahrenheit and bake for 20 minutes, turning them every 10 minutes. Take cauliflower out of the oven, sprinkle with ¼ cup cheese and bake for 5 minutes. Set the Instant Pot on Sauté mode, add 1 tablespoon oil and heat it up. Add the onion, stir, and cook for 5 minutes. Add the garlic, stir, and cook for 1 minute. Add the stock, thyme, and barley, stir, cover the Instant Pot, and cook on the Manual setting for 25 minutes. Release the pressure, uncover, the Instant Pot, stir the barley, discard the thyme, add the butter, the rest of the cheese, cauliflower, salt, pepper, and parsley. Stir the risotto, divide among plates, and serve.

Nutrition:

- Calories: 350
- Fat: 16
- Fiber: 10
- Carbs: 25
- Protein: 14.6

Garlicky Potatoes

Preparation time: 10 minutes
Cooking time: 6 minutes
Servings: 4

Ingredients:

- 1 pound new potatoes, peeled and sliced thin
- 1 cup water
- Salt and ground black pepper, to taste
- ¼ teaspoon dried rosemary
- 1 tablespoon extra virgin olive oil
- 2 garlic cloves, peeled and minced

Directions:

Put the potatoes and the water in the steamer basket of the Instant Pot, cover and cook on the Manual setting for 4 minutes. In a heat-proof dish, mix the rosemary with oil and garlic, cover and microwave for 1 minute. Release the pressure from the Instant Pot, drain the potatoes and spread them on a lined baking sheet. Add the oil mix, salt and pepper, toss to coat, divide among plates, and serve.

Nutrition:

- Calories: 94
- Fat: 1
- Fiber: 2.2
- Carbs: 21
- Protein: 2.5

Lemon Parmesan and Peas Risotto

I

Preparation time: 10 minutes
Cooking time: 17 minutes
Servings: 6

Ingredients:
- 1½ cup rice
- 2 tablespoons butter
- 1 yellow onion, peeled and chopped
- 1 tablespoon extra virgin olive oil
- 2 tablespoons lemon juice
- 1 teaspoon lemon zest, grated
- 3½ cups chicken stock
- 2 tablespoons parsley, diced
- Salt and ground black pepper, to taste
- 1½ cup peas
- 2 tablespoons Parmesan cheese, finely grated

Directions:
Set the Instant Pot on Sauté mode, add 1 tablespoon butter and the oil and heat them up. Add the onions, stir and cook for 5 minutes. Add the rice, stir and cook for 3 more minutes. Add 3 cups stock and the lemon juice, stir, cover, and cook on the Rice setting for 5 minutes. Release the pressure, set the Instant Pot on Manual mode, add the peas and the rest of the stock, stir, and cook for 2 minutes. Add the cheese, parsley, the rest of the butter, lemon zest, salt, and pepper to taste and stir. Divide among plates, and serve.

Nutrition:
- Calories: 140
- Fat: 1.5
- Fiber: 1
- Carbs: 27
- Protein: 5

Spinach and Goat Cheese Risotto

Preparation time: 10 minutes
Cooking time: 10 minutes
Servings: 6

Ingredients:
- 2 garlic cloves, peeled and minced
- 2 tablespoons extra virgin olive oil
- ¾ cup yellow onion, chopped
- 1½ cups Arborio rice
- ½ cup white wine
- 12 ounces spinach, chopped
- 3½ cups hot vegetable stock
- Salt and ground black pepper, to taste
- 4 ounces goat cheese, soft and crumbled
- 2 tablespoons lemon juice
- ⅓ cup pecans, toasted and chopped

Directions:
Set the Instant Pot on Sauté mode, add the oil and heat it up. Add the garlic and onions, stir, and cook for 5 minutes. Add the rice, stir and cook for 1 minute. Add the wine, stir, and cook until it's absorbed. Add 3 cups stock, cover the Instant Pot and cook on the Rice setting for 4 minutes. Release the pressure, uncover the Instant Pot, add spinach, stir and cook on Manual mode for 3 minutes. Add the salt, pepper, the rest of the stock, lemon juice, and goat cheese and stir. Divide among plates, garnish with pecans, and serve.

Nutrition:
- Calories: 340
- Fat: 23
- Fiber: 4.5
- Carbs: 24
- Protein: 18.9

Rice and Artichokes

Preparation time: 10 minutes
Cooking time: 20 minutes
Servings: 4

Ingredients:

- 1 tablespoon extra virgin olive oil
- 5 ounces Arborio rice
- 2 garlic cloves, peeled and crushed
- 1¼ cups chicken broth
- 1 tablespoon white wine
- 6 ounces graham cracker crumbs
- 1¼ cups water
- 15 ounces canned artichoke hearts, chopped
- 16 ounces cream cheese
- 1 tablespoon grated Parmesan cheese
- 1½ tablespoons fresh thyme, chopped
- Salt and ground black pepper, to taste

Directions:

Set the Instant Pot on Sauté mode, add the oil, heat up, add the rice and cook for 2 minutes. Add the garlic, stir and cook for 1 minute. Transfer this to a heat-proof dish. Add the stock, crumbs, salt, pepper, and wine, stir and cover the dish with aluminum foil. Place the dish in the steamer basket of the Instant Pot, add the water, cover and cook on the Rice setting for 8 minutes. Release the pressure, take the dish out, uncover, add the cream cheese, Parmesan cheese, artichoke hearts, and thyme. Mix well, and serve.

Nutrition:

- Calories: 240
- Fat: 7.2
- Fiber: 5.1
- Carbs: 34
- Protein: 6

Potatoes Au Gratin

Preparation time: 10 minutes
Cooking time: 17 minutes
Servings: 6

Ingredients:

- 1 cup chicken stock
- ½ cup yellow onion, chopped
- 2 tablespoons butter
- 6 potatoes, peeled and sliced
- Salt and ground black pepper, to taste
- ½ cup sour cream
- 1 cup Monterey jack cheese, shredded

For the topping:
- 3 tablespoons melted butter
- 1 cup bread crumbs

Directions:

Set the Instant Pot on Sauté mode, add the butter, and melt it. Add the onion, stir and cook for 5 minutes. Add the stock, salt, and pepper, and put the steamer basket in the Instant Pot as well. Add the potatoes, cover the Instant Pot and cook on the Manual setting for 5 minutes. In a bowl, mix 3 tablespoons butter with bread crumbs and stir well. Release the pressure from the Instant Pot fast, take the steamer basket out, and transfer potatoes to a baking dish. Pour the cream and cheese into Instant Pot and stir. Add the potatoes and stir gently. Spread the bread crumbs mix all over, introduce under a preheated broiler, and broil for 7 minutes. Let it cool for a couple of minutes and serve.

Nutrition:

- Calories: 340
- Fat: 22
- Fiber: 2
- Carbs: 32
- Protein: 11

Mashed Squash

Preparation time: 10 minutes
Cooking time: 20 minutes
Servings: 4

Ingredients:

- ½ cup water
- 2 acorn squashes, cut into halves and seeded
- Salt and ground black pepper, to taste
- ¼ teaspoon baking soda
- 2 tablespoons butter
- ½ teaspoon fresh nutmeg, grated
- 2 tablespoons brown sugar

Directions:

Sprinkle the squash halves with salt, pepper, and baking soda and place them in the steamer basket of the Instant Pot. Add the water to the Instant Pot, cover and cook on the Manual setting for 20 minutes. Release the pressure, take the squash and set aside on a plate to cool down. Scrape the flesh from the squash and put in a bowl. Add the salt, pepper, butter, sugar, and nutmeg and mash everything with a potato masher. Stir well, and serve.

Nutrition:

- Calories: 140
- Fat: 1
- Fiber: 0.5
- Carbs: 10.5
- Protein: 1.7

Potato Casserole

Preparation time: 15 minutes
Cooking time: 10 minutes
Servings: 4

Ingredients:

- 3 pounds sweet potatoes, scrubbed
- 1 cup water
- ¼ cup coconut milk
- ⅓ cup brown sugar
- ½ teaspoon fresh nutmeg, ground
- 2 tablespoons coconut flour
- 1 teaspoon ground cinnamon
- ¼ teaspoon allspice
- Salt, to taste

For the topping:
- ½ cup almond flour

- ½ cup walnuts, soaked, drained, and ground
- ¼ cup pecans, soaked, drained, and ground
- ¼ cup shredded coconut
- 1 tablespoon chia seeds
- ¼ cup brown sugar
- Salt, to taste
- 1 teaspoon ground cinnamon
- 5 tablespoons salted butter

Directions:

Prick the potatoes with a fork, place them in the steamer basket of the Instant Pot, add the water to the Instant Pot, cover, and cook on the Manual setting for 20 minutes. In a bowl, mix the almond flour with pecans, walnuts, coconut, ¼ cup brown sugar, chia seeds, 1 teaspoon cinnamon, a pinch of salt, and the butter and stir everything. Release the pressure naturally from the Instant Pot, take the potatoes and peel them and add ½ cup water to the Instant Pot. Chop the potatoes and place them in a baking dish. Add the crumble mix, stir everything, spread evenly in the dish, cover, place in the steamer basket, cover the Instant Pot again and cook on the Manual setting for 10 minutes. Release the pressure, take the dish out of the Instant Pot, uncover, let it cool briefly, cut, and serve.

Nutrition:

- Calories: 150
- Fat: 9
- Fiber: 3
- Carbs: 25
- Sugar: 10
- Protein: 4

French Fries

Preparation time: 10 minutes
Cooking time: 10 minutes
Servings: 4

Ingredients:
- 8 medium potatoes, peeled, cut into medium matchsticks, and patted dry
- 1 cup water
- Salt, to taste
- ¼ teaspoon baking soda
- Oil for frying

Directions:
Put the water into the Instant Pot, add salt and the baking soda and stir. Put potatoes in the steamer basket and introduce it in the Instant Pot. Cover and cook on the Manual setting for 3 minutes. Release the pressure naturally, take the fries out of the Instant Pot and put them in a bowl. Heat up a pan with enough oil over medium-high heat, add the fries, spread them, and cook until they become golden. Transfer the fries to paper towels to drain excess grease and then put them in a bowl. Add salt, toss to coat, and serve.

Nutrition:
- Calories: 300
- Fat: 10
- Fiber: 3.7
- Carbs: 41
- Protein: 3.4

Green Beans and Mushrooms

Preparation time: 10 minutes
Cooking time: 6 minutes
Servings: 4

Ingredients:
- 1 pound fresh green beans, trimmed
- 1 small yellow onion, peeled and chopped
- 6 ounces bacon, chopped
- 1 garlic clove, peeled and minced
- 8 ounces mushrooms, sliced
- Salt and ground black pepper, to taste
- Balsamic vinegar

Directions:
Put the beans into the Instant Pot, add water to cover them, cover the Instant Pot and cook on the Manual setting for 3 minutes. Release the pressure naturally, drain the beans and set aside. Set the Instant Pot on Sauté mode, add the bacon and brown it for 1-2 minutes, stirring often. Add the garlic and onion, stir, and cook 2 minutes. Add the mushrooms, stir and cook until they are soft. Add the drained beans, salt, pepper and a splash of vinegar, stir, take off the heat, divide among plates, and serve.

Nutrition:
- Calories: 120
- Fat: 3.7
- Fiber: 3.3
- Carbs: 7.5
- Protein: 2.4

Easy Refried Beans

Preparation time: 10 minutes
Cooking time: 20 minutes
Servings: 4

Ingredients:

- 3 cups pinto beans, soaked for 4 hours and drained
- 1 yellow onion, peeled and cut into halves
- 1 jalapeño, chopped
- 2 tablespoons garlic, minced
- Salt and ground black pepper, to taste
- 9 cups vegetable stock
- 1/8 teaspoon cumin

Directions:

In the Instant Pot, mix the beans with salt, pepper, stock, onion, jalapeño, garlic, and cumin. Stir, cover and cook on the Bean/Chili setting for 20 minutes. Release the pressure naturally, discard the onion halves, strain beans, transfer them to your blender and reserve cooking liquid. Blend well, adding some of the liquid as needed, transfer to a bowl, and serve.

Nutrition:

- Calories: 100
- Fat: 2
- Fiber: 5
- Carbs: 15
- Protein: 6

Three Bean Medley

Preparation time: 10 minutes
Cooking time: 15 minutes
Servings: 4

Ingredients:

- 1 cup garbanzo beans, soaked overnight and drained
- 1 cup cranberry beans, soaked overnight and drained
- 1½ cups green beans
- 4 cups water
- 1 garlic clove, peeled and crushed
- 1 bay leaf
- 2 celery stalks, chopped
- 1 bunch parsley, chopped
- 1 small red onion, peeled and chopped
- 1 tablespoon sugar
- 5 tablespoons apple cider vinegar
- 4 tablespoons extra virgin olive oil
- Salt and ground black pepper, to taste

Directions:

Put the water into the Instant Pot. Add the bay leaf, garlic and garbanzo beans. Put the steamer basket into the pot as well and add the cranberry beans to it. Wrap the green beans in aluminum foil and also place in the steamer basket. Cover the Instant Pot and cook on the Bean/Chili setting for 15 minutes. Release the pressure naturally for 10 minutes, uncover the Instant Pot, drain beans, unwrap the green beans and put them all in a bowl. In another bowl, mix onion with vinegar and sugar, stir well and set aside for a few minutes. Add the onions to beans and toss to coat. Also add the celery, olive oil, salt, pepper to taste and parsley, toss to coat, divide among plates, and serve.

Nutrition:

- Calories: 200
- Fat: 1
- Fiber: 6
- Carbs: 45
- Protein: 4

Black Beans

Preparation time: 10 minutes
Cooking time: 5 minutes
Servings: 8

Ingredients:

- 1 cup black beans, soaked overnight, drained and rinsed
- 1 piece dried seaweed
- ⅔ cup water
- Salt, to taste
- 1 teaspoon coriander seeds
- 2 garlic cloves, peeled and minced
- ½ teaspoon cumin seeds

Directions:

In the Instant Pot, mix beans with seaweed, water, garlic, coriander, and cumin. Stir, cover the Instant Pot and cook on the Bean/Chili setting for 5 minutes. Release the pressure, discard seaweed and coriander seeds, divide beans among plates, season with salt, and serve.

Nutrition:

- Calories: 330
- Fat: 1
- Fiber: 16
- Carbs: 23
- Protein: 21

Pineapple and Cauliflower Rice

Preparation time: 10 minutes
Cooking time: 20 minutes
Servings: 6

Ingredients:

- 2 cups rice
- 4 cups water
- 1 cauliflower, separated into florets and chopped
- ½ pineapple, peeled and chopped
- Salt and ground black pepper, to taste
- 2 teaspoons extra virgin olive oil

Directions:

In the Instant Pot, mix rice with pineapple, cauliflower, water, oil, salt, and pepper, stir, cover and cook for 20 minutes on Manual mode. Release the pressure naturally for 10 minutes, uncover the Instant Pot, fluff with a fork, add more salt and pepper, divide among plates, and serve.

Nutrition:

- Calories: 100
- Fat: 2.7
- Fiber: 2.9
- Carbs: 12
- Protein: 4.9

Red Beans and Rice

Preparation time: 20 minutes
Cooking time: 25 minutes
Servings: 6

Ingredients:

- 1 pound red kidney beans, soaked overnight and drained
- Salt, to taste
- 1 teaspoon vegetable oil
- 1 pound smoked sausage, cut into wedges
- 1 yellow onion, peeled and chopped
- 1 celery stalk, chopped
- 4 garlic cloves, peeled and chopped
- 1 green bell pepper, seeded and chopped
- 1 teaspoon dried thyme
- 2 bay leaves
- 5 cups water
- Long grain rice already cooked
- 2 green onions, minced, for serving
- 2 tablespoons parsley, minced, for serving
- Hot sauce, for serving

Directions:

Set the Instant Pot on Sauté mode, add the oil and heat it up. Add the sausage, onion, bell pepper, celery, garlic, thyme, and salt, stir, and cook for 8 minutes. Add the beans, bay leaves, and the water, stir, cover the Instant Pot and cook on the Bean/Chili setting for 15 minutes. Release the pressure naturally for 20 minutes, discard the bay leaves, and put 2 cups of beans and some liquid into the blender. Pulse them well and return to pot. Divide the rice among plates, add the beans, sausage, and vegetables on top, sprinkle with green onions and parsley, and serve with hot sauce.

Nutrition:

- Calories: 160
- Fat: 3.8
- Fiber: 3.4
- Carbs: 24
- Protein: 4.6

Savory Stuffing

Preparation time: 10 minutes
Cooking time: 20 minutes
Servings: 4

Ingredients:

- 1½ cups water
- ½ cup butter
- 1¼ cup turkey stock
- 1 bread loaf, cubed and toasted
- 1 cup celery, chopped
- 1 yellow onion, peeled and chopped
- Salt and ground black pepper, to taste
- 1 teaspoon sage
- 1 teaspoon poultry seasoning

Directions:

Set the Instant Pot on Sauté mode, add the butter, and melt it. Add the stock, onion, celery, salt, pepper, sage, and poultry seasoning and stir well. Add the bread cubes, stir, and cook for 1 minute. Transfer this to a Bundt pan and cover it with aluminum foil. Clean the Instant Pot, add the water and place the pan in the steamer basket, cover the Instant Pot and cook on the Manual setting for 15 minutes. Release the pressure, uncover the pan, place it in the oven at 350°F, and bake for 5 minutes. Serve hot.

Nutrition:

- Calories: 230
- Fat: 3.4
- Fiber: 3.2
- Carbs: 23
- Protein: 11

Parsnips and Onions

Preparation time: 10 minutes
Cooking time: 30 minutes
Servings: 4

Ingredients:
- 2½ pounds parsnips, peeled and chopped
- 4 tablespoons vegetable shortening
- Salt and ground black pepper, to taste
- 1½ cups beef stock
- 1 thyme sprig
- 1 yellow onion, peeled and sliced thin

Directions:
Set the Instant Pot on Sauté mode, add 3 tablespoons of the shortening and heat it up. Add the parsnips, stir and cook for 15 minutes. Add the stock and thyme, stir, cover, and cook on the Manual setting for 3 minutes. Release the pressure, transfer the parsnips mixture to a blender, add salt and pepper to taste, and pulse. Set the Instant Pot on Sauté mode again, add the rest of the shortening and heat it up. Add the onion, stir, and cook for 10 minutes. Transfer the parsnips to plates, top with sautéed onions, and serve.

Nutrition:
- Calories: 130
- Fat: 2
- Fiber: 3
- Carbs: 6.7
- Protein: 10.1

Cauliflower Mash

Preparation time: 10 minutes
Cooking time: 6 minutes
Servings: 4

Ingredients:
- 1 cauliflower, separated into florets
- Salt and ground black pepper, to taste
- 1½ cups water
- ½ teaspoon turmeric
- 1 tablespoon butter
- 3 chives, diced

Directions:
Put the water into the Instant Pot, place the cauliflower in the steamer basket, cover the Instant Pot and cook on the Steam setting for 6 minutes. Release the pressure naturally for 2 minutes and then release the rest quickly. Transfer cauliflower to a bowl and mash it with a potato masher. Add the salt, pepper, butter, and turmeric, stir, transfer to a blender, and pulse well. Serve with chives sprinkled on top.

Nutrition:
- Calories: 70
- Fat: 5
- Fiber: 2
- Carbs: 5
- Protein: 2

Mashed Turnips

Preparation time: 10 minutes
Cooking time: 5 minutes
Servings: 4

Ingredients:

- 4 turnips, peeled and chopped
- Salt and ground black pepper, to taste
- 1 yellow onion, peeled and chopped
- ¼ cup sour cream
- ½ cup chicken stock

Directions:

In the Instant Pot, mix the turnips with the stock and onion. Stir, cover, and cook on the Manual setting for 5 minutes. Release the pressure naturally, drain the turnips, and transfer them to a bowl. Puree them using a food processor and add salt and pepper to taste and sour cream. Blend again, and serve.

Nutrition:

- Calories: 70
- Fat: 1
- Fiber: 4.6
- Carbs: 11.2
- Protein: 1.6

Sweet Carrot Puree

Preparation time: 5 minutes
Cooking time: 5 minutes
Servings: 4

Ingredients:

- 1½ pounds carrots, peeled and chopped
- 1 tablespoon butter, softened
- Salt, to taste
- 1 cup water
- 1 tablespoon honey
- 1 teaspoon brown sugar

Directions:

Put carrots into the Instant Pot, add the water, cover and cook on the Manual setting for 4 minutes. Release the pressure naturally, drain the carrots, and place them in a bowl. Puree them using an immersion blender, add the butter, salt, and honey. Blend again, add sugar on top, and serve.

Nutrition:

- Calories: 50
- Fat: 1
- Fiber: 3
- Carbs: 11
- Protein: 1

Butternut and Apple Mash

Preparation time: 10 minutes
Cooking time: 15 minutes
Servings: 4

Ingredients:
- 1 cup water
- 1 butternut squash, peeled and cut into medium chunks
- 2 apples, cored and sliced
- 2 tablespoons butter, browned
- 1 yellow onion, thinly sliced
- ½ teaspoon apple pie spice
- Salt, to taste

Directions:
Put the squash, onion, and apple pieces in the steamer basket of the Instant Pot, add the water to the Instant Pot, cover, and cook on the Manual setting for 8 minutes. Release the pressure quickly and transfer the squash, onion, and apple to a bowl. Mash everything using a potato masher, add the salt, apple pie spice, and brown butter, stir well, and serve warm.

Nutrition:
- Calories: 140
- Fat: 2.3
- Fiber: 6.5
- Carbs: 24
- Protein: 2.5

Glazed Carrots

Preparation time: 10 minutes
Cooking time; 6 minutes
Servings: 4

Ingredients:
- ½ cup water
- 1 pound baby carrots
- ½ cup honey
- 1 teaspoon dried thyme
- 1 teaspoon dried dill
- Salt, to taste
- 2 tablespoons butter

Directions:
Put the water into the Instant Pot, place the carrots in the steamer basket, cover, and cook on the Manual setting for 3 minutes. Release the pressure, drain the carrots and put them in a bowl. Set the Instant Pot on Sauté mode, add the butter and melt it. Add the dill, thyme, honey, and salt and stir well. Add the carrots, toss to coat, cook for 1 minute, transfer them to plates, and serve.

Nutrition:
- Calories: 200
- Fat: 11
- Fiber: 4
- Carbs: 12
- Protein: 1.4

Sweet Brussels Sprouts

Preparation time: 10 minutes
Cooking time: 4 minutes
Servings: 8

Ingredients:
- 2 pounds Brussels sprouts
- Salt and ground black pepper, to taste
- ¼ cup orange juice
- 1 teaspoon orange zest, grated
- 1 tablespoon butter
- 2 tablespoons maple syrup

Directions:
In the Instant Pot, mix the Brussels sprouts with the orange juice, orange zest, butter, maple syrup, salt, and pepper, stir, cover and cook on the Manual setting for 4 minutes. Release the pressure naturally, transfer sprouts mixture to plates, and serve them.

Nutrition:
- Calories: 65
- Fat: 2
- Fiber: 3
- Carbs: 12
- Protein: 3

Lemony Broccoli

Preparation time: 5 minutes
Cooking time: 15 minutes
Servings: 6

Ingredients:
- 1 head of broccoli, separated into florets
- 1 cup water
- 5 lemon slices
- Salt and ground black pepper, to taste

Directions:
Pour the water into the Instant Pot. Season the broccoli with salt and pepper to taste and add it to the Instant Pot. Add the lemon slices and stir gently. Cover the Instant Pot and cook on the Steam setting for 15 minutes. Release the pressure, divide broccoli among plates and serve.

Nutrition:
- Calories: 55
- Fat: 0.5
- Fiber: 5
- Carbs: 11
- Protein: 3.4

Garlic and Parmesan Asparagus

Preparation time: 5 minutes
Cooking time: 8 minutes
Servings: 4

Ingredients:

- 3 garlic cloves, peeled and minced
- 1 bunch asparagus, trimmed
- 1 cup water
- 3 tablespoons butter
- 3 tablespoons Parmesan cheese, grated

Directions:

Put the water into the Instant Pot. Place the asparagus on aluminum foil, add the garlic and butter and seal the edges of the foil. Place this into the pot, cover it and cook on the Manual setting for 8 minutes. Release the pressure, arrange the asparagus on plates, sprinkle with cheese, and serve.

Nutrition:

- Calories: 70
- Fat: 5.2
- Fiber: 1.8
- Carbs: 3.8
- Protein: 4

Poached Fennel

Preparation time: 5 minutes
Cooking time: 6 minutes
Servings: 3

Ingredients:

- 2 big fennel bulbs, sliced
- 2 tablespoons butter
- 1 tablespoon white flour
- 2 cups milk
- Ground nutmeg
- Salt, to taste

Directions:

Set the Instant Pot on Sauté mode, add the butter, and melt it. Add the fennel slices, stir, and cook until slightly browned. Add the flour, salt, pepper, nutmeg, and milk, stir, cover, and cook on Manual for 6 minutes. Release the pressure, transfer the fennel to plates, and serve.

Nutrition:

- Calories: 140
- Fat: 5
- Fiber: 4.7
- Carbs: 12
- Protein: 4.4

Drunken Peas

Preparation time: 10 minutes
Cooking time: 7 minutes
Servings: 4

Ingredients:

- 4 ounces smoked pancetta, chopped
- 1 pound fresh peas
- 1 green onion, sliced
- 1 tablespoon fresh mint, chopped
- ¼ cup beer
- 1 tablespoon butter
- Salt and ground black pepper, to taste
- 2 cups water

Directions:

Put the water into the Instant Pot, place the steamer basket inside, and set aside. In a heat-proof pan, mix the pancetta with half of the onion and spread on the bottom. Heat this up on the stove over medium-high heat for 3 minutes, add the beer, peas, and salt, stir, and take off the heat. Cover this pan with some aluminum foil, place in the steamer basket, cover the Instant Pot and cook on the Manual setting for 1 minute. Release the pressure, uncover the pan, add the salt, pepper, mint, and butter, stir, divide among plates, and serve with the rest of the onions sprinkled on top.

Nutrition:

- Calories: 134
- Fat: 2
- Fiber: 2.5
- Carbs: 10
- Protein: 4.3

Artichokes

Preparation time: 10 minutes
Cooking time: 25 minutes
Servings: 4

Ingredients:

- 1 cup water
- 2 medium artichokes, trimmed
- 1 lemon wedges
- Salt, to taste

Directions:

Rub the artichokes with the lemon wedges, place them in the steamer basket of the Instant Pot, add the water to the Instant Pot, cover, and cook on the Manual setting for 20 minutes. Release the pressure for 10 minutes, divide the artichokes among plates, add salt on top, and serve.

Nutrition:

- Calories: 78
- Fat: 0.4
- Fiber: 3
- Carbs: 2
- Protein: 4

Harvest Vegetables

Preparation time: 10 minutes
Cooking time: 6 minutes
Servings: 4

Ingredients:
- 2 yellow bell peppers, seeded and sliced thin
- 1 green bell pepper, seeded and sliced thin
- 2 red bell peppers, seeded and sliced, thin
- 2 tomatoes, cored and chopped
- 2 garlic cloves, peeled and minced
- 1 red onion, peeled and sliced thin
- Salt and ground black pepper, to taste
- 1 bunch parsley, diced
- Extra virgin olive oil

Directions:
Set the Instant Pot on Sauté mode, add a drizzle of oil, and heat it up. Add the onions, stir, and cook for 3 minutes. Add the red, yellow and green peppers, stir, and cook for 5 minutes. Add the tomatoes, salt and pepper, stir, cover and cook on the Manual setting for 6 minutes. Release the pressure, uncover the Instant Pot, transfer the peppers and tomatoes to a bowl, add more salt and pepper with the garlic, parsley, and a drizzle of oil. Toss to coat, and serve.

Nutrition:
- Calories: 146
- Fat: 2.2
- Fiber: 8.1
- Carbs: 28.1
- Protein: 4.5

Eggplant

Preparation time: 40 minutes
Cooking time: 13 minutes
Servings: 4

Ingredients:
- 2 eggplants, cubed
- Salt and ground black pepper, to taste
- 2 tablespoons extra virgin olive oil
- 1 garlic clove, peeled and crushed
- Red pepper flakes
- 1 bunch oregano, chopped
- ½ cup water
- 2 anchovies, chopped

Directions:
Sprinkle the eggplant pieces with salt, place them in a strainer, press them with a plate, set aside for 30 minutes, and then drain them. Set the Instant Pot on Sauté mode, add the oil and the garlic and heat it up. Add the anchovies, oregano, and a pinch of pepper flakes, stir and cook for 5 minutes. Discard the garlic, add the eggplant, salt and pepper, toss to coat, and cook for 5 minutes. Add the water, stir, cover the Instant Pot and cook on the Manual setting for 3 minutes. Release the pressure, transfer the eggplant mixture to plates, and serve.

Nutrition:
- Calories: 130
- Fat: 5
- Fiber: 10
- Carbs: 12
- Protein: 15

Calamari and Tomatoes

Preparation time: 10 minutes
Cooking time: 32 minutes
Servings: 4

Ingredients:

- 1½ pounds calamari, washed, tentacles separated, and cut into strips
- Salt and ground black pepper, to taste
- 14 ounces canned tomatoes, chopped
- 1 bunch parsley, chopped
- 1 garlic clove, peeled and crushed
- ½ cup white wine
- 1 cup water
- 2 anchovies
- Juice of 1 lemon
- 2 tablespoons extra virgin olive oil
- Red pepper flakes

Directions:

Set the Instant Pot on Sauté mode, add oil, pepper flakes, garlic and anchovies, stir, and cook for 3 minutes. Add the calamari, stir, and cook for 5 minutes. Add the wine, stir, and cook 3 minutes. Add tomatoes, 1 cup water, half of the parsley, salt, and pepper. Stir, cover the Instant Pot and cook on the Manual setting for 20 minutes. Release the pressure, add the rest of the parsley, lemon juice, salt, and pepper, stir, divide among plates, and serve.

Nutrition:

- Calories: 230
- Fat: 6.5
- Fiber: 1.2
- Carbs: 11
- Protein: 24

Cauliflower, Broccoli, and Citrus

Preparation time: 10 minutes
Cooking time: 6 minutes
Servings: 4

Ingredients:

- 1 cauliflower, florets separated
- 1 pound broccoli, florets separated
- 1 romanesco cauliflower, florets separated
- 2 oranges, peeled and sliced
- Zest from 1 orange
- Juice from 1 orange
- Red pepper flakes
- 4 anchovies
- 1 tablespoon capers, chopped
- Salt and ground black pepper, to taste
- 4 tablespoons extra virgin olive oil
- 1 cup water

Directions:

In a bowl, mix the orange zest with orange juice, pepper flakes, anchovies, capers, salt, pepper, and olive oil, stir well and set the dish aside. Place the cauliflower and broccoli in the steamer basket of you Instant Pot, add 1 cup water to the Instant Pot, cover and cook on Steam mode for 6 minutes. Release the pressure, uncover the Instant Pot, transfer florets to a bowl and mix with orange slices. Add the orange vinaigrette, toss to coat, and divide among plates and serve.

Nutrition:

- Calories: 260
- Fat: 2.9
- Fiber: 6.5
- Carbs: 33
- Protein: 4.2

Beets and Garlic

Preparation time: 10 minutes
Cooking time: 15 minutes
Servings: 4

Ingredients:
- 3 beets, greens cut off and washed
- Water to cover
- 1 tablespoon extra virgin olive oil
- Salt, to taste
- 2 garlic cloves, peeled and minced
- 1 teaspoon lemon juice

Directions:

Put beets into the Instant Pot, add enough water to cover, add salt, cover the Instant Pot, and cook on the Manual setting for 15 minutes. Release the pressure naturally for 10 minutes, strain the beets, peel them, and chop them. Heat up a pan with the oil over medium-high heat, add the beets, stir, and cook for 3 minutes. Add the garlic, lemon juice, and salt, stir, take off heat, divide among plates, and serve.

Nutrition:
- Calories: 70
- Fat: 1
- Fiber: 3.8
- Carbs: 13
- Protein: 2.2

Fava Bean Sauté

Preparation time: 10 minutes
Cooking time: 7 minutes
Servings: 4

Ingredients:
- 3 pounds fava beans, shelled
- 1 teaspoon extra virgin olive oil
- Salt and ground black pepper, to taste
- 4 ounces bacon, chopped
- ½ cup white wine
- 3 parsley sprigs, chopped
- ¾ cup water

Directions:

Set the Instant Pot on Sauté mode, add the oil and heat up. Add the bacon, stir, and cook until it browns. Add the wine, stir and cook for 2 minutes. Add the water and fava beans, stir, cover, and cook on the Bean/Chili setting for 7 minutes. Release pressure, transfer the beans to plates, add the parsley, salt and pepper, stir, and serve.

Nutrition:
- Calories: 140
- Fat: 3
- Fiber: 1
- Carbs: 23
- Protein: 13

Green Beans

Preparation time: 10 minutes
Cooking time: 5 minutes
Servings: 4

Ingredients:

- 2 cups tomatoes, cored and chopped
- 1 tablespoon extra virgin olive oil
- 1 garlic clove, peeled and crushed
- 1 pound green beans, trimmed
- 1 teaspoon extra virgin olive oil
- Salt, to taste
- ½ cup basil leaves, chopped

Directions:

Set the Instant Pot on Sauté mode, add 1 tablespoon of oil and heat it up. Add the garlic, stir, and cook for 1 minute. Add the tomatoes, stir, and cook for 1 minute. Place the green beans in the steamer basket and place it in the Instant Pot. Add the salt, cover the Instant Pot and cook on the Manual setting for 5 minutes. Release the pressure, transfer the green beans from the basket into the Instant Pot, and toss to coat. Transfer to plates, sprinkle with the basil, and drizzle 1 teaspoon oil on them and serve.

Nutrition:

- Calories: 55
- Fat: 3.2
- Fiber: 2.6
- Carbs: 1.6
- Protein: 1.6

Savory Bok Choy

Preparation time: 10 minutes
Cooking time: 10 minutes
Servings: 4

Ingredients:

- 5 bok choy bunches, ends cut off
- 5 cups water
- 2 garlic cloves, peeled and minced
- 1 teaspoon ginger, grated
- 1 tablespoon coconut oil
- Salt, to taste

Directions:

Put the bok choy into the Instant Pot, add the water, cover the Instant Pot and cook on the Manual setting for 7 minutes. Release the pressure, drain the bok choy, chop it, and put them in a bowl. Heat up a pan with the oil over medium heat, add the bok choy, stir, and cook for 3 minutes. Add more salt, garlic, and ginger, stir, and cook for 2 minutes. Divide among plates, and serve.

Nutrition:

- Calories: 60
- Fat: 0.4
- Fiber: 1.3
- Carbs: 6.5
- Protein: 2.4

Israeli Couscous

Preparation time: 10 minutes
Cooking time: 5 minutes
Servings: 10
Ingredients:

- 16 ounces harvest grains blend
- Salt and ground black pepper, to taste
- 2½ cups chicken stock
- 2 tablespoons butter
- Parsley leaves, chopped, for serving

Directions:

Set the Instant Pot on Sauté mode, add the butter, and melt it. Add the grains and stock and stir. Cover the Instant Pot and cook on the Multigrain setting for 5 minutes. Release the pressure, fluff the couscous with a fork, season with salt and pepper, divide among plates, sprinkle parsley on top, and serve.

Nutrition:

- Calories: 190
- Fat: 1
- Fiber: 2
- Carbs: 34
- Protein: 6

Red Cabbage

Preparation time: 10 minutes
Cooking time: 10 minutes
Servings: 4

Ingredients:

- 4 garlic cloves, peeled and minced
- ½ cup yellow onion, peeled and chopped
- 1 tablespoon vegetable oil
- 6 cups red cabbage, chopped
- 1 cup water
- 1 tablespoon apple cider vinegar
- 1 cup applesauce
- Salt and ground black pepper, to taste

Directions:

Set the Instant Pot on Sauté mode, add the oil and heat it up. Add the onions, stir, and cook for 4 minutes. Add the garlic, stir, and cook for 1 minute. Add the cabbage, water, applesauce, vinegar, salt, and pepper, stir, cover, and cook on the Manual setting for 10 minutes. Release the pressure, uncover the Instant Pot, stir the cabbage, add more vinegar, salt, and pepper, if needed, divide among plates, and serve.

Nutrition:

- Calories: 160
- Fat: 12
- Fiber: 2.2
- Crabs 10.2
- Protein: 5.6

Instant Pot Poultry Recipes

Lemongrass Chicken

Preparation time: 10 minutes
Cooking time: 20 minutes
Servings: 5

Ingredients:
- 1 bunch lemongrass, bottom removed and trimmed
- 1-inch piece ginger root, peeled and chopped
- 4 garlic cloves, peeled and crushed
- 2 tablespoons fish sauce
- 3 tablespoons coconut aminos
- 1 teaspoon Chinese five spice powder
- 10 chicken drumsticks
- 1 cup coconut milk
- Salt and ground black pepper, to taste
- 1 teaspoon butter
- ¼ cup cilantro, diced
- 1 yellow onion, peeled and chopped
- 1 tablespoon lime juice

Directions:

In a food processor, mix the lemongrass with the ginger, garlic, aminos, fish sauce, and five spice powder, and pulse well. Add the coconut milk and pulse again. Set the Instant Pot on Sauté mode, add the butter and melt it. Add the onion, stir, and cook for 5 minutes. Add the chicken, salt, and pepper, stir, and cook for 1 minute. Add the coconut milk and lemongrass mix, stir, cover, set on Poultry mode, and cook for 15 minutes. Release the pressure, uncover, add more salt and pepper and lime juice, stir, divide among plates, and serve with cilantro sprinkled on top.

Nutrition:
- Calories: 400
- Fat: 18
- Fiber: 2
- Carbs: 6
- Protein: 20

Salsa Chicken

Preparation time: 10 minutes
Cooking time: 25 minutes
Servings: 5

Ingredients:
- 1 pound chicken breast, skinless and boneless
- ¾ teaspoon cumin
- Salt and ground black pepper, to taste
- Dried oregano
- 1 cup chunky salsa

Directions:

Season the chicken with salt and pepper to taste and add it to the Instant Pot. Add the oregano, cumin, and the salsa, stir, cover, set the Instant Pot on Poultry mode and cook for 25 minutes. Release the pressure, transfer the chicken and salsa to a bowl, shred meat with a fork, and serve with some tortillas on the side.

Nutrition:
- Calories: 125
- Fat: 3
- Fiber: 1
- Carbs: 3
- Protein: 22

Chicken and Potatoes

Preparation time: 15 minutes
Cooking time: 15 minutes
Servings: 4

Ingredients:
- 2 tablespoons extra virgin olive oil
- 2 pounds chicken thighs, skinless and boneless
- ¾ cup chicken stock
- ¼ cup lemon juice
- 2 pounds red potatoes, peeled, and cut into quarters
- 3 tablespoons Dijon mustard
- 2 tablespoons Italian seasoning
- Salt and ground black pepper, to taste

Directions:
Set the Instant Pot on Sauté mode, add the oil, and heat it up. Add the chicken thighs, salt, and pepper, stir, and brown for 2 minutes. In a bowl, mix the stock with mustard, Italian seasoning, and lemon juice, and stir well. Pour this over the chicken, add the potatoes, stir, cover the Instant Pot and cook on the Poultry setting for 15 minutes. Release the pressure, uncover the Instant Pot, stir the chicken, divide among plates, and serve.

Nutrition:
- Calories: 190
- Fat: 6
- Fiber: 3.3
- Carbs: 23
- Protein: 18

Chicken Sandwiches

Preparation time: 10 minutes
Cooking time: 15 minutes
Servings: 8

Ingredients:
- 6 chicken breasts, skinless and boneless
- 12 ounces orange juice
- 2 tablespoons lemon juice
- 15 ounces canned peaches with juice
- 1 teaspoon soy sauce
- 20 ounces canned pineapple with juice, chopped
- 1 tablespoon cornstarch
- ¼ cup brown sugar
- 8 hamburger buns
- 8 grilled pineapple slices, for serving

Directions:
In a bowl, mix the orange juice with the soy sauce, lemon juice, canned pineapple, peaches, and sugar and stir well. Pour half of this mixture into the Instant Pot, add the chicken and pour the rest of the sauce over meat. Cover the Instant Pot and cook on the Poultry setting for 12 minutes. Release the pressure, take out the chicken and put it on a cutting board. Shred the meat and set the dish aside. In a bowl, mix the cornstarch with 1 tablespoon cooking juice and stir well. Transfer the sauce to a pot, add the cornstarch mix and chicken, stir, and cook for a few minutes. Divide this chicken mix onto hamburger buns, top with grilled pineapple pieces, and serve.

Nutrition:
- Calories: 240
- Fat: 4.6
- Fiber: 4
- Carbs: 21
- Protein: 14

Moroccan Chicken

Preparation time: 10 minutes
Cooking time: 25 minutes
Servings: 4

Ingredients:

- 6 chicken thighs
- 2 tablespoons extra virgin olive oil
- 10 cardamom pods
- 2 bay leaves
- ½ teaspoon coriander
- 1 teaspoon cloves
- ½ teaspoon cumin
- ½ teaspoon ground ginger
- ½ teaspoon turmeric
- ½ teaspoon ground cinnamon
- 1 teaspoon paprika
- 2 yellow onions, peeled and chopped
- 2 tablespoons tomato paste
- 5 garlic cloves, peeled and chopped
- ¼ cup white wine
- 1 cup green olives
- 1 cup chicken stock
- ¼ cup dried cranberries
- Juice of 1 lemon
- ½ cup parsley, diced

Directions:

In a bowl, mix the bay leaf with the cardamom, cloves, coriander, ginger, cumin, cinnamon, turmeric, and paprika and stir. Set the Instant Pot on Sauté mode, add the oil and heat up. Add the chicken thighs, brown for a few minutes, and transfer to a plate. Add the onion to the Instant Pot, stir, and cook for 4 minutes. Add the garlic, stir and cook for 1 minute. Add the wine, tomato paste, spices from the bowl, stock, and chicken. Stir, cover and cook on the Poultry setting for 15 minutes. Release the pressure, discard bay leaf, cardamom, and cloves, add the olives, cranberries, lemon juice, and parsley, stir, divide the chicken mixture among plates, and serve.

Nutrition:

- Calories: 381
- Fat: 10.2
- Fiber: 7.8
- Carbs: 4
- Fiber: 32

Cacciatore Chicken

Preparation time: 10 minutes
Cooking time: 15 minutes
Servings: 4

Ingredients:

- 1 cup chicken stock
- Salt, to taste
- 8 chicken drumsticks
- 1 bay leaf
- 1 teaspoon garlic powder
- 1 yellow onion, peeled chopped
- 28 ounces canned crushed tomatoes
- 1 teaspoon dried oregano
- ½ cup black olives, pitted and sliced

Directions:

Set the Instant Pot on Sauté mode, add the stock, bay leaf, and salt and stir. Add the chicken, garlic powder, onion, oregano, and crushed tomatoes, stir, cover the Instant Pot and cook on the Poultry setting for 15 minutes. Release the pressure naturally, uncover the Instant Pot, discard the bay leaf, divide the cacciatore chicken among plates, drizzle cooking liquid on top, sprinkle with the olives, and serve.

Nutrition:

- Calories: 210
- Fat: 2.9
- Fiber: 2.4
- Carbs: 9.5
- Protein: 25.9

Honey Barbecue Chicken Wings

Preparation time: 10 minutes
Cooking time: 25 minutes
Servings: 4

Ingredients:

- 2 pounds chicken wings
- Salt and ground black pepper, to taste
- ¾ cup honey barbecue sauce
- Cayenne pepper
- ½ cup apple juice
- 1 teaspoon red pepper flakes
- 2 teaspoons paprika
- ½ cup water
- ½ teaspoon dried basil
- ½ cup brown sugar

Directions:

Put the chicken wings into the Instant Pot. Add the barbecue sauce, apple juice, salt, pepper, red pepper, paprika, basil, sugar, and water. Stir, cover, and cook on the Poultry setting for 10 minutes. Release the pressure, uncover the Instant Pot, transfer chicken to a baking sheet, add the sauce all over, place under a preheated broiler, broil for 7 minutes, turn the chicken wings, broil for 7 minutes, divide among plates, and serve.

Nutrition:

- Calories: 147.5
- Fat: 2.2
- Fiber: 1
- Carbs: 8
- Protein: 21.8

Sweet and Tangy Chicken

Preparation time: 10 minutes
Cooking time: 10 minutes
Servings: 4

Ingredients:

- 2 pounds chicken thighs, boneless and skinless
- ½ cup fish sauce
- 1 cup lime juice
- 2 tablespoons coconut nectar
- ¼ cup extra virgin olive oil
- 1 teaspoon ginger, grated
- 2 teaspoons cilantro, diced
- 1 teaspoon fresh mint, chopped

Directions:

Put chicken thighs into the Instant Pot. In a bowl, mix the lime juice with the fish sauce, olive oil, coconut nectar, ginger, mint, and cilantro and whisk well. Pour this over the chicken, cover the Instant Pot and cook on the Poultry setting for 10 minutes. Release the pressure, divide the chicken among plates, and serve.

Nutrition:

- Calories: 300
- Fat: 5
- Fiber: 4
- Carbs: 23
- Protein: 32

Turkey Chili

Preparation time: 10 minutes
Cooking time: 10 minutes
Servings: 4

Ingredients:

- 1 pound turkey meat, ground
- Salt and ground black pepper, to taste
- 5 ounces water
- 15 ounces chickpeas, already cooked
- 1 yellow onion, peeled and chopped
- 1 yellow bell pepper, seeded and chopped
- 3 garlic cloves, peeled and chopped
- 2½ tablespoons chili powder
- 1½ teaspoons cumin
- Cayenne pepper
- 12 ounces vegetable stock

Directions:

Put the turkey meat into the Instant Pot. Add the water, stir, cover and cook on the Poultry setting for 5 minutes. Release the pressure, uncover the Instant Pot and add the chickpeas, bell pepper, onion, garlic, chili powder, cumin, salt, pepper, cayenne pepper, and stock. Stir, cover the Instant Pot, and cook on the Bean/Chili setting for 5 minutes. Release the pressure for 10 minutes, uncover the Instant Pot again, stir the chili, divide it among plates, and serve.

Nutrition:

- Calories: 224
- Fat: 7.7
- Fiber: 6.1
- Carbs: 18
- Protein: 19.7

Chicken Romano

Preparation time: 10 minutes
Cooking time: 15 minutes
Servings: 4

Ingredients:

- 6 chicken thighs, boneless and skinless and cut into medium chunks
- Salt and ground black pepper, to taste
- ½ cup white flour
- 2 tablespoons vegetable oil
- 10 ounces tomato sauce
- 1 teaspoon white wine vinegar
- 4 ounces mushrooms, sliced
- 1 tablespoon sugar
- 1 tablespoon dried oregano
- 1 teaspoon garlic, minced
- 1 teaspoon dried basil
- 1 teaspoon chicken bouillon granules
- 1 yellow onion, peeled and chopped
- 1 cup Romano cheese, grated

Directions:

Set the Instant Pot on Sauté mode, add the oil and heat it up. Add the chicken pieces, stir, and brown them for 2 minutes. Add the onion and garlic, stir, and cook for 3 minutes. Add the salt, pepper, flour, and stir well. Add the tomato sauce, vinegar, mushrooms, sugar, oregano, basil and bouillon granules, stir, cover, and cook on the Poultry setting for 10 minutes. Release the pressure for 10 minutes, uncover the Instant Pot, add the cheese, stir, divide among plates, and serve.

Nutrition:

- Calories: 450
- Fat: 11
- Fiber: 1
- Carbs: 24.2
- Protein: 61.2

Filipino Chicken

Preparation time: 10 minutes
Cooking time: 15 minutes
Servings: 4

Ingredients:

- 5 pounds chicken thighs
- Salt and ground black pepper, to taste
- ½ cup white vinegar
- 1 teaspoon black peppercorns, crushed
- 4 garlic cloves, minced
- 3 bay leaves
- ½ cup soy sauce

Directions:

Set the Instant Pot on Poultry mode, add the chicken, vinegar, soy sauce, salt, pepper, garlic, peppercorns, and bay leaves, stir, cover, and cook for 15 minutes. Release the pressure for 10 minutes, uncover the Instant Pot, discard the bay leaves, stir, divide the chicken between plates, and serve.

Nutrition:

- Calories: 430
- Fat: 19.2
- Fiber: 1
- Carbs: 2.4
- Protein: 76

Chicken in Tomatillo Sauce

Preparation time: 10 minutes
Cooking time: 15 minutes
Servings: 6

Ingredients:

- 1 pound chicken thighs, skinless and boneless
- 2 tablespoons extra virgin olive oil
- 1 yellow onion, peeled and sliced thinly
- 1 garlic clove, peeled and crushed
- 4 ounces canned chopped green chilies
- ½ cup cilantro, diced
- Salt and ground black pepper, to taste
- 15 ounces canned tomatillos, chopped
- 5 ounces canned garbanzo beans, drained
- 15 ounces rice, already cooked
- 5 ounces tomatoes, cored and chopped
- 15 ounces cheddar cheese, grated
- 4 ounces black olives, pitted and chopped

Directions:

Set the Instant Pot on Sauté mode, add the oil, and heat it up. Add the onions, stir, and cook for 5 minutes. Add the garlic, stir, and cook for 15 seconds. Add the chicken, chilies, salt, pepper, cilantro, and tomatillos, stir, cover the Instant Pot, and cook on Poultry mode for 8 minutes. Release the pressure, uncover the Instant Pot, take the chicken out and shred it. Return the chicken to pot, add rice, beans, set the Instant Pot on Sauté mode, and cook for 1 minute. Add the cheese, tomatoes, and olives, stir, cook for 2 minutes, divide among plates, and serve.

Nutrition:

- Calories: 245
- Fat: 11.4
- Fiber: 1.3
- Carbs: 14.2
- Protein: 20

Braised Duck and Potatoes

Preparation time: 10 minutes
Cooking time: 20 minutes
Servings: 4

Ingredients:

- 2 duck breasts, boneless, skinless, and cut into small chunks
- Ground black pepper, to taste
- 1 potato, cut into cubes
- 1-inch ginger root, peeled and sliced
- 4 garlic cloves, peeled and minced
- 4 tablespoons sugar
- 4 tablespoons soy sauce
- 2 green onions, roughly chopped
- 4 tablespoons sherry wine
- Salt, to taste
- ¼ cup water

Directions:

Set the Instant Pot on Sauté mode, add the duck, stir, and brown it for a few minutes. Add the garlic, ginger, green onions, soy sauce, sugar, wine, water, and a pinch of salt and black pepper, stir, cover, set the Instant Pot to Poultry mode, and cook for 18 minutes. Release the pressure, uncover the Instant Pot, add the potatoes, stir, cover, and cook on the Steam setting for 5 minutes. Release the pressure, divide the braised duck among plates, and serve.

Nutrition:

- Calories: 238
- Fat: 18
- Fiber: 0
- Carbs: 1
- Protein: 19

Duck and Vegetables

Preparation time: 10 minutes
Cooking time: 40 minutes
Servings: 8

Ingredients:

- 1 duck, chopped into eight pieces
- 1 cucumber, chopped
- 1 tablespoon wine
- 2 carrots, peeled and chopped
- 2 cups water
- Salt and ground black pepper, to taste
- 1-inch ginger piece, peeled and chopped

Directions:

Put the duck pieces into the Instant Pot. Add the cucumber, carrots, wine, water, ginger, salt, and pepper, stir, cover, and cook on Poultry mode for 40 minutes. Release the pressure, divide the mix among plates, and serve.

Nutrition:

- Calories: 189
- Fat: 2
- Fiber: 1
- Carbs: 4
- Protein: 22

Turkey Meatballs

Preparation time: 10 minutes
Cooking time: 40 minutes
Servings: 8

Ingredients:

- 1 pound turkey meat, ground
- 1 yellow onion, peeled and minced
- ¼ cup Parmesan cheese, grated
- ½ cup panko bread crumbs
- 4 garlic cloves, peeled and minced
- ¼ cup parsley, chopped
- Salt and ground black pepper, to taste
- 1 teaspoon dried oregano
- 1 egg, whisked
- ¼ cup milk
- 2 teaspoons soy sauce
- 1 teaspoon fish sauce
- 12 cremini mushrooms, chopped
- 3 dried shiitake mushrooms, soaked in water, drained, and chopped
- 1 cup chicken stock
- 2 tablespoons extra virgin olive oil
- 2 tablespoons butter
- Sherry
- 2 tablespoons cornstarch mixed with 2 tablespoons water

Directions:

In a bowl, mix the turkey meat with Parmesan cheese, salt, pepper, onion, garlic, bread crumbs, parsley, oregano, egg, milk, fish sauce, and 1 teaspoon soy sauce, stir well, and shape 16 meatballs. Heat up a pan with 1 tablespoon oil over medium-high heat, add the meatballs, brown them for 1 minutes on each side, and transfer them to a plate. Pour the chicken stock into the pan, stir, and take off heat. Set the Instant Pot on Sauté mode, add 1 tablespoon oil, 2 tablespoons butter, and heat them up. Add the cremini mushrooms, salt, and pepper, stir, and cook for 10 minutes. Add the dried mushrooms, sherry, and the rest of the soy sauce and stir well. Add the meatballs, cover the Instant Pot and cook on the Manual setting for 6 minutes. Release the pressure, uncover the Instant Pot, add the cornstarch slurry, stir well, divide everything between plates, and serve.

Nutrition:

- Calories: 330
- Fat: 16
- Fiber: 3
- Carbs: 21
- Protein: 28

Turkey Mix and Mashed Potatoes

Preparation time: 10 minutes
Cooking time: 50 minutes
Servings: 3

Ingredients:

- 2 turkey quarters
- 1 yellow onion, peeled and chopped
- 1 carrot, peeled and chopped
- 3 garlic cloves, peeled and minced
- 1 celery stalk, chopped
- 1 cup chicken stock
- Salt and ground black pepper, to taste
- White wine
- 2 tablespoons extra virgin olive oil
- Dried rosemary

- 2 bay leaves
- Dried sage
- Dried thyme
- 3 tablespoons cornstarch mixed with 2 tablespoons water
- 5 Yukon gold potatoes, cut into halves
- 2 tablespoons Parmesan cheese, grated
- 3.5 ounces cream
- 2 tablespoons butter

Directions:

Season the turkey with salt and pepper. Put 1 tablespoon oil into the Instant Pot, set the Instant Pot on Sauté mode, and heat it up. Add the turkey, brown the pieces for 4 minutes, transfer them to a plate set aside. Add ½ cup stock to the Instant Pot and stir well. Add the 1 tablespoon oil and heat it up. Add the onion, stir, and cook for 1 minute. Add the garlic, stir, and cook for 20 seconds. Add the salt and pepper, carrot and celery, stir and cook for 7 minutes. Add the bay leaves, thyme, sage, and rosemary, stir and cook everything 1 minute. Add the wine, turkey and the rest of the stock. Put the potatoes in the steamer basket and also introduce it in the Instant Pot, cover and cook for 20 minutes on Steam mode. Release the pressure for 10 minutes, uncover the Instant Pot, transfer the potatoes to a bowl and mash them. Add the salt, pepper, butter, Parmesan cheese, and cream and stir well. Divide the turkey quarters to plates and set the Instant Pot on Sauté mode. Add the cornstarch mixture to pot, stir well, and cook for 2-3 minutes. Drizzle the sauce over the turkey, add the mashed potatoes on the side, and serve.

Nutrition:

- Calories: 200
- Fat: 5
- Fiber: 4

- Carbs: 19
- Protein: 18

Stuffed Chicken Breasts

Preparation time: 10 minutes
Cooking time: 30 minutes
Servings: 2

Ingredients:

- 2 chicken breasts, skinless, boneless, and butterflied
- 1 piece ham, cut in half and cooked
- 6 asparagus spears
- 16 bacon strips
- 4 mozzarella cheese slices
- Salt and ground black pepper, to taste
- 2 cup water

Directions:

In a bowl, mix the chicken breasts with salt and 1 cup water, stir, cover, and keep in the refrigerator for 30 minutes. Pat chicken breasts dry and place them on a working surface. Add 2 slices of mozzarella, 1 piece ham, and 3 asparagus pieces onto each. Add salt and pepper and roll up each chicken breast. Place 8 bacon strips on a working surface, add the chicken and wrap them in bacon. Repeat this with the rest of the bacon strips and the other chicken breast. Put rolls in the steamer basket of the Instant Pot, add 1 cup water to the Instant Pot, cover and cook on the Poultry setting for 10 minutes. Release the pressure, pat dry rolls with paper towels and leave them on a plate. Set the Instant Pot on Sauté mode, add the chicken rolls and brown them for a few minutes. Divide among plates, and serve.

Nutrition:

- Calories: 270
- Fat: 11
- Fiber: 1
- Carbs: 6
- Protein: 37

Simple Chicken Salad

Preparation time: 55 minutes
Cooking time: 10 minutes
Servings: 2

Ingredients:

- 1 chicken breast, skinless and boneless
- 3 cups water
- Salt and ground black pepper, to taste
- 1 tablespoon mustard
- 3 garlic cloves, peeled and minced
- 1 tablespoon balsamic vinegar
- 1 tablespoon honey
- 3 tablespoons extra virgin olive oil
- Mixed salad greens
- A handful cherry tomatoes, cut into halves

Directions:

In a bowl, mix 2 cups water with a pinch of salt. Add the chicken to the mixture, stir, and keep in the refrigerator for 45 minutes. Add the remaining water to the Instant Pot, place the chicken breast in the steamer basket of the Instant Pot, cover and cook on the Poultry setting for 5 minutes. Release the pressure naturally, set the chicken breast aside to rest, then cut into thin strips. In a bowl, mix the garlic with salt and pepper, mustard, honey, vinegar, and olive oil and whisk well. In a salad bowl, mix chicken strips with the salad greens and tomatoes. Drizzle the vinaigrette on top, and serve.

Nutrition:

- Calories: 140
- Fat: 2.5
- Fiber: 4
- Carbs: 11
- Protein: 19

Chicken and Rice

Preparation time: 15 minutes
Cooking time: 35 minutes
Servings: 2

Ingredients:

- 3 chicken quarters, cut into small pieces
- 2 carrots, cut into chunks
- 2 potatoes, cut into quarters
- 1 shallot, peeled and sliced
- 1 yellow onion, peeled and sliced
- 3 garlic cloves, peeled and minced
- Salt and ground black pepper, to taste
- 1 green bell pepper, seeded and chopped
- 7 ounces coconut milk
- 2 bay leaves
- 1 tablespoon soy sauce
- 1 tablespoon peanut oil
- 1½ teaspoon turmeric
- 1 teaspoon cumin
- 1½ tablespoons cornstarch mixed with 2 tablespoons water

For the marinade:

- 1 tablespoon soy sauce
- ½ teaspoon sugar
- 1 tablespoon white wine
- Ground white pepper
- 1½ cups water
- 1½ cups rice

Directions:

In a bowl, mix the chicken with the sugar, white pepper, 1 tablespoon soy sauce, and 1 tablespoon white wine, stir, and keep in the refrigerator for 20 minutes. Set the Instant Pot on Sauté mode, add the peanut oil, and heat it up. Add the onion and shallot, stir, and cook for 3 minutes. Add the garlic, salt, and pepper, stir, and cook for 2 minutes. Add the chicken, stir, and brown for 2 minutes. Add the turmeric and cumin, stir, and cook for 1 minute. Add the bay leaves, carrots, potatoes, bell pepper, coconut milk, and 1 tablespoon soy sauce. Stir everything, place the steamer basket in the Instant Pot, place the rice in a bowl in the basket. Add 1½ cups water in the bowl, cover the Instant Pot and cook on the Poultry setting for 4 minutes. Release the pressure naturally, take the rice out of the Instant Pot and divide among plates, add the cornstarch to pot and stir. Add the chicken on the plates with to rice, and serve.

Nutrition:

- Calories: 200
- Fat: 9
- Fiber: 1
- Carbs: 22
- Protein: 26

Crispy Chicken

Preparation time: 10 minutes
Cooking time: 40 minutes
Servings: 4

Ingredients:

- 4 garlic cloves, peeled and chopped
- 6 chicken thighs
- 1 yellow onion, peeled and sliced thin
- Dried rosemary
- 1 cup cold water
- 1 tablespoon soy sauce
- Salt and ground black pepper, to taste
- 2 tablespoons cornstarch mixed with 2½ tablespoons water
- 1½ cups panko breadcrumbs
- 2 tablespoons extra virgin olive oil
- 2 tablespoons butter
- 1 cup white flour
- 2 eggs, whisked

Directions:

In the Instant Pot, mix the garlic with onion, rosemary, and water. Place the chicken things in the steamer basket and place in the Instant Pot. Cover and cook on the Poultry setting for 9 minutes. Release the pressure naturally for 10 minutes and uncover the Instant Pot. Heat up a pan with the butter and oil over medium-high heat. Add the breadcrumbs, stir, toast them, and take them off heat. Remove the chicken from the Instant Pot; pat them dry, season with salt and pepper, coat them with the flour, dip them in whisked egg, and then coat them in toasted breadcrumbs. Place the chicken thighs on a lined baking sheet, place in the oven at 300°F, and bake for 10 minutes. Set the Instant Pot on Sauté mode and heat up the cooking liquid. Add the soy sauce, salt, pepper, and cornstarch, stir, and transfer to a bowl. Take the chicken thighs out of the oven, divide them between plates, and serve with the sauce from the Instant Pot on the side.

Nutrition:

- Calories: 360
- Fat: 7
- Fiber: 4
- Carbs: 18
- Protein: 15

Braised Quail

Preparation time: 10 minutes
Cooking time: 15 minutes
Servings: 2

Ingredients:

- 2 cups water
- 2 quails, cleaned
- 3.5 ounces smoked pancetta, chopped
- ½ cup champagne
- 2 shallots, peeled and chopped
- 1 bunch thyme,
- 1 bay leaf
- Salt and ground black pepper, to taste
- 1 bunch rosemary
- ½ fennel bulb, cut into matchsticks
- 4 carrots, peeled and cut into thin matchsticks
- ½ cup arugula
- Juice of 1 lemon
- Olive oil

Directions:

Put fennel and carrot in the steamer basket of the Instant Pot, add the water to the Instant Pot, cover, cook on the Steam setting for 1 minute, release the pressure, rinse the vegetables with cold water, and transfer them to a bowl. Place the cooking liquid in a separate bowl. Chop half of the thyme and rosemary and set aside. Set the Instant Pot on Sauté mode, add the shallots, pancetta, rosemary, thyme, bay leaf, salt and pepper, stir and cook for 4 minutes. Stuff the quail with whole rosemary and thyme and add to the Instant Pot. Brown on all sides, add the champagne, stir, and cook for 2 minutes. Add the cooking liquid from the vegetables, stir, cover, and cook on the Poultry setting for 9 minutes. Release the pressure, take the quail out of the Instant Pot and set aside. Strain the liquid from the Instant Pot into a pan, heat up over medium heat and simmer until it reduces by half. Arrange the arugula on a platter, add the steamed fennel and carrots, a drizzle of oil, lemon juice and top with quail. Drizzle the sauce from the pan all over, and serve.

Nutrition:

- Calories: 300
- Fat: 17
- Fiber: 0.2
- Carbs: 0.2
- Protein: 40

Braised Turkey Wings

Preparation time: 10 minutes
Cooking time: 20 minutes
Servings: 4

Ingredients:

- 4 turkey wings
- 2 tablespoons butter
- 2 tablespoons vegetable oil
- 1½ cups fresh cranberries
- Salt and ground black pepper, to taste
- 1 yellow onions, peeled and sliced
- 1 cup walnuts
- 1 cup orange juice
- 1 bunch thyme, chopped

Directions:

Set the Instant Pot on Sauté mode, add the butter and oil and heat up. Add the turkey wings, salt, and pepper and brown them on all sides. Take the wings out of the Instant Pot, add the onion, walnuts, cranberries and thyme, stir, and cook for 2 minutes. Add the orange juice and return the wings to the Instant Pot, stir, cover and cook on the Poultry setting for 20 minutes. Release the pressure naturally, uncover the Instant Pot and divide the wings among plates. Transfer the cranberry mixture to a pan, heat up over medium heat and simmer for 5 minutes. Drizzle the sauce over turkey wings, and serve.

Nutrition:

- Calories: 320
- Fat: 15.3
- Fiber: 2.1
- Carbs: 16.4
- Protein: 29

Roasted Chicken

Preparation time: 10 minutes
Cooking time: 35 minutes
Servings: 8

Ingredients:
- 1 whole chicken
- 1 tablespoon extra virgin olive oil
- 1½ tablespoons lemon zest
- 1 cup chicken stock
- 1 tablespoon fresh thyme
- ½ teaspoon ground cinnamon
- Salt and ground black pepper, to taste
- 1 tablespoon cumin
- 2 teaspoons garlic powder
- 1 tablespoon coriander

Directions:
In a bowl, mix the cinnamon with cumin, garlic, coriander, salt, pepper, and lemon zest and stir well. Rub chicken with half of the oil, then rub it inside and out with spice mix. Set the Instant Pot on Sauté mode, add the rest of the oil and heat it up. Add the chicken and brown it on all sides for 5 minutes. Add the stock and thyme, stir, cover and cook on the Poultry setting for 25 minutes. Release the pressure naturally and transfer chicken to a platter. Add the cooking liquid over it, and serve.

Nutrition:
- Calories: 260
- Fat: 3.1
- Fiber: 1
- Carbs: 4
- Protein: 26.7

Party Chicken Wings

Preparation time: 10 minutes
Cooking time: 25 minutes
Servings: 6

Ingredients:
- 12 chicken wings, cut into 24 pieces
- 1 pound celery, cut into thin matchsticks
- ¼ cup honey
- 4 tablespoons hot sauce
- Salt, to taste
- 1 cup water
- ¼ cup tomato puree
- 1 cup yogurt
- 1 tablespoon fresh parsley, diced

Directions:
Put water into the Instant Pot. Place the chicken wings in the steamer basket of the Instant Pot, cover and cook on the Poultry setting for 19 minutes. In a bowl, mix the tomato puree with the hot sauce, salt, and honey and stir well. Release the pressure from the Instant Pot, add the chicken wings to the honey mix and toss them to coat. Arrange the chicken wings on a lined baking sheet and place under a preheated broiler for 5 minutes. Arrange the celery sticks on a platter and add the chicken wings next to it. In a bowl, mix the yogurt with the parsley, stir well, place next to the platter, and serve.

Nutrition:
- Calories: 300
- Fat: 3.1
- Fiber: 2
- Carbs: 14
- Protein: 33

Chicken Delight

Preparation time: 10 minutes
Cooking time: 37 minutes
Servings: 4
Ingredients:

- 6 chicken thighs
- 1 teaspoon vegetable oil
- Salt and ground black pepper, to taste
- 1 yellow onion, peeled and chopped
- 1 celery stalk, chopped
- ¼ pound baby carrots, cut into halves
- ½ teaspoon dried thyme
- 2 tablespoons tomato paste
- ½ cup white wine
- 15 ounces canned diced tomatoes
- 2 cups chicken stock
- 1½ pounds potatoes, chopped

Directions:

Set the Instant Pot on Sauté mode, add the oil and heat it up. Add the chicken pieces, salt, and pepper to taste, and brown them for 4 minutes on each side. Take the chicken out of the Instant Pot and set aside. Add the onion, carrots, celery, thyme, and tomato paste to the Instant Pot, stir, and cook for 5 minutes. Add the white wine and salt, stir and cook for 3 minutes. Add the chicken stock, chicken pieces and chopped tomatoes and stir. Place the steamer basket in the Instant Pot, add potatoes in it, cover the Instant Pot and cook on the Poultry setting for 30 minutes. Release the pressure, take potatoes out of the Instant Pot and also remove the chicken pieces. Shred the chicken meat and add it to a bowl with the potatoes and more salt and pepper, stir, divide among plates, and serve.

Nutrition:

- Calories: 237
- Fat: 12
- Fiber: 0
- Carbs: 1
- Protein: 30

Chicken Gumbo

Preparation time: 10 minutes
Cooking time: 45 minutes
Servings: 4

Ingredients:

- 1 pound smoked sausage, sliced
- 1 tablespoon vegetable oil
- 1 pound chicken thighs, cut into halves
- Salt and ground black pepper, to taste

For the roux:

- ½ cup flour
- ¼ cup vegetable oil
- 1 teaspoon Cajun spice

Aromatics:

- 1 bell pepper, seeded and chopped
- 1 yellow onion, peeled and chopped
- 1 celery stalk, chopped
- Salt, to taste
- 4 garlic cloves, peeled and minced
- 2 quarts chicken stock
- 15 ounces canned tomatoes, chopped
- ½ pound okra
- Tabasco sauce

For serving:

- White rice, already cooked
- ½ cup fresh parsley, chopped

Directions:

Set the Instant Pot on Sauté mode, add 1 tablespoon oil and heat it up. Add the sausage, stir, brown for 4 minutes, and transfer to a plate. Add the chicken pieces, stir, brown for 6 minutes, and transfer next to the sausage. Add the remaining vegetable oil to the Instant Pot and heat it up. Add the Cajun spice, stir, and cook for 5 minutes. Add the bell pepper, onion, garlic, celery, salt and pepper, stir and cook for 5 minutes. Return the chicken and sausage to the Instant Pot and stir. Add the stock and tomatoes and stir everything. Cover the Instant Pot and cook on the Meat/Stew setting for 10 minutes. Release the pressure naturally for 15 minutes, uncover the Instant Pot, add the okra, set the Instant Pot to Manual mode and cook for 10 minutes. Add more salt and pepper and the Tabasco sauce, stir, and divide gumbo among bowls. Serve with rice on the side and with parsley sprinkled on top.

Nutrition:

- Calories: 208
- Fat: 15
- Fiber: 1
- Carbs: 8
- Protein: 10

Duck Chili

Preparation time: 10 minutes
Cooking time: 1 hour
Servings: 4

Ingredients:

- 1 pound northern beans, soaked and rinsed
- 1 yellow onion, peeled and cut into half
- 1 garlic head, top trimmed off
- Salt, to taste
- 2 cloves
- 1 bay leaf
- 6 cups water
For the duck:
- 1 pound duck, ground

- 1 tablespoon vegetable oil
- 1 yellow onion, peeled and minced
- 2 carrots, peeled and chopped
- Salt and ground black pepper, to taste
- 4 ounces canned green chilies
- 1 teaspoon brown sugar
- 15 ounces diced canned tomatoes
- ½ cup fresh cilantro, chopped

Directions:

Put the beans into the Instant Pot. Add the onion halves, garlic head, cloves, bay leaf, water, and salt, stir, cover and cook on the Bean/Chili setting for 25 minutes. Release the pressure, uncover the Instant Pot, discard the solids and transfer beans to a bowl. Heat up a pan with the oil over medium high heat, add the carrots and chopped onion, season with salt and pepper, stir, and cook for 5 minutes. Add the duck, stir, and cook for 5 minutes. Add the chilies and tomatoes, bring to a simmer, and take off heat. Pour this into the Instant Pot, cover and cook on the Manual setting for 5 minutes. Release pressure naturally for 15 minutes, uncover the Instant Pot, add more salt and pepper, the beans and brown sugar, stir, and divide among plates. Serve with cilantro on top.

Nutrition:

- Calories: 270
- Fat: 13
- Fiber: 26

- Carbs: 15
- Protein: 25

Coca-Cola Chicken

Preparation time: 10 minutes
Cooking time: 10 minutes
Servings: 4

Ingredients:

- 1 yellow onion, peeled and minced
- 4 chicken drumsticks
- 1 tablespoon balsamic vinegar
- 1 chili pepper, chopped

- 15 ounces Coca-Cola
- Salt and ground black pepper, to taste
- 2 tablespoons extra virgin olive oil

Directions:

Set the Instant Pot on Sauté mode, add the oil and heat it up. Add the chicken pieces, stir, and brown them on all sides, and then transfer them to a plate. Add the vinegar, Coca-Cola, and chili pepper to the Instant Pot, stir and simmer for 2 minutes. Return the chicken, add the salt and pepper, stir, cover, and cook on the Poultry setting for 10 minutes. Release the pressure, uncover the Instant Pot, divide the chicken among plates, and serve.

Nutrition:

- Calories: 410
- Fat: 23
- Fiber: 1

- Carbs: 24
- Sugar: 21
- Protein: 27

Chicken Curry

Preparation time: 10 minutes
Cooking time: 20 minutes
Servings: 4

Ingredients:

- 15 ounces boneless and skinless chicken breast, chopped
- 1 tablespoon extra virgin olive oil
- 1 yellow onion, peeled and sliced thin
- 6 potatoes, cut into halves
- 5 ounces canned coconut cream
- 2 tablespoons curry powder
- ½ bunch fresh cilantro, chopped

Directions:

Set the Instant Pot on Sauté mode, add the oil and heat it up. Add the chicken, stir and brown for 2 minutes. Add the onion, stir and cook for 1 minute. In a bowl, mix the curry powder with coconut cream and stir. Pour this over the chicken, add the potatoes, stir, cover, and cook on the Manual setting for 15 minutes. Release the pressure, uncover the Instant Pot, divide the chicken among plates, and serve with cilantro on top.

Nutrition:

- Calories: 120
- Fat: 8.6
- Fiber: 1.2
- Carbs: 6.11
- Protein: 14.8

Coq au Vin

Preparation time: 10 minutes
Cooking time: 50 minutes
Servings: 4

Ingredients:

- 2 pounds chicken drumsticks and thighs
- 4 ounces bacon, chopped
- ¼ cup peanut oil
- 2 onions, peeled and sliced
- 2 garlic cloves, peeled and crushed
- 14 ounces red wine
- 1 bay leaf
- 2 tablespoons flour
- 7 ounces white mushrooms, sliced
- 1 cup fresh parsley, diced
- Salt and ground black pepper, to taste
- 12 small potatoes, cut into halves
- 2 tablespoons cognac

Directions:

Set the Instant Pot on Sauté mode, add the oil and heat it up. Add the chicken pieces, brown them on all sides, and transfer them to a bowl. Add the bacon and onions to the Instant Pot, stir, and cook for 5 minutes. Add the garlic, stir, and cook for 1 minute. Return the chicken to pot, add the flour and cognac, stir, and cook for 1 minute. Add the salt, pepper, bay leaf, and red wine, stir, bring to a boil, cover the Instant Pot and cook on the Poultry setting for 30 minutes. Release the pressure, add the mushrooms to the Instant Pot, add the potatoes in the steamer basket, cover the Instant Pot again, and cook for 15 minutes. Release the pressure, take the potatoes and divide them among plates. Add the chicken on top, sprinkle with parsley, and serve.

Nutrition:

- Calories: 281
- Fat: 12.4
- Fiber: 2.2
- Carbs: 15
- Protein: 23

Italian Chicken

Preparation time: 10 minutes
Cooking time: 20 minutes
Servings: 6

Ingredients:

- 1 tablespoon extra virgin olive oil
- 2 pounds chicken breasts, skinless and boneless
- Salt and ground black pepper, to taste
- ¾ cup yellow onion, diced
- ½ cup green bell pepper, chopped
- ½ cup red bell pepper, chopped
- ¾ cup marinara sauce
- 2 tablespoons pesto
- ¾ cup mushrooms, sliced
- Mozzarella cheese, shredded for serving

Directions:

Set the Instant Pot on Sauté mode, add the oil, and heat it up. Add the onion, bell pepper, salt, and pepper, stir, and cook for 4 minutes. Add the pesto, marinara sauce, and chicken, stir, cover, and cook on the Poultry setting for 12 minutes. Release the pressure, uncover the Instant Pot, remove the chicken, place on a cutting board, and shred. Discard ⅔ cup of the cooking liquid, add the mushrooms to the Instant Pot, set it on Sauté mode and cook them for 3 minutes. Return the chicken, stir, divide among plates, and serve with shredded cheese on top.

Nutrition:

- Calories: 340
- Fat: 15
- Fiber: 3.5
- Carbs: 10.1
- Protein: 34

Teriyaki Chicken

Preparation time: 10 minutes
Cooking time: 12 minutes
Servings: 6

Ingredients:

- 2 pounds chicken breasts, skinless and boneless
- ⅔ cup teriyaki sauce
- 1 tablespoon honey
- ½ cup chicken stock
- Salt and ground black pepper, to taste
- Green onions, chopped

Directions:

Set the Instant Pot on the Sauté mode, add the teriyaki sauce, and honey, stir and simmer for 1 minute. Add the stock, chicken, salt and pepper, stir, cover and cook on the Poultry setting for 12 minutes. Release the pressure, place the chicken breasts on a work surface, and shred with 2 forks. Remove ½ cup of the cooking liquid, put the chicken serving dishes, top with green onions, , and serve.

Nutrition:

- Calories: 240
- Fat: 13
- Fiber: 1
- Carbs: 8
- Protein: 34

Creamy Chicken

Preparation time: 10 minutes
Cooking time: 20 minutes
Servings: 6

Ingredients:
- 2 slices bacon, chopped
- 1 cup chicken stock
- 4 ounces cream cheese
- 1 ounce ranch seasoning
- 2 pounds chicken breasts, skinless and boneless
- Green onions, chopped, for serving

Directions:
Set the Instant Pot on Sauté mode, add the bacon and cook for 4 minutes. Add the chicken, stock and seasoning, stir, cover, and cook on the Poultry setting for 12 minutes. Release the pressure, uncover the Instant Pot, transfer the chicken to a work surface, and shred it. Remove ⅔ cup liquid from the Instant Pot, add the cream cheese, set the Instant Pot to Manual mode and cook for 3 minutes. Return the chicken to the Instant Pot, stir, divide among plates, add the green onions, and serve.

Nutrition:
- Calories: 300
- Fat: 7
- Fiber: 3
- Carbs: 23
- Protein: 22

Buffalo Chicken

Preparation time: 10 minutes
Cooking time: 15 minutes
Servings: 6

Ingredients:
- 2 pounds chicken breasts, skinless and boneless , cut into thin strips
- ½ cup celery, chopped
- 1 small yellow onion, peeled and chopped
- ½ cup buffalo sauce
- ½ cup chicken stock
- ¼ cup bleu cheese, crumbled

Directions:
In the Instant Pot, mix the onion with the celery, buffalo sauce, stock, and chicken, stir, cover, and cook on the Poultry setting for 12 minutes. Release the pressure, uncover the Instant Pot, discard ⅔ cup of cooking liquid, add the cheese, stir well, divide among plates, and serve.

Nutrition:
- Calories: 190
- Fat: 9
- Fiber: 1
- Carbs: 20
- Protein: 14

Colombian Chicken

Preparation time: 10 minutes
Cooking time: 25 minutes
Servings: 4

Ingredients:

- 4 Yukon gold potatoes, cut into medium chunks
- 1 yellow onion, peeled and sliced thin
- 4 tomatoes, cut into medium chunks
- 1 chicken, cut into 8 pieces
- Salt and ground black pepper, to taste
- 2 bay leaves
- Salt and ground black pepper, to taste

Directions:

In the Instant Pot, mix the potatoes with the onion, chicken, tomato, bay leaves, salt, and pepper, stir well, cover and cook on the Manual setting for 25 minutes. Release the pressure naturally, uncover the Instant Pot, add more salt and pepper, discard the bay leaves, divide the chicken among plates, and serve.

Nutrition:

- Calories: 270
- Fat: 12
- Fiber: 1
- Carbs: 23
- Protein: 14

Chicken and Lentils

Preparation time: 10 minutes
Cooking time: 25 minutes
Servings: 4

Ingredients:

- 8 ounces bacon, chopped
- 2 tablespoons extra virgin olive oil
- Olive oil for serving
- 1 cup yellow onion, chopped
- 8 ounces lentils, dried
- 2 carrots, chopped
- 12 parsley sprigs, chopped
- Salt and ground black pepper, to taste
- 2 bay leaves
- 2½ pounds chicken pieces
- 1-quart chicken stock
- 2 teaspoons sherry vinegar

Directions:

Set the Instant Pot on Sauté mode, add the oil, and heat it up. Add the bacon, stir, and cook for 1 minute. Add the onions, stir, and cook 2 minutes. Add the lentils, carrots, chicken, parsley, bay leaves, stock, salt and pepper, stir, cover, and cook on the Manual setting for 20 minutes. Release the pressure, take chicken pieces, and place them on a cutting board. Discard the skin and bones, shred chicken, and return it to the Instant Pot. Set the Instant Pot on Sauté mode and cook for 7 minutes. Add more salt and pepper and the vinegar, stir, and divide among plates. Drizzle some olive oil over the whole mix, and serve.

Nutrition:

- Calories: 340
- Fat: 3.3
- Fiber: 23
- Carbs: 30
- Protein: 29

Chicken Curry with Eggplant and Squash

Preparation time: 10 minutes
Cooking time: 25 minutes
Servings: 4

Ingredients:

- 3 garlic cloves, peeled and crushed
- 2 tablespoons vegetable oil
- 3 arbol chilies, cut into halves
- 1-inch piece ginger, peeled and sliced
- 2 tablespoons green curry paste
- ⅛ teaspoon cumin
- ¼ teaspoon coriander
- 14 ounces canned coconut milk
- 6 cups butternut squash, peeled and cubed
- 8 chicken pieces
- 1 eggplant, peeled and cubed
- Salt and ground black pepper, to taste
- 1 tablespoon fish sauce
- 4 cups spinach, chopped
- ½ cup fresh cilantro, chopped
- ½ cup fresh basil, chopped
- Cooked barley for serving
- Lime wedges, for serving

Directions:

Set the Instant Pot on Sauté mode, add the oil, and heat it up. Add the garlic, ginger, chilies, cumin, and coriander, stir, and cook for 1 minute. Add the curry paste, stir, and cook 3 minutes. Add the coconut milk, stir, and simmer for 1 minute. Add the chicken, squash, eggplant, salt, and pepper, stir, cover and cook on the Poultry setting for 20 minutes. Release the pressure, uncover the Instant Pot, add spinach, fish sauce, more salt and pepper, basil, and cilantro, stir and divide among plates. Serve with cooked barley on the side and lime wedges.

Nutrition:

- Calories: 160
- Fat: 8.2
- Fiber: 4.1
- Carbs: 13.2
- Protein: 6

Chicken and Chickpea Masala

Preparation time: 10 minutes
Cooking time: 25 minutes
Servings: 4

Ingredients:
- 1 yellow onion, peeled and diced
- 2 tablespoons butter
- 4 garlic cloves, peeled and minced
- 1 tablespoon ginger, grated
- 1½ teaspoon paprika
- 1 tablespoon cumin
- 1½ teaspoons coriander
- 1 teaspoon turmeric
- Salt and ground black pepper, to taste
- Cayenne pepper
- 15 ounces canned crushed tomatoes
- ¼ cup lemon juice
- 1 pound spinach, chopped
- 3 pounds chicken drumsticks and thighs
- ½ cup fresh cilantro, chopped
- ½ cup chicken stock
- 15 ounces canned chickpeas, drained
- ½ cup heavy cream

Directions:

Set the Instant Pot on Sauté mode, add the butter and melt it. Add the ginger, onion, and garlic, stir and cook for 5 minutes. Add the paprika, cumin, coriander, cayenne, turmeric, salt, and pepper, stir and cook for 30 seconds. Add the tomatoes and spinach, stir and cook for 2 minutes. Add half of the cilantro, chicken pieces, and stock, stir, cover the Instant Pot and cook on the Poultry setting for 15 minutes. Release the pressure, uncover the Instant Pot, add the heavy cream, chickpeas, lemon juice, more salt, and pepper, stir, set the Instant Pot on Sauté mode again and simmer for 3 minutes. Sprinkle the rest of the cilantro on top, stir, divide among plates, and serve.

Nutrition:
- Calories: 270
- Fat: 8
- Fiber: 7.6
- Carbs: 30
- Protein: 31

Sesame Chicken

Preparation time: 10 minutes
Cooking time: 8 minutes
Servings: 4

Ingredients:
- 2 pounds chicken breasts, skinless, boneless, and chopped
- ½ cup yellow onion, peeled and chopped
- Salt and ground black pepper, to taste
- 1 tablespoon vegetable oil
- 2 garlic cloves, peeled and minced
- ½ cup soy sauce
- ¼ cup ketchup
- 2 teaspoons sesame oil
- ½ cup honey
- 2 tablespoons cornstarch
- ¼ teaspoon red pepper flakes
- 3 tablespoons water
- 2 green onions, chopped
- 1 tablespoons sesame seeds, toasted

Drections:

Set the Instant Pot on the Sauté mode, add the oil, and heat it up. Add the garlic, onion, chicken, salt and pepper, stir, and cook for 3 minutes. Add the pepper flakes, soy sauce, and ketchup, stir, cover and cook on the Manual setting for 3 minutes. Release pressure, uncover the Instant Pot, add the sesame oil and honey and stir. In a bowl, mix the cornstarch with the water and stir well. Add this to the Instant Pot with the green onions and sesame seeds, stir well, divide among plates, and serve.

Nutrition:
- Calories: 170
- Fat: 3.5
- Fiber: 2.9
- Carbs: 16
- Protein: 7

Chicken with Duck Sauce

Preparation time: 10 minutes
Cooking time: 20 minutes
Servings: 4

Ingredients:

- 1 chicken, cut into medium-sized pieces
- Salt and ground black pepper, to taste
- 1 tablespoon extra virgin olive oil
- ½ teaspoon paprika
- ¼ cup white wine
- ½ teaspoon dried marjoram
- ¼ cup chicken stock

For the duck sauce:

- 2 tablespoons white vinegar
- ¼ cup apricot preserves
- 1½ teaspoon ginger root, grated
- 2 tablespoons honey

Directions:

Set the Instant Pot on Sauté mode, add the oil, and heat it up. Add the chicken pieces, brown them on all sides, and transfer to a bowl. Season them with salt, pepper, marjoram, and paprika and toss to coat. Drain the fat from pot, add the stock and wine, stir, and simmer for 2 minutes. Return the chicken, cover the Instant Pot and cook on the Poultry setting for 9 minutes. Release the pressure, transfer the chicken to serving dishes and set the dish aside. Add the apricot preserves to the Instant Pot, ginger, vinegar, and honey, set on the Sauté mode, stir, and simmer sauce for 10 minutes. Drizzle over chicken, and serve.

Nutrition:

- Calories: 170
- Fat: 4
- Fiber: 3
- Carbs: 9
- Protein: 23

Chicken and Dumplings

Preparation time: 10 minutes
Cooking time: 20 minutes
Servings: 6

Ingredients:

- 2 pounds chicken breasts, skinless and bone-in
- 4 carrots, peeled and chopped
- 1 yellow onion, peeled and chopped
- 3 celery stalks, chopped
- ¾ cup chicken stock
- Salt and ground black pepper, to taste
- ½ teaspoon thyme, dried
- 2 eggs
- ⅔ cup milk
- 1 tablespoon baking powder
- 2 cups flour
- 1 tablespoon chives

Directions:

In the Instant Pot, add the chicken, onion, carrots, celery, stock, thyme, salt, and pepper, stir, cover, and cook on poultry mode for 15 minutes. Release the pressure, transfer chicken to a bowl and keep warm for now. In a bowl, mix the eggs with salt, milk and baking powder and stir. Add the flour gradually and stir very well. Set the Instant Pot to Sauté mode and bring the liquid to a boil. Shape dumplings from the egg mixture, drop them into stock, cover the Instant Pot and cook on the Manual setting for 7 minutes. Shred the chicken and add to the Instant Pot after you've released the pressure, stir, divide everything among plates, and serve with chives sprinkled on top.

Nutrition:

- Calories: 380
- Fat: 4.2
- Fiber: 2.9
- Carbs: 40
- Protein: 43

Chicken and Noodles

Preparation time: 10 minutes
Cooking time: 20 minutes
Servings: 6

Ingredients:

- 8 chicken thighs, skinless and boneless
- 3 carrots, chopped
- 2 garlic cloves, minced
- 1 yellow onion, chopped
- 3 celery stalks, chopped
- 6 cups chicken stock
- 1 bay leaf
- 2 sage leaves, chopped
- 1 rosemary sprig
- 5 thyme sprigs
- Salt and ground black pepper, to taste
- 1 teaspoon chicken seasoning
- 1 pound egg noodles
- 2 tablespoons cornstarch
- 3 tablespoons water
- 1 cup peas, frozen
- Juice of 1 lemon
- ¼ cup parsley, chopped

Directions:

Set the Instant Pot on Sauté mode, add onion, garlic, and celery, stir and brown for 4 minutes. Add carrot, chicken, stock, bay leaf, thyme, rosemary, sage, chicken seasoning, salt and pepper, stir, cover the Instant Pot and cook on Low for 10 minutes. Release the pressure naturally, uncover the Instant Pot, add egg noodles, cornstarch mixed with water, peas, lemon juice, parsley and more salt and pepper if needed. Discard herbs, stir everything, divide among plates, and serve.

Nutrition:

- Calories: 560
- Fat: 11.2
- Fiber: 5.2
- Carbs: 77
- Protein: 39

Chicken and Pomegranate

Preparation time: 10 minutes
Cooking time: 15 minutes
Servings: 6

Ingredients:
- 10 chicken pieces
- 2 cups walnuts
- Salt and ground black pepper, to taste
- 3 tablespoons extra virgin olive oil
- 1 yellow onion, peeled and chopped
- ¼ teaspoon cardamom
- ½ teaspoon ground cinnamon
- ½ cup pomegranate juice
- ½ cup molasses
- ¾ cup water
- 2 tablespoons sugar
- Juice of ½ lemon
- Pomegranate seeds for serving

Directions:

Heat up a pan over medium-high heat, add the walnuts, stir, and toast for 5 minutes. Transfer them to a food processor, blend well, transfer to a bowl and set aside. Set the Instant Pot on Sauté mode, add the 2 tablespoons oil and heat it up. Add the chicken pieces, salt and pepper, brown them on all sides, and transfer them to a plate. Add the rest of the oil to the Instant Pot, add onion, stir, and cook for 3 minutes. Add the cardamom and cinnamon, stir, and cook for 1 minute. Add the walnuts, pomegranate juice, molasses, lemon juice, chicken and sugar, stir, cover and cook on the Poultry setting for 7 minutes. Release the pressure, uncover the Instant Pot, add more salt and pepper, stir, divide among plates, and serve with the sauce from the Instant Pot and with pomegranate seeds on top.

Nutrition:
- Calories: 200
- Fat: 1
- Fiber: 4
- Carbs: 27
- Protein: 17

Goose with Cream

Preparation time: 10 minutes
Cooking time: 1 hour
Servings: 5

Ingredients:
- 1 goose breast, fat trimmed off and cut into pieces
- 1 goose leg, skinless
- 1 goose thigh, skinless
- Salt and ground black pepper, to taste
- 3½ cups water
- 2 teaspoons garlic, minced
- 1 yellow onion, peeled and chopped
- 12 ounces canned cream of mushroom soup

Directions:

Put the goose meat into the Instant Pot. Add the onion, salt, pepper, water, and garlic, stir, cover and cook on Poultry mode for 1 hour. Release the pressure, uncover the Instant Pot, add the soup, set the Instant Pot on Manual mode and cook everything for 5 minutes. Divide into bowls, and serve with toasted bread.

Nutrition:
- Calories: 345
- Fat: 7.8
- Fiber: 1Carbs: 1
- Protein: 28.4

Goose with Chili Sauce

Preparation time: 10 minutes
Cooking time: 15 minutes
Servings: 4

Ingredients:

- 1 goose breast half, skinless, boneless, and cut into thin slices
- ¼ cup extra virgin olive oil
- 1 sweet onion, peeled and chopped
- 2 teaspoons garlic, chopped
- Salt and ground black pepper, to taste
- ¼ cup chili sauce

Directions:

Set the Instant Pot on Sauté mode, add the oil and heat it up. Add the onion and garlic, stir, and cook for 2 minutes. Add the goose breast slices, salt and pepper, stir and cook for 2 minutes on each side. Add the chili sauce, stir, cover and cook on the Manual setting for 5 minutes. Release pressure, divide among plates, and serve.

Nutrition:

- Calories: 190
- Fat: 8
- Fiber: 1
- Carbs: 1
- Protein: 29

Chicken and Shrimp

Preparation time: 10 minutes
Cooking time: 15 minutes
Servings: 4

Ingredients:

- 8 ounces shrimp, peeled and deveined
- 8 ounces sausages, sliced
- 8 ounces chicken breasts, skinless, boneless, and chopped
- 2 tablespoons extra virgin olive oil
- 1 teaspoon Creole seasoning
- 2 teaspoons dried thyme
- Cayenne pepper
- 2 teaspoons Worcestershire sauce
- Tabasco sauce
- 3 garlic cloves, peeled and minced
- 1 yellow onion, peeled and chopped
- 1 green bell pepper, seeded and chopped
- 3 celery stalks, chopped
- 1 cup white rice
- 1 cup chicken stock
- 2 cups canned diced tomatoes
- 3 tablespoons fresh parsley, chopped

Directions:

In a bowl, mix the Creole seasoning with thyme and cayenne and stir. Set the Instant Pot on Sauté mode, add the oil and heat it up. Add the chicken and brown for a few minutes. Add the sausage slices, stir, and cook for 3 minutes. Add the shrimp and half of the seasoning mix, stir, and cook for 2 minutes. Transfer everything to a bowl and set the dish aside. Add the garlic, onions, celery, and bell peppers to the Instant Pot. Add the rest of the seasoning mix, stir, and cook for 10 minutes. Add the rice, stock, tomatoes, Tabasco sauce, and Worcestershire sauce, stir, cover, and cook on Rice mode for 8 minutes. Release the pressure, return the chicken, sausage and shrimp, stir, cover, and leave Instant Pot aside for 5 minutes. Divide everything among plates, and serve.

Nutrition:

- Calories: 269
- Fat: 5.9
- Fiber: 2.4
- Carbs: 23.5
- Protein: 28.4

Indian Butter Chicken

Preparation time: 10 minutes
Cooking time: 15 minutes
Servings: 6

Ingredients:

- 10 chicken thighs, skinless and boneless
- 2 jalapeño peppers, chopped
- 28 ounces canned diced tomatoes
- 2 teaspoons cumin
- 2 tablespoons ginger, chopped
- ½ cup butter
- Salt and ground black pepper, to taste
- ¾ cup heavy cream
- 2 teaspoons garam masala
- ¾ cup Greek yogurt
- 2 teaspoons cumin seeds, toasted and ground
- 2 tablespoons cornstarch
- 2 tablespoons water
- ¼ cup fresh cilantro, chopped

Directions:

In a food processor, mix the tomatoes with ginger and jalapeños and blend well. Set the Instant Pot on Sauté mode, add the butter and melt it. Add the chicken, stir, and brown for 3 minutes on each side. Transfer the chicken pieces to a bowl and set aside. Add the paprika and cumin to the Instant Pot, stir, and cook for 10 seconds. Add the tomato mix, salt, pepper, yogurt, heavy cream, and chicken pieces, stir, cover, and cook on the Manual setting for 5 minutes. Release the pressure naturally for 15 minutes, uncover the Instant Pot, add cornstarch mixed with the water, garam masala, and cumin seeds and stir well. Add the cilantro, stir, divide among plates, and serve with naan bread.

Nutrition:

- Calories: 380
- Fat: 29
- Fiber: 2
- Carbs: 8
- Sugar: 2
- Protein: 24

Chicken and Broccoli

Preparation time: 10 minutes
Cooking time: 15 minutes
Servings: 6

Ingredients:

- 2 chicken breasts, skinless and boneless
- 1 tablespoon butter
- 1 tablespoon extra virgin olive oil
- ½ cup yellow onion, chopped
- 14 ounces canned chicken stock
- Salt and ground black pepper, to taste
- Red pepper flakes
- 1 tablespoon dried parsley
- 2 tablespoons water
- 2 tablespoons cornstarch
- 3 cups broccoli, steamed and chopped
- 1 cup cheddar cheese, shredded
- 4 ounces cream cheese, cubed

Directions:

Set the Instant Pot on Sauté mode, add butter and oil and heat up. Add chicken breasts, salt and pepper, brown on all sides and transfer to a bowl. Add onion to the Instant Pot, stir and cook for 5 minutes. Add more salt, pepper, stock, parsley, pepper flakes and return chicken breasts as well. Stir, cover the Instant Pot and cook on the Manual setting for 5 minutes. Release the pressure, transfer chicken to a cutting board, chop it and return to pot. Add cornstarch mixed with the water, shredded cheese and cream cheese and stir until all cheese dissolves. Add broccoli, stir, set the Instant Pot on Manual mode and cook for 5 minutes. Divide among plates, and serve.

Nutrition:

- Calories: 280
- Fat: 13
- Fiber: 4
- Carbs: 23
- Protein: 30

Chicken with Corn

Preparation time: 10 minutes
Cooking time: 25 minutes
Servings: 4

Ingredients:

- 8 chicken drumsticks
- Salt and ground black pepper, to taste
- 1 teaspoon extra virgin olive oil
- ½ teaspoon garlic powder
- 3 scallions, chopped
- ½ yellow onion, peeled and chopped
- 1 tomato, cored and chopped
- ¼ cup fresh cilantro, chopped
- 1 garlic clove, peeled and minced
- 2 cups water
- 8 ounces tomato sauce
- 1 tablespoon chicken bouillon
- 2 corn on the cob, husked and cut into halves
- ½ teaspoon cumin

Directions:

Set the Instant Pot on Sauté mode, add the oil, and heat up. Add the onions, tomato, scallions, and garlic, stir, and cook for 3 minutes. Add the cilantro, stir, and cook for 1 minute. Add the tomato sauce, water, bouillon, cumin, garlic powder, chicken, salt, and pepper and top with the corn. Cover the Instant Pot and cook on the Poultry setting for 20 minutes. Release the pressure, uncover the Instant Pot, add more salt and pepper, if needed, divide chicken, and corn among plates, and serve.

Nutrition:

- Calories: 320
- Fat: 10
- Fiber: 3
- Carbs: 18
- Protein: 42

Chicken and Cabbage

Preparation time: 10 minutes
Cooking time: 30 minutes
Servings: 3

Ingredients:

- 1½ pounds chicken thighs, boneless
- 1 green cabbage, roughly chopped
- 1 tablespoon vegetable oil
- Salt and ground black pepper, to taste
- 2 chili peppers, chopped
- 1 yellow onion, peeled and chopped
- 4 garlic cloves, peeled and chopped
- 3 tablespoons curry
- Cayenne pepper
- ½ cup white wine
- 10 ounces coconut milk
- 1 tablespoon fish sauce

Directions:

Set the Instant Pot on Sauté mode, add the oil, and heat it up. Add the chicken, season with salt and pepper, stir, brown for a few minutes, and transfer to a bowl. Add the garlic, chili peppers and onions to the Instant Pot, stir, and cook for 4 minutes. Add the curry, stir, and cook for 2 minutes. Add the wine, cabbage, coconut milk, cayenne, fish sauce, chicken pieces, salt and pepper, stir, cover and cook on the Poultry setting for 20 minutes. Release the pressure naturally, uncover the Instant Pot, stir your mix, divide it among plates, and serve.

Nutrition:

- Calories: 260
- Fat: 5.5
- Fiber: 4.9
- Carbs: 15.2
- Protein: 30.2

Instant Pot Meat Recipes

Corned Beef

Preparation time: 10 minutes
Cooking time: 60 minutes
Servings: 6

Ingredients:

- 4 pounds beef brisket
- 2 oranges, sliced
- 2 garlic cloves, peeled and minced
- 2 yellow onions, peeled and sliced thin
- 11 ounces celery, sliced thin

- 1 tablespoon dried dill
- 3 bay leaves
- 4 cinnamon sticks, cut into halves
- Salt and ground black pepper, to taste
- 17 ounces water

Directions:

Put the beef in a bowl, add some water to cover, set aside to soak for a few hours, drain and transfer to the Instant Pot. Add the celery, orange slices, onions, garlic, bay leaves, dill, cinnamon, dill, salt, pepper, and water. Stir, cover the Instant Pot and cook on the Meat/Stew setting for 50 minutes. Release the pressure, set the beef aside to cool for 5 minutes, transfer to a cutting board, slice, and divide among plates. Drizzle the juice and vegetables from the Instant Pot over beef, and serve.

Nutrition:

- Calories: 251
- Fat: 3.14
- Fiber: 0

- Carbs: 1
- Protein: 7

Beef Bourguignon

Preparation time: 15 minutes
Cooking time: 30 minutes
Servings: 6

Ingredients:

- 10 pounds round steak, cut into small cubes
- 2 carrots, peeled and sliced
- ½ cup beef stock
- 1 cup dry red wine
- 3 bacon slices, chopped
- 8 ounces mushrooms, cut into quarters

- 2 tablespoons white flour
- 12 pearl onions
- 2 garlic cloves, peeled and minced
- ¼ teaspoon dried basil
- Salt and ground black pepper, to taste

Directions:

Set the Instant Pot on Sauté mode, add the bacon, and brown it for 2 minutes. Add the beef pieces, stir, and brown for 5 minutes. Add the flour and stir very well. Add the salt, pepper, wine, stock, onions, garlic, and basil, stir, cover and cook on the Meat/Stew setting for 20 minutes. Release the pressure, uncover the Instant Pot, add the mushrooms and carrots, cover the Instant Pot again and cook on the Manual setting for 5 minutes. Release the pressure again, divide the beef bourguignon among plates, and serve.

Nutrition:

- Calories: 442
- Fat: 17.2
- Fiber: 3

- Carbs: 16
- Protein: 39

Beef Curry

Preparation time: 10 minutes
Cooking time: 20 minutes
Servings: 4

Ingredients:

- 2 pounds beef steak, cubed
- 2 tablespoons extra virgin olive oil
- 3 potatoes, diced
- 1 tablespoon Dijon mustard
- 2½ tablespoons curry powder
- 2 yellow onions, peeled and chopped
- 2 garlic cloves, peeled and minced
- 10 ounces canned coconut milk
- 2 tablespoons tomato sauce
- Salt and ground black pepper, to taste

Directions:

Set the Instant Pot on Sauté mode, add the oil, and heat it up. Add the onions and garlic, stir and cook for 4 minutes. Add the potatoes and mustard, stir, and cook for 1 minute. Add the beef, stir and brown on all sides. Add the curry powder, salt and pepper, stir, and cook for 2 minutes. Add the coconut milk and tomato sauce, stir, cover the Instant Pot and cook on the Meat/Stew setting for 10 minutes. Release the pressure, uncover the Instant Pot, divide curry among plates, and serve.

Nutrition:

- Calories: 434
- Fat: 20
- Fiber: 2.9
- Carbs: 14
- Protein: 27.5

Beef Stroganoff

Preparation time: 10 minutes
Cooking time: 25 minutes
Servings: 4

Ingredients:

- 10 pounds beef, cut into small cubes
- 1 yellow onion, peeled and chopped
- 2½ tablespoons vegetable oil
- 1½ tablespoons white flour
- 2 garlic cloves, peeled and minced
- 4 ounces mushrooms, sliced
- 1½ tablespoon tomato paste
- Salt and ground black pepper, to taste
- 3 tablespoons Worcestershire sauce
- 13 ounces beef stock
- 8 ounces sour cream
- Egg noodles, already cooked, for serving

Directions:

Put the beef, salt, pepper and flour in a bowl and toss to coat. Set the Instant Pot on Sauté mode, add the oil, and heat it up. Add the meat and brown it on all sides. Add the onion, garlic, mushrooms, Worcestershire sauce, stock, and tomato paste, stir well, cover the Instant Pot and cook on the Meat/Stew setting for 20 minutes. Release the pressure, uncover the Instant Pot, add the sour cream, more salt and pepper, stir well, divide among plates on top of egg noodles and serve.

Nutrition:

- Calories: 335
- Fat: 18.4
- Fiber: 1.3
- Carbs: 22.5
- Protein: 20.1

Beef Chili

Preparation time: 10 minutes
Cooking time: 40 minutes
Servings: 6

Ingredients:

- 1½ pounds ground beef
- 1 sweet onion, peeled and chopped
- Salt and ground black pepper, to taste
- 16 ounces mixed beans, soaked overnight and drained
- 28 ounces canned diced tomatoes
- 17 ounces beef stock
- 12 ounces beer
- 6 garlic cloves, peeled and chopped
- 7 jalapeño peppers, diced
- 2 tablespoons vegetable oil
- 4 carrots, peeled and chopped
- 3 tablespoons chili powder
- 1 bay leaf
- 1 teaspoon chili powder

Directions:

Set the Instant Pot on Sauté mode, add half of the oil and heat it up. Add the beef, stir, brown for 8 minutes and transfer to a bowl. Add the rest of the oil to the Instant Pot and heat it up. Add the carrots, onion, jalapeños and garlic, stir, and sauté for 4 minutes. Add the beer and tomatoes and stir. Add the beans, bay leaf, stock, chili powder, chili powder, salt, pepper, and beef, stir, cover and cook on the Bean/Chili setting for 25 minutes. Release the pressure naturally, uncover the Instant Pot, stir chili, transfer to bowls, and serve.

Nutrition:

- Calories: 272
- Fat: 5
- Fiber: 0
- Carbs: 32
- Protein: 25

Chili Con Carne

Preparation time: 10 minutes
Cooking time: 30 minutes
Servings: 4

Ingredients:

- 1 pound ground beef
- 1 yellow onion, peeled and chopped
- 4 tablespoons extra virgin olive oil
- Salt and ground black pepper, to taste
- 2 garlic cloves, peeled and minced
- 1 bay leaf
- 4 ounces kidney beans, soaked overnight and drained
- 1 teaspoon tomato paste
- 8 ounces canned diced tomatoes
- 1 tablespoon chili powder
- ½ teaspoon cumin
- 5 ounces water

Directions:

Set the Instant Pot on Sauté mode, add 1 tablespoon oil and heat it up. Add the meat, brown for a few minutes and transfer to a bowl. Add the rest of the oil to the Instant Pot and also heat it up. Add the onion and garlic, stir, and cook for 3 minutes. Return the beef to pot, add the bay leaf, beans, tomato paste, tomatoes, chili powder, cumin, salt, pepper, and water, stir, cover, and cook on the Bean/Chili setting for 18 minutes. Release the pressure, uncover the Instant Pot, discard bay leaf, divide chili among bowls, and serve.

Nutrition:

- Calories: 256
- Fat: 8
- Fiber: 1
- Carbs: 22
- Protein: 25

Beef Pot Roast

Preparation time: 10 minutes
Cooking time: 1 hour
Servings: 6

Ingredients:

- 3 pounds beef roast
- Salt and ground black pepper, to taste
- 17 ounces beef stock
- 3 ounces red wine
- ½ teaspoon chicken salt
- ½ teaspoon smoked paprika
- 1 yellow onion, peeled and chopped
- 4 garlic cloves, peeled and minced
- 3 carrots, peeled and chopped
- 5 potatoes, chopped

Directions:

In a bowl, mix the salt, pepper, chicken, salt, and paprika and stir. Rub the beef with this mixture and put it into the Instant Pot. Add the onion, garlic, stock, and wine, toss to coat, cover the Instant Pot and cook on Meat Stew for 50 minutes. Release the pressure, uncover the Instant Pot, add the carrots and potatoes, cover again, and cook on the Steam setting for 10 minutes. Release the pressure again, uncover the Instant Pot, transfer the roast to a platter, drizzle cooking juices all over, and serve with the vegetables on the side.

Nutrition:

- Calories: 290
- Fat: 20
- Fiber: 0
- Carbs: 2
- Protein: 25

Beef and Vegetables

Preparation time: 10 minutes
Cooking time: 30 minutes
Servings: 4

Ingredients:

- 2 tablespoons extra virgin olive oil
- 1½ pounds, beef chuck roast, cubed
- 4 tablespoons flour
- 1 yellow onion, peeled and chopped
- 2 tablespoons red wine
- 2 garlic cloves, peeled and minced
- 2 cups water
- 2 cups beef stock
- Salt and ground black pepper, to taste
- 1 bay leaf
- ½ teaspoon dried thyme
- 2 celery stalks, chopped
- 2 carrots, peeled and chopped
- 4 potatoes, chopped
- ½ bunch parsley, chopped

Directions:

Season the beef with salt and pepper and mix with half of the flour. Set the Instant Pot on Sauté mode, add the oil and heat it up. Add the beef, brown for 2 minutes, and transfer to a bowl. Add the onion to the Instant Pot, stir, and cook for 3 minutes. Add the garlic, stir, and cook for 1 minute. Add the wine, stir well, and cook for 15 seconds. Add the rest of the flour and stir well for 2 minutes. Return the meat to the Instant Pot, add the stock, water, bay leaf, and thyme, stir, cover and cook on the Meat/Stew setting for 12 minutes. Release the pressure, uncover the Instant Pot, add the carrots, celery, and potatoes, stir, cover the Instant Pot and cook on the Steam setting for 5 minutes. Release the pressure naturally for 10 minutes, uncover the Instant Pot, divide among plates, and serve with parsley sprinkled on top.

Nutrition:

- Calories: 221
- Fat: 5.3
- Fiber: 1
- Carbs: 20.2
- Protein: 22.7

Veal with Mushrooms

Preparation time: 10 minutes
Cooking time: 35 minutes
Servings: 4

Ingredients:

- 3.5 ounces button mushrooms, sliced
- 3.5 ounces shiitake mushrooms, sliced
- 2 pounds veal shoulder, cut into medium chunks
- 17 ounces potatoes, chopped
- 16 ounces shallots, peeled and chopped
- 9 ounces beef stock
- 2 ounces white wine
- 1 tablespoon white flour
- 2 garlic cloves, peeled and minced
- 2 tablespoons chives, chopped
- 1 teaspoon dried sage
- 1/8 teaspoon dried thyme
- Salt and ground black pepper, to taste
- 3½ tablespoons extra virgin olive oil

Directions:

Set the Instant Pot on Sauté mode, add 1½ tablespoons oil, and heat it up. Add the veal, season with salt and pepper, stir, brown for 5 minutes, and transfer to a bowl. Add the rest of the oil to the Instant Pot and heat it up. Add the mushrooms, stir, and cook for 3 minutes. Add the garlic, stir, cook for 1 minute, and transfer everything to a bowl. Add the wine and flour to the Instant Pot, stir, and cook for 1 minute. Add the stock, sage, and thyme and return the meat to the Instant Pot. Stir, cover and cook on the Meat/Stew setting for 20 minutes. Release the pressure, uncover the Instant Pot, return the mushrooms and garlic, and stir. Add the potatoes and shallots, stir, cover, and cook on the Manual setting for 4 minutes. Release the pressure again, uncover the Instant Pot, add more salt and pepper, if needed, add the chives, stir, divide among bowls, and serve.

Nutrition:

- Calories: 395
- Fat: 18
- Fiber: 1.4
- Carbs: 7.1
- Protein: 47.8

Beef and Pasta Casserole

Preparation time: 10 minutes
Cooking time: 20 minutes
Servings: 4

Ingredients:

- 17 ounces pasta
- 1 pound ground beef
- 13 ounces mozzarella cheese, shredded
- 16 ounces tomato puree
- 1 celery stalk, chopped
- 1 yellow onion, peeled and chopped
- 1 carrot, peeled and chopped
- 1 tablespoon red wine
- 2 tablespoons butter
- Salt and ground black pepper, to taste

Directions:

Set the Instant Pot on Sauté mode, add the butter and melt it. Add the carrot, onion, and celery, stir, and cook for 5 minutes. Add the beef, salt and pepper, and cook for 10 minutes. Add the wine, stir and cook for 1 minute. Add the pasta, tomato puree, and water to cover pasta, stir, cover and cook on the Manual setting for 6 minutes. Release the pressure, uncover the Instant Pot, add the cheese, stir, divide everything among plates, and serve.

Nutrition:

- Calories: 182
- Fat: 1
- Fiber: 1.4
- Carbs: 31
- Protein: 12

Korean Beef

Preparation time: 10 minutes
Cooking time: 25 minutes
Servings: 6

Ingredients:

- ¼ cup soybean paste
- 1 cup chicken stock
- 2 pounds beefsteak, cut into thin strips
- ¼ teaspoon red pepper flakes
- Salt and ground black pepper, to taste
- 1 yellow onion, peeled and sliced thin
- 1 zucchini, cubed
- 1 ounce shiitake mushroom caps, cut into quarters
- 12 ounces extra firm tofu, cubed
- 1 chili pepper, sliced
- 1 scallion, chopped

Directions:

Set the Instant Pot on Sauté mode, add the stock and soybean paste, stir, and simmer for 2 minutes. Add the beef, salt, pepper, and pepper flakes stir, cover the Instant Pot, and cook on the Meat/Stew setting for 15 minutes. Release the pressure, add the tofu, onion, zucchini and mushrooms, stir, bring to a boil, cover the Instant Pot, and cook on the Manual setting for 4 minutes. Release the pressure again, uncover the Instant Pot, add more salt and pepper, add the chili pepper and scallion, stir, divide into bowls, and serve.

Nutrition:

- Calories: 310
- Fat: 9.3
- Fiber: 0.2
- Carbs: 18.4
- Protein: 35.3

Beef and Broccoli

Preparation time: 10 minutes
Cooking time: 10 minutes
Servings: 4

Ingredients:

- 3 pounds beef chuck roast, cut into thin strips
- 1 tablespoon peanut oil
- 1 yellow onion, peeled and chopped
- ½ cup beef stock
- 1 pound broccoli florets
- 2 teaspoons toasted sesame oil
- 2 tablespoons potato starch

For the marinade:
- 1 cup soy sauce
- 1 tablespoon sesame oil
- 2 tablespoons fish sauce
- 5 garlic cloves, peeled and minced
- 3 red peppers, dried and crushed
- ½ teaspoon Chinese five spice powder
- White rice, already cooked, for serving
- Toasted sesame seeds, for serving

Directions:

In a bowl, mix the soy sauce with the fish sauce, 1 tablespoon sesame oil, garlic, five spice powder, and crushed red peppers and stir well. Add the beef strips, toss to coat, and set aside for 10 minutes. Set the Instant Pot on Sauté mode, add the peanut oil and heat it up. Add the onions, stir, and cook for 4 minutes. Add the beef and marinade, stir, and cook for 2 minutes. Add the stock, stir, cover the Instant Pot and cook on the Meat/Stew setting for 5 minutes. Release the pressure naturally for 10 minutes, uncover the Instant Pot, add the cornstarch with ¼ cup liquid from the Instant Pot, add the broccoli to the steamer basket, cover the Instant Pot again, and cook for 3 minutes on Manual mode. Release the pressure, uncover the Instant Pot, divide the beef into bowls on top of rice, add the broccoli on the side, drizzle the toasted sesame oil, sprinkle with sesame seeds, and serve.

Nutrition:

- Calories: 338
- Fat: 18
- Fiber: 5
- Carbs: 50
- Protein: 20

Beef and Cabbage

Preparation time: 10 minutes
Cooking time: 1 hour and 20 minutes
Servings: 6

Ingredients:

- 2½ pounds beef brisket
- 4 cups water
- 2 bay leaves
- 3 garlic cloves, peeled and chopped
- 4 carrots, peeled and chopped
- 1 cabbage head, cut into 6 wedges
- 6 potatoes, cut into quarters
- Salt and ground black pepper, to taste
- 3 turnips, cut into quarters
- Horseradish sauce, for serving

Directions:

Put the beef brisket and water into the Instant Pot, add the salt, pepper, garlic, and bay leaves, cover the Instant Pot and cook on the Meat/Stew setting for 1 hour and 15 minutes. Release the pressure, uncover the Instant Pot, add the carrots, cabbage, potatoes, and turnips, stir, cover the Instant Pot, and cook on the Manual setting for 6 minutes. Release the pressure naturally, uncover the Instant Pot, divide among plates, and serve with horseradish sauce on top.

Nutrition:

- Calories: 340
- Fat: 24
- Fiber: 1
- Carbs: 14
- Protein: 26

Lamb Shanks

Preparation time: 10 minutes
Cooking time: 45 minutes
Servings: 4

Ingredients:

- 4 lamb shanks
- 2 tablespoons extra virgin olive oil
- 2 tablespoons white flour
- 1 yellow onion, peeled and diced
- 3 carrots, peeled and chopped
- 2 garlic cloves, peeled and minced
- 2 tablespoons tomato paste
- 1 teaspoon dried oregano
- 1 tomato, cored and chopped
- 2 tablespoons water
- 4 ounces red wine
- Salt and ground black pepper, to taste
- 1 beef bouillon cube

Directions:

In a bowl, mix the flour with salt and pepper. Add the lamb shanks and toss to coat. Set the Instant Pot on Sauté mode, add the oil and heat it up. Add the lamb, brown on all sides, and transfer to a bowl. Add the onion, oregano, carrots, and garlic to the Instant Pot, stir and cook for 5 minutes. Add the tomato, tomato paste, water, wine, and bouillon cube, stir and bring to a boil. Return the lamb to pot, stir, cover, and cook on Manual mode for 25 minutes. Release the pressure, uncover the Instant Pot, divide the lamb among plates, pour cooking sauce all over, and serve.

Nutrition:

- Calories: 430
- Fat: 17
- Fiber: 2.5
- Carbs: 11.3
- Protein: 50

Lamb Ribs

Preparation time: 15 minutes
Cooking time: 20 minutes
Servings: 8

Ingredients:

- 8 lamb ribs
- 4 garlic cloves, peeled and minced
- 2 carrots, peeled and chopped
- 13 ounces veggie stock
- 4 rosemary sprigs
- 2 tablespoons extra virgin olive oil
- Salt and ground black pepper, to taste
- 3 tablespoons white flour

Directions:

Set the Instant Pot on Sauté mode, add the oil, and heat it up. Add the lamb, garlic, salt and pepper, and brown it on all sides. Add the flour, stock, rosemary, and carrots, stir well, cover the Instant Pot and cook on the Meat/Stew setting for 20 minutes. Release the pressure, uncover the Instant Pot, discard the rosemary, divide the lamb on plates, and serve with the cooking liquid drizzled on top.

Nutrition:

- Calories: 234
- Fat: 8.4
- Fiber: 1
- Carbs: 3
- Protein: 35

Mediterranean Lamb

Preparation time: 15 minutes
Cooking time: 60 minutes
Servings: 4

Ingredients:

- 6 pound lamb leg, boneless
- 2 tablespoons extra virgin olive oil
- Salt and ground black pepper, to taste
- 1 bay leaf
- 1 teaspoon marjoram
- 1 teaspoon dried sage
- 1 teaspoon ginger, grated
- 3 garlic cloves, peeled and minced
- 1 teaspoon dried thyme
- 2 cups vegetable stock
- 3 pounds potatoes, chopped
- 3 tablespoons arrowroot powder, mixed with ⅓ cup water

Directions:

Set the Instant Pot on Sauté mode, add the oil, and heat it up. Add the lamb leg and brown on all sides. Add the salt, pepper, bay leaf, marjoram, sage, ginger, garlic, thyme, and stock, stir, cover the Instant Pot, and cook on the Meat/Stew setting for 50 minutes. Release the pressure, add the potatoes, arrowroot mix, more salt and pepper, if needed, stir, cover the Instant Pot, and cook on Manual for 10 minutes. Release the pressure, uncover the Instant Pot, divide lamb among plates, and serve.

Nutrition:

- Calories: 238
- Fat: 5
- Fiber: 4
- Carbs: 17
- Protein: 7.3

Lamb Curry

Preparation time: 10 minutes
Cooking time: 25 minutes
Servings: 6

Ingredients:

- 1½ pounds lamb shoulder, cut into medium chunks
- 2 ounces coconut milk
- 3 ounces dry white wine
- 3 tablespoons pure cream
- 3 tablespoons curry powder
- 2 tablespoons vegetable oil
- 3 tablespoons water
- 1 yellow onion, peeled and chopped
- 1 tablespoon parsley, chopped
- Salt and ground black pepper, to taste

Directions:

In a bowl, mix half of the curry powder with the salt, pepper, and coconut milk, and stir well. Set the Instant Pot on Sauté mode, add the oil and heat it up. Add the onion, stir, and cook for 4 minutes. Add the rest of the curry powder, stir, and cook for 1 minute. Add the lamb, brown them for 3 minutes, and mix with water, salt, pepper, and wine. Stir, cover the Instant Pot and cook on the Meat/Stew setting for 20 minutes. Release the pressure, set the Instant Pot to Manual mode, add the coconut milk mixture, stir, and boil for 5 minutes. Divide among plates, sprinkle parsley on top, and serve.

Nutrition:

- Calories: 378
- Fat: 8
- Fiber: 3
- Carbs: 18
- Protein: 22

Lamb Chops

Preparation time: 15 minutes
Cooking time: 35 minutes
Servings: 6

Ingredients:

- 3 pounds lamb chops
- Salt and ground black pepper, to taste
- 2 tablespoons flour
- 2 tablespoons extra virgin olive oil
- 2 yellow onions, peeled and chopped
- 3 ounces red wine
- 2 garlic cloves, peeled and crushed
- 2 carrots, peeled and sliced
- 2 celery sticks, chopped
- 2 tablespoons tomato sauce
- 2 bay leaves
- 1 cup green peas
- 14 ounces canned diced tomatoes
- 4 ounces green beans
- 2 tablespoons fresh parsley, diced
- Beef stock

Directions:

Put the flour in a bowl and mix with salt and pepper. Add the lamb chops and toss to coat. Set the Instant Pot on Sauté mode, add the oil, and heat it up. Add the lamb, stir, brown for 3 minutes on all sides, and transfer to a plate. Add the garlic and onion, stir, and cook for 2 minutes. Add the wine and cook for 2 minutes. Add the bay leaves, carrots, celery, and return the lamb to the Instant Pot. Add the tomato sauce, tomatoes, green beans, and peas and stir. Add enough stock to cover everything, cover the Instant Pot and cook on the Meat/Stew setting for 20 minutes. Release the pressure, uncover the Instant Pot, add the parsley, more salt and pepper, if needed, divide among plates, and serve.

Nutrition:

- Calories: 435
- Fat: 31
- Fiber: 4
- Carbs: 6
- Protein: 22

Moroccan Lamb

Preparation time: 10 minutes
Cooking time: 25 minutes
Servings: 8

Ingredients:

- 2½ pounds lamb shoulder, chopped
- 3 tablespoons honey
- 3 ounces almonds, peeled and chopped
- 9 ounces prunes, pitted
- 8 ounces vegetable stock
- 2 yellow onions, peeled and chopped
- 2 garlic cloves, peeled and minced
- 1 bay leaf
- Salt and ground black pepper, to tastes
- 1 cinnamon stick
- 1 teaspoon cumin
- 1 teaspoon turmeric
- 1 teaspoon ground ginger
- 1 teaspoon ground cinnamon
- Sesame seeds, for serving
- 3 tablespoons extra virgin olive oil

Directions:

In a bowl, mix the ground cinnamon with ginger, cumin, turmeric, garlic, and 2 tablespoons olive oil, and stir well. Add the meat and toss to coat. Put the prunes in a bowl, cover them with hot water and set aside. Set the Instant Pot on Sauté mode, add the rest of the oil, and heat it up. Add the onions, stir, cook for 3 minutes, transfer to a bowl and set aside. Add the meat to the Instant Pot, and brown it for 10 minutes. Add the stock, cinnamon stick, and bay leaf, and return the onions, stir, cover the Instant Pot and cook on the Meat/Stew setting for 25 minutes. Release the pressure naturally, uncover the Instant Pot, add the prunes, salt, pepper, and honey, and stir. Set the Instant Pot on Manual mode, cook everything for 5 minutes, and discard the bay leaf and cinnamon stick. Divide among plates, and serve with almonds and sesame seeds on top.

Nutrition:

- Calories: 434
- Fat: 21
- Fiber: 4
- Carbs: 41
- Protein: 20
- Sugar: 9

Lamb Ragout

Preparation time: 15 minutes
Cooking time: 1 hour
Servings: 8

Ingredients:
- 1½ pounds mutton, bone-in
- 2 carrots, peeled and sliced
- ½ pounds mushrooms, sliced
- 4 tomatoes, cored and chopped
- 1 yellow onion, peeled and chopped
- 6 garlic cloves, peeled and minced
- 2 tablespoons tomato paste
- 1 teaspoon vegetable oil
- Salt and ground black pepper, to taste
- 1 teaspoon dried oregano
- ½ cup parsley, diced

Directions:

Set the Instant Pot on Sauté mode, add the oil, and heat it up. Add the meat and brown it on all sides. Add the tomato paste, tomatoes, onion, garlic, mushrooms, oregano, carrots, and water to cover everything. Add the salt and pepper, stir, cover the Instant Pot, and cook on the Meat/Stew setting for 1 hour. Release the pressure, take the meat out of the Instant Pot , discard the bones, and shred it. Return the meat to pot, add the parsley and stir. Add more salt and pepper, if needed, and serve.

Nutrition:
- Calories: 360
- Fat: 14
- Fiber: 3
- Carbs: 15.1
- Protein: 30

Lamb and Barley Dish

Preparation time: 15 minutes
Cooking time: 45 minutes
Servings: 4

Ingredients:
- 6 ounces barley
- 5 ounces peas
- 1 lamb leg, already cooked, boneless and chopped
- 3 yellow onions, peeled and chopped
- 5 carrots, peeled and chopped
- 6 ounces beef stock
- 12 ounces water
- Salt and ground black pepper, to taste

Directions:

In the Instant Pot, mix the stock with water and barley, cover and cook on the Meat/Stew setting for 20 minutes. Release the pressure, uncover the Instant Pot, add the onions, peas, and carrots, stir, cover, and cook on the Manual setting for 10 minutes. Release the pressure, add the meat, salt, and pepper, stir, divide into bowls, and serve.

Nutrition:
- Calories: 324
- Fat: 9
- Fiber: 4
- Carbs: 21
- Protein: 15

Lamb and White Beans

Preparation time: 10 minutes
Cooking time: 40 minutes
Servings: 4

Ingredients:

- 4 lamb chops
- 1½ cups white beans, soaked overnight and drained
- 1 cup onion, peeled and chopped
- 2 cups canned diced tomatoes
- 1 cup leeks, chopped
- 2 tablespoons garlic, minced
- 1 teaspoon herbs de Provence
- Salt and ground black pepper, to taste
- 3 cups water
- 2 teaspoons Worcestershire sauce

Directions:

Put the lamb chops into the Instant Pot. Add the beans, onion, tomatoes, leeks, garlic, salt, pepper, herbs de Provence, Worcestershire sauce and water. Stir, cover and cook on the Meat/Stew setting for 40 minutes. Release the pressure, uncover the Instant Pot, divide among plates, and serve.

Nutrition:

- Calories: 520
- Fat: 17
- Fiber: 7
- Carbs: 35
- Protein: 56

Mexican-style Lamb

Preparation time: 10 minutes
Cooking time: 50 minutes
Servings: 4

Ingredients:

- 3 pounds lamb shoulder, cubed
- 19 ounces enchilada sauce
- 3 garlic cloves, peeled and minced
- 1 yellow onion, peeled and chopped
- 2 tablespoons extra virgin olive oil
- Salt, to taste
- ½ bunch fresh cilantro, diced
- warm corn tortillas, for serving
- lime wedges, for serving
- refried beans, for serving

Directions:

Put the enchilada sauce in a bowl, add the lamb and marinade for 24 hours. Set the Instant Pot on Sauté mode, add the oil, and heat it up. Add the onions and garlic, stir, and cook for 5 minutes. Add the lamb, salt, and marinade, stir, bring to a boil, cover the Instant Pot, and cook on the Meat/Stew setting for 45 minutes. Release the pressure, take the meat and put it on a cutting board and set aside to cool down for a few minutes. Shred the meat and put it in a bowl. Add the cooking sauce to it and stir. Divide the meat on tortillas, sprinkle cilantro on each, add the beans, sprinkle with lime juice, roll, and serve.

Nutrition:

- Calories: 484
- Fat: 19
- Fiber: 9
- Carbs: 28
- Protein: 44

Goat with Roasted Tomatoes

Preparation time: 10 minutes
Cooking time: 60 minutes
Servings: 4

Ingredients:
- 17 ounces goat meat, cubed
- 1 carrot, peeled and chopped
- 1 celery rib, chopped
- 4 ounces tomato paste
- 1 yellow onion, peeled and chopped
- 3 garlic cloves, peeled and crushed
- Sherry
- ½ cup water
- Salt and ground black pepper, to taste
- 1 cup chicken stock
- 2 tablespoons extra virgin olive oil
- 1 tablespoon cumin
- Dried rosemary
- 2 roasted tomatoes, cored chopped

Directions:
Set the Instant Pot on Sauté mode, add 1 tablespoon oil, and heat it up. Add the goat, salt, and pepper, and brown for a few minutes on each side. Add the cumin and rosemary, stir, cook for 2 minutes, and transfer to a bowl. Add the rest of the oil to the Instant Pot and heat it up. Add onion, garlic, salt, and pepper, stir, and cook for 1 minute. Add the carrot and celery, stir, and cook 2 minutes. Add the sherry, stock, water, goat, tomato paste, more salt and pepper, stir, cover and cook on Meat/Stew for 40 minutes. Release the pressure naturally, uncover the Instant Pot, add the tomatoes, stir, divide among plates, and serve.

Nutrition:
- Calories: 340
- Fat: 3.8
- Fiber: 4.1
- Carbs: 30
- Protein: 12.6

Goat and Potatoes

Preparation time: 10 minutes
Cooking time: 50 minutes
Servings: 5

Ingredients:

- 2½ pounds goat meat, cut into small cubes
- Salt and ground black pepper, to taste
- 5 tablespoons vegetable oil
- 3 teaspoons turmeric
- 3 potatoes, cut into halves
- 1 teaspoon sugar
- 4 cloves
- 3 cardamom pods
- 3 onions, peeled and chopped
- 2-inch cinnamon stick
- 1-inch piece of ginger, grated
- 2 tomatoes, cored and chopped
- 4 garlic cloves, peeled and minced
- 2 green chilies, chopped
- ¾ teaspoon chili powder
- 2½ cups water
- 1 teaspoon fresh cilantro, chopped

Directions:

Put the goat in a bowl, add the salt, pepper, and turmeric, toss to coat, and set aside for 10 minutes. Set the Instant Pot on Sauté mode, add the oil and half of the sugar, stir, and heat up. Add the potatoes, fry them a bit, and transfer to a bowl. Add the cloves, cinnamon stick, and cardamom to the Instant Pot, and stir. Add the ginger, onion, chilies, and garlic, stir, and cook for 3 minutes. Add the tomatoes and chili powder, stir, and cook for 5 minutes. Add the meat, stir, and cook for 10 minutes. Add the 2 cups water, stir, cover, and cook on the Meat/Stew setting for 15 minutes. Release the pressure, uncover the Instant Pot, add more salt and pepper, the rest of the sugar, potatoes and ½ cup water, cover, and cook on the Manual setting for 5 minutes. Release the pressure again, uncover the Instant Pot, divide among plates, sprinkle the cilantro on top, and serve.

Nutrition:

- Calories: 300
- Fat: 17
- Fiber: 1
- Carbs: 5
- Protein: 30

Apple Cider Pork

Preparation time: 10 minutes
Cooking time: 25 minutes
Servings: 4

Ingredients:

- 2 pounds pork loin
- 2 cups apple cider
- 2 tablespoons extra virgin olive oil
- Salt and ground black pepper, to taste
- 1 yellow onion, peeled and chopped
- 2 apples, cored and chopped
- 1 tablespoon dried onion flakes

Directions:

Set the Instant Pot on Sauté mode, add the oil, and heat it up. Add the pork loin, salt, pepper, and dried onion, stir, and brown the meat on all sides and transfer to a plate. Add the onion to the Instant Pot, stir, and cook for 2 minutes. Return the meat to Instant Pot, add the cider, apples, more salt and pepper, stir, cover, and cook on Manual mode for 20 minutes. Release the pressure, uncover the Instant Pot, transfer pork to a cutting board, slice it, and divide among plates. Add the sauce and mix from the Instant Pot on the side, and serve.

Nutrition:

- Calories: 450
- Fat: 22
- Fiber: 2.2
- Carbs: 29
- Protein: 37.2

Pork Chops and Onion

Preparation time: 10 minutes
Cooking time: 15 minutes
Servings: 4

Ingredients:
- 4 pork chops
- 2 tablespoons fresh parsley, chopped
- 1 garlic clove, peeled and minced
- 2 tablespoons lime juice
- 2 tablespoons extra virgin olive oil
- 1 pound onions, peeled and sliced
- ½ cup milk
- Salt and ground black pepper, to taste
- 2 tablespoons butter
- 2 tablespoons cornstarch mixed with 3 tablespoons water
- 1 tablespoon white flour
- ½ cup white wine

Directions:
Set the Instant Pot on Sauté mode, add the oil and butter and heat it up. Add the pork chops, salt, and pepper, brown on all sides, and transfer to a bowl. Add the garlic and onion to pot, stir, and cook for 2 minutes. Add the wine, lime juice, milk, parsley, and return pork chops to pot. Stir, cover and cook on the Manual setting for 15 minutes. Release the pressure, uncover the Instant Pot, add the cornstarch slurry and flour, stir well and cook, on Manual mode for 3 minutes. Divide the pork chops and onions on plates, drizzle the cooking sauce all over, and serve.

Nutrition:
- Calories: 222
- Fat: 7
- Fiber: 3
- Carbs: 9
- Protein: 22.2

Creamy Pork Chops

Preparation time: 10 minutes
Cooking time: 20 minutes
Servings: 4

Ingredients:
- 4 pork chops, boneless
- 1 cup water
- 2 tablespoons extra virgin olive oil
- 2 teaspoons chicken bouillon
- 10 ounces canned cream of mushroom soup
- 1 cup sour cream
- Salt and ground black pepper, to taste
- ½ small bunch fresh parsley, chopped

Directions:
Set the Instant Pot on Sauté mode, add the oil and heat it up. Add the pork chops, salt, and pepper, brown them on all sides, transfer to a plate and set the dish aside. Add the water and bouillon to the Instant Pot and stir well. Return the pork chops, stir, cover and cook on the Manual setting for 9 minutes. Release the pressure naturally, transfer the pork chops to a platter and set aside. Set the Instant Pot on Manual mode and heat up the cooking liquid. Add the mushroom soup, stir, cook for 2 minutes, and take off heat. Add the parsley and sour cream, stir, and pour over pork chops.

Nutrition:
- Calories: 284
- Fat: 16
- Fiber: 1
- Carbs: 10.5
- Protein: 23.2

Pulled Pork

Preparation time: 10 minutes
Cooking time: 1 hour and 20 minutes
Servings: 6

Ingredients:

- 3 pounds pork shoulder, boneless and cut into large chinks
- 11 ounces beer
- 8 ounces water
- 3 ounces white sugar
- Salt, to taste
- 2 teaspoons dry mustard
- 2 teaspoons smoked paprika

For the sauce:
- 4 ounces hot water
- 12 ounces apple cider vinegar
- 2 tablespoons brown sugar
- Salt and ground black pepper, to taste
- Cayenne pepper
- 2 teaspoons dry mustard

Directions:

In a bowl, mix the white sugar with smoked paprika, 2 teaspoons dry mustard, and salt. Rub the pork with this mixture and put pieces into the Instant Pot. Add the beer and 3 ounces water, stir, cover the Instant Pot and cook on the Meat/Stew setting for 75 minutes. Release the pressure, uncover the Instant Pot, transfer the pork to a cutting board, shred with 2 forks and set the dish aside. Discard half of the cooking liquid from the Instant Pot. In a bowl, mix the brown sugar with 4 ounces hot water, vinegar, cayenne, salt, pepper, and 2 teaspoons dry mustard, and stir well. Pour this over cooking sauce from the Instant Pot, stir, cover and cook on the Manual setting for 3 minutes. Release the pressure, divide pork among plates, drizzle the sauce all over, and serve.

Nutrition:

- Calories: 440
- Fat: 12
- Fiber: 4
- Carbs: 40
- Protein: 32

Pork Roast with Fennel

Preparation time: 10 minutes
Cooking time: 1 hour and 20 minutes
Servings: 4

Ingredients:

- 2 pounds pork meat, boneless
- 2 tablespoons extra virgin olive oil
- Salt and ground black pepper, to taste
- 2 garlic cloves, peeled and minced
- 1 yellow onion, peeled and chopped
- 5 ounces white wine
- 5 ounces chicken stock
- 1 pound fennel bulbs, sliced

Directions:

Set the Instant Pot on Sauté mode, add the oil and heat it up. Add the pork, salt and pepper, stir, brown on all sides, and transfer to a plate. Add the garlic, wine, and stock to the Instant Pot, stir, and cook for 2 minutes. Return pork to pot, cover, and cook on the Manual setting for 40 minutes. Release the pressure, uncover the Instant Pot, add the onion and fennel, stir, cover and cook on the Manual setting for 15 minutes. Release the pressure again, stir your mix, transfer the pork to a cutting board, slice, and divide among plates. Serve with onion and fennel on the side with the cooking sauce all over.

Nutrition:

- Calories: 428
- Fat: 16
- Fiber: 1.1
- Carbs: 29
- Protein: 38

Chinese Barbecue Pork

Preparation time: 10 minutes
Cooking time: 50 minutes
Servings: 6

Ingredients:
- 2 pounds pork belly
- 4 tablespoons soy sauce
- 2 tablespoons dry sherry
- 1-quart chicken stock
- 8 tablespoons char siu sauce
- 2 teaspoons sesame oil
- 2 tablespoons honey
- 1 teaspoon peanut oil

Directions:

Set the Instant Pot on Manual mode, add the sherry, stock, soy sauce and half of char siu sauce, stir, and cook for 8 minutes. Add the pork, stir, cover and cook on the Meat/Stew setting for 30 minutes. Release the pressure naturally, transfer the pork to a cutting board, set aside to cool down and chop into small pieces. Heat up a pan with the peanut oil over medium-high heat, add the pork, stir, and cook for a few minutes. In a bowl, mix the sesame oil with the rest of the char siu sauce and honey. Brush the pork with the sauce, stir, and cook for 10 minutes. Heat up another pan over medium-high heat, add the cooking liquid from the Instant Pot and bring to a boil. Simmer for 3 minutes and take off the heat. Divide the pork on plates, drizzle the sauce over it, and serve.

Nutrition:
- Calories: 400
- Fat: 23
- Fiber: 1
- Carbs: 15
- Sugar: 14
- Protein: 41

Braised Pork

Preparation time: 10 minutes
Cooking time: 75 minutes
Servings: 6

Ingredients:
- 4 pounds pork butt, chopped
- 16 ounces chicken stock
- 16 ounces red wine
- 4 ounces lemon juice
- 2 tablespoons extra virgin olive oil
- ¼ cup onion, chopped
- ¼ cup garlic powder
- 1 tablespoon paprika
- Salt and ground black pepper, to taste

Directions:

In the Instant Pot, mix the pork with the stock, wine, lemon juice, onion, garlic powder, oil, paprika, salt, and pepper, stir, cover, and cook on the Meat/Stew mode for 45 minutes. Release the pressure naturally for 15 minutes, stir the pork, divide into bowls, and serve.

Nutrition:
- Calories: 454
- Fat: 45
- Fiber: 1
- Carbs: 2
- Protein: 8

Pork Chops and Brown Rice

Preparation time: 10 minutes
Cooking time: 25 minutes
Servings: 6

Ingredients:

- 2 cups water
- ⅓ cup brown sugar
- ⅓ cup salt
- 2 cups ice
- 2 hot peppers, minced
- 1 tablespoon peppercorns, crushed
- 4 garlic cloves, peeled and crushed
- 2 bay leaves
- 2 pounds pork chops
- 2 cups brown rice
- 1 cup onion, peeled and chopped
- 3 tablespoons butter
- 2½ cups beef stock
- Salt and ground black pepper, to taste

Directions:

Heat up a pan over medium-high heat with the water. Add the salt and brown sugar, stir until it dissolves, take off heat, and add the ice. Add the hot peppers, garlic, peppercorns, and bay leaves and stir. Add the pork chops, toss to coat, cover, and keep in the refrigerator for 4 hours. Rinse the pork chops and pat them dry with paper towels. Set the Instant Pot on Sauté mode, add the butter and melt it. Add the pork chops, brown them on all sides, transfer to a plate and set the dish aside. Add the onion to the Instant Pot and cook for 2 minutes. Add the rice, stir, and cook for 1 minute. Add the stock, pork chops, cover the Instant Pot and cook on the Meat/Stew setting for 22 minutes. Release the pressure naturally for 10 minutes, uncover the Instant Pot, add salt and pepper, divide the pork chops and rice among plates, and serve.

Nutrition:

- Calories: 430
- Fat: 12.3
- Fiber: 4.3
- Carbs: 53
- Protein: 30

Pork Chops and Smashed Potatoes

Preparation time: 15 minutes
Cooking time: 20 minutes
Servings: 6
Ingredients:

- 6 pork chops, boneless
- 2 pounds potatoes, cut into chunks
- 2 cups chicken stock
- 3 garlic cloves, peeled and chopped
- 1 yellow onion, peeled and cut into chunks
- 1 bunch mixed rosemary, sage, oregano, and thyme
- Salt and ground black pepper, to taste
- 2 tablespoons butter
- 1 teaspoon smoked paprika
- 2 tablespoons white flour

Directions:

Put the potatoes into the Instant Pot. Add the garlic and half of the onion. Add the herbs and stock. Place the pork chops on top, add salt, pepper, and paprika. Cover and cook on the Meat/Stew setting for 15 minutes. Meanwhile, heat up a pan over medium heat, add butter, and heat it up. Add the flour, stir well, cook for 2 minutes, and take off heat. Release the pressure, transfer the pork to a platter and discard the herbs. Transfer the potatoes to a bowl, add some of the cooking liquid, add the salt and pepper, and stir using a hand mixer. Set the Instant Pot on Manual mode, and cook the cooking liquid for 2 minutes. Add the butter mix and stir until it thickens. Divide the pork chops on plates, add the mashed potatoes on the side, and drizzle the gravy from the Instant Pot all over.

Nutrition:

- Calories: 510
- Fat: 22
- Fiber: 5.7
- Carbs: 47
- Protein: 30.2

Country-style Ribs

Preparation time: 2 hours
Cooking time: 20 minutes
Servings: 8

Ingredients:

- 5 pounds country style ribs, boneless
For the brine:
- ½ cup brown sugar
- ½ cup salt
- 4 cups water
- 2 tablespoons liquid smoke
- 3 garlic cloves, peeled and crushed
For the ribs:
- 2 tablespoons butter
- ½ tablespoons water
- 1 cup onion, peeled and chopped
- 1 pound apples, cored, peeled and sliced
- ½ teaspoon ground cinnamon
- 1 teaspoon chili powder
- Cayenne pepper
For the sauce:
- 1 tablespoons liquid smoke
- 2 tablespoons yellow mustard
- 2 tablespoons Dijon mustard
- 2 tablespoons brown sugar
- 1 teaspoon hot sauce
- 1 tablespoon Worcestershire sauce
- 1 tablespoon soy sauce
- ¼ cup honey
- 2 tablespoons water
- 2 tablespoons cornstarch

Directions:

In a bowl, mix the 4 cups water with ½ cup salt, ½ cup sugar, 2 tablespoons liquid smoke, and garlic. Stir, add the pork ribs and keep in the refrigerator for 2 hours. Set the Instant Pot on Sauté mode, add 2 tablespoons butter and melt it. Add the ribs, brown them on all sides, and transfer to a plate. Add the onions½ tablespoon water, stir, and cook for 2 minutes. Add the cinnamon, cayenne, chili powder, and apples. Return the ribs, cover the Instant Pot, and cook on the Meat/Stew setting for 15 minutes. Release the pressure, transfer the ribs to a plate and set aside. Puree the onions and apples using a food processor, and set the Instant Pot on Sauté mode again. Add the yellow mustard, Dijon mustard, 1 tablespoon liquid smoke, 2 tablespoons sugar, Worcestershire sauce, hot sauce, soy sauce, and honey and stir well. Add the cornstarch mixed with 2 tablespoons water, stir, and cook for 2 minutes. Divide the ribs on plates, drizzle the gravy all over, and serve.

Nutrition:

- Calories: 470
- Fat: 34
- Fiber: 3
- Carbs: 11
- Protein: 29

Ribs and Coleslaw

Preparation time: 15 minutes
Cooking time: 35 minutes
Servings: 4

Ingredients:

- 2½ pounds pork baby back ribs
- Salt and ground black pepper, to taste
- 1 teaspoon onion powder
- ½ teaspoon paprika
- ½ teaspoon dry mustard
- ½ teaspoon chili powder
- ½ teaspoon garlic powder

For the sauce:

- 1 small yellow onion, peeled and chopped
- 2 bacon slices, chopped
- 6 ounces tomato paste
- ¾ cup tomato sauce
- 2 garlic cloves, peeled and minced
- Salt and ground black pepper, to taste
- ¼ cup coconut aminos

- ½ teaspoon smoked paprika
- Cayenne pepper
- ⅓ cup apple cider vinegar
- 1 tablespoon vegetable oil
- ½ cup apple juice

For the coleslaw:

- 1 cup red cabbage, shredded
- 3 cups green cabbage, shredded
- 1 cup raisins
- 2½ teaspoons caraway seeds
- ¼ cup apple cider vinegar
- ¾ cup mayonnaise
- Salt and ground black pepper, to taste
- 2 carrots, peeled and grated
- 2 green onions, chopped

Directions:

In a salad bowl, mix the cabbage with the green onions, carrots, and raisins. In a small bowl, mix the caraway seeds with the mayonnaise, salt, pepper¼ cup vinegar, and stir well. Pour this over the coleslaw, toss to coat and keep in the refrigerator until ready to serve. In a bowl, mix the onion powder with paprika, salt, pepper, dry mustard, garlic powder, and chili powder. Rub the ribs with this mixture and place them into the Instant Pot. Add some water, cover the Instant Pot and cook on the Meat/Stew setting for 15 minutes. Heat up a pan with the oil over medium heat, add the bacon and cook for 2 minutes. Add the onion and garlic, stir, and cook for 5 minutes. Add the tomato sauce and tomato paste, apple juice, coconut aminos, ⅓ cup vinegar, paprika, and a pinch of cayenne pepper, salt, and pepper, stir, and cook for 10 minutes. Release the pressure from the Instant Pot, uncover, and transfer the ribs to a plate. Add some of the sauce to the bottom of the Instant Pot , add a layer of ribs, then a layer of sauce, then another layer of ribs until all of the ribs are in the Instant Pot. Cover the Instant Pot and cook on the Manual setting for 10 minutes. Release the pressure again, divide the ribs and sauce among plates, and serve with the coleslaw.

Nutrition:

- Calories: 360
- Fat: 15
- Fiber: 1

- Carbs: 4
- Sugar: 3
- Protein: 17

Asian Short Ribs

Preparation time: 10 minutes
Cooking time: 60 minutes
Servings: 4

Ingredients:
- 2 green onions, chopped
- 1 teaspoon vegetable oil
- 3 garlic cloves, peeled and minced
- 3 ginger slices
- 4 pounds short ribs
- ½ cup water
- ½ cup soy sauce
- ¼ cup rice wine
- ¼ cup pear juice
- 2 teaspoons sesame oil

Directions:
Set the Instant Pot on Sauté mode, add the oil, and heat it up. Add the green onions, ginger, and garlic, stir, and cook for 1 minute. Add the ribs, water, wine, soy sauce, sesame oil, and pear juice, stir, and cook for 2-3 minutes. Cover the Instant Pot and cook on the Meat/Stew setting for 45 minutes. Release the pressure naturally for 15 minutes, uncover the Instant Pot, and transfer the ribs to a plate. Strain the liquid from the Instant Pot, divide the ribs among plates and drizzle the sauce all over.

Nutrition:
- Calories: 300
- Fat: 11
- Fiber: 1
- Carbs: 5
- Protein: 10

Short Ribs and Beer

Preparation time: 15 minutes
Cooking time: 60 minutes
Servings: 6

Ingredients:
- 4 pounds short ribs, cut into small pieces
- 1 teaspoon vegetable oil
- 1 yellow onion, peeled and chopped
- Salt and ground black pepper, to taste
- ¼ cup tomato paste
- 1 cup dark beer
- 1 cup chicken stock
- 1 thyme sprig
- 1 bay leaf
- 6 thyme sprigs
- 1 Portobello mushroom, dried

Directions:
Set the Instant Pot on Sauté mode, add the oil, and heat it up. Add the ribs, salt, and pepper, brown for 3 minutes on each side, and transfer to a bowl. Add the tomato paste and onion to the Instant Pot, stir, and cook for 5 minutes. Add the stock and beer, stir, and cook 30 seconds. Add the mushroom, bay leaves, thyme, and ribs, stir, cover the Instant Pot and cook on the Meat/Stew setting for 35 minutes. Release the pressure naturally for 15 minutes, uncover the Instant Pot, discard the thyme, mushroom, and bay leaves and strain the sauce. Divide the ribs among plates, and serve with beer sauce drizzled all over.

Nutrition:
- Calories: 240
- Fat: 8.1
- Fiber: 1
- Carbs: 11
- Protein: 24

Pork Carnitas

Preparation time: 10 minutes
Cooking time: 1 hour and 10 minutes
Servings: 8

Ingredients:

- 2 tablespoons extra virgin olive oil
- 3 pounds pork shoulder, chopped
- Salt and ground black pepper, to taste
- 1 jalapeño pepper, chopped
- 1 poblano pepper, seeded and chopped
- 1 green bell pepper, seeded and chopped
- 3 garlic cloves, peeled and minced
- 1 yellow onion, peeled and chopped
- 1 pound tomatillos, cut into quarters
- 1 teaspoon dried oregano
- 1 teaspoon cumin
- 2 cups chicken stock
- 2 bay leaves
- Flour tortillas, for serving
- 1 red onion, chopped, for serving
- Shredded cheddar cheese, for serving

Directions:

Set the Instant Pot on Sauté mode, add the oil and heat it up. Add the pork, salt, and pepper and brown them for 3 minutes. Add the bell pepper, jalapeño pepper, poblano pepper, tomatillos, onion, garlic, oregano, cumin, bay leaves, and stock. Stir, cover, and cook on the Meat/Stew setting for 55 minutes. Release the pressure naturally for 10 minutes, uncover and transfer meat to a cutting board. Puree the mix from the Instant Pot using an immersion blender. Shred the meat with a fork and mix with the puree. Divide the pork mixture onto flour tortillas, add the onion and cheese, and serve.

Nutrition:

- Calories: 355
- Fat: 23
- Fiber: 1
- Carbs: 10
- Protein: 23

Pork with Orange and Honey

Preparation time: 10 minutes
Cooking time: 1 hour
Servings: 4

Ingredients:

- 1½ pounds pork shoulder, chopped
- 3 garlic cloves, peeled and minced
- 1 cinnamon stick
- Juice from 1 orange
- Salt and ground black pepper, to taste
- 1 yellow onion, peeled and sliced
- 1 tablespoon ginger, sliced
- 2 cloves
- ½ cup water
- 1 teaspoon dried rosemary
- 1 tablespoon maple syrup
- 2 tablespoons soy sauce
- 1 tablespoon vegetable oil
- 1 tablespoon honey
- 1 tablespoon water
- 1½ tablespoons cornstarch

Directions:

Set the Instant Pot on Sauté mode, add the oil, and heat it up. Add the pork, salt and pepper, stir, brown for 5 minutes on each side, and transfer to a plate. Add the onions, ginger, salt, and pepper to the Instant Pot, stir, and cook for 1 minute. Add the garlic and cook for 30 seconds. Add the orange juice, water, soy sauce, honey, maple syrup, cinnamon, cloves, rosemary, and pork pieces. Cover the Instant Pot, cook on the Meat/Stew setting for 50 minutes and release the pressure naturally. Uncover the Instant Pot, discard the cinnamon and cloves, add the cornstarch mixed with water, stir, set the Instant Pot on Sauté mode, and cook until the sauce thickens. Divide the pork and sauce among plates, and serve.

Nutrition:

- Calories: 300
- Fat: 7.4
- Fiber: 1
- Carbs: 33
- Protein: 20

Pork Tamales

Preparation time: 10 minutes
Cooking time: 1 hour and 35 minutes
Servings: 24 pieces

Ingredients:

- 8 ounces dried corn husks, soaked for 1 day and drained
- 4 cups water
- 3 pounds pork shoulder, boneless and chopped
- 1 yellow onion, peeled and chopped
- 2 garlic cloves, peeled and crushed
- 3 tablespoons chili powder
- Salt and ground black pepper, to taste
- 1 teaspoon cumin
- 4 cups masa
- ¼ cup corn oil
- ¼ cup shortening
- 1 teaspoon baking powder

Directions:

In the Instant Pot, mix 2 cups of the water with the salt, pepper, onion, garlic, chili powder, and cumin. Add the pork, stir, cover the Instant Pot, and cook on the Meat/Stew setting for 75 minutes. Release the pressure naturally for 10 minutes, uncover the Instant Pot, transfer meat to a cutting board, and shred it with 2 forks. Put the pork in a bowl, add 1 tablespoon of the cooking liquid and more salt and pepper, stir and set aside. In a bowl, mix the masa with salt, pepper, baking powder, shortening, and oil and combine using a hand mixer. Add the cooking liquid from the Instant Pot and blend again well. Add 2 cups of water to the Instant Pot and place the steamer basket inside. Unfold 2 of the corn husks, place them on a work surface, add ¼ cup of the masa mixture near the top of the husk, press into a square and leaves 2 inches at the bottom. Add 1 tablespoon pork in the center of the masa, wrap the husk around the dough and place standing up in the steamer basket. Repeat with the rest of the husks, cover the Instant Pot and cook on the Steam setting for 20 minutes. Release the pressure for 15 minutes, uncover the Instant Pot, transfer the tamales to plates, and serve.

Nutrition:

- Calories: 150
- Fat: 7.2
- Fiber: 2
- Carbs: 11
- Protein: 7

Pork Tostadas

Preparation time: 10 minutes
Cooking time: 30 minutes
Servings: 4

Ingredients:

- 4 pounds pork shoulder, boneless and cubed
- Salt and ground black pepper, to taste
- 2 cups cola
- ⅓ cup brown sugar
- ½ cup picante sauce
- 2 teaspoons chili powder
- 2 tablespoons tomato paste
- ¼ teaspoon cumin
- 1 cup enchilada sauce
- Corn tortillas, for serving
- Mexican cheese, shredded for serving
- Shredded lettuce, for serving
- Salsa, for serving
- Guacamole, for serving

Directions:

In the Instant Pot, mix 1 cup of the cola with picante sauce, salsa, sugar, tomato paste, chili powder, and cumin and stir. Add the pork, stir, cover, and cook on Meat/Stew mode for 25 minutes. Release the pressure for 15 minutes, uncover the Instant Pot, drain juice from the Instant Pot, transfer the meat to a cutting board and shred it. Return the meat to Instant Pot, add the rest of the cola and enchilada sauce, stir, set the Instant Pot on Sauté mode and heat thoroughly. Brown tortillas in the oven at 350°F for 5 minutes and place them on a working surface. Add the lettuce leaves, cheese and guacamole, fold, and serve.

Nutrition:

- Calories: 160
- Fat: 3
- Fiber: 3
- Carbs: 13
- Protein: 9

Pork with Hominy

Preparation time: 10 minutes
Cooking time: 30 minutes
Servings: 6

Ingredients:

- 1¼ pounds pork shoulder, boneless and cut into medium pieces
- 2 tablespoons vegetable oil
- Salt and ground black pepper, to taste
- 2 tablespoons chili powder
- 1 white onion, peeled and chopped
- 4 garlic cloves, peeled and minced
- 30 ounces canned hominy, drained
- 4 cups chicken stock
- Avocado slices, for serving
- Lime wedges, for serving
- ¼ cup water
- 2 tablespoons cornstarch

Directions:

Set the Instant Pot on Sauté mode, add 1 tablespoon oil and heat it up. Add the pork, salt, and pepper, brown on all sides, and transfer to a bowl. Add the rest of the oil to the Instant Pot and heat it up. Add the garlic, onion, and chili powder, stir, and sauté for 4 minutes. Add half of the stock, stir, and cook for 1 minute. Add the rest of the stock and return pork to pot, stir, cover, and cook on the Manual setting for 30 minutes. Release the pressure naturally for 10 minutes, transfer the pork to a cutting board, and shred with 2 forks. Add the cornstarch mixed with water to the Instant Pot and set on Sauté mode. Add the hominy, more salt and pepper, and shredded pork, stir, and cook for 2 minutes. Divide among bowls, and serve with avocado slices on top and lime wedges on the side.

Nutrition:

- Calories: 250
- Fat: 8.7
- Fiber: 7.7
- Carbs: 29
- Protein: 12

Kalua Pork

Preparation time: 10 minutes
Cooking time: 90 minutes
Servings: 5

Ingredients:

- 4 pounds pork shoulder, cut into half
- ½ cup water
- 2 tablespoons vegetable oil
- Salt and ground black pepper, to taste
- 1 tablespoon liquid smoke
- Steamed green beans, for serving

Directions:

Set the Instant Pot on Sauté mode, add the oil, and heat it up. Add the pork, salt, and pepper, brown for 3 minutes on each side, and transfer to a plate. Add the water and liquid smoke to the Instant Pot and stir. Return the meat, stir, cover the Instant Pot and cook on the Meat/Stew setting for 90 minutes. Release the pressure for 15 minutes, transfer the meat to a cutting board and shred it with 2 forks. Divide the pork on plates, add some of the sauce on top, and serve with steamed green beans on the side.

Nutrition:

- Calories: 243
- Fat: 15
- Fiber: 1
- Carbs: 1
- Protein: 26

Sausage and Red Beans

Preparation time: 15 minutes
Cooking time: 30 minutes
Servings: 8

Ingredients:

- 1 pound smoked sausage, sliced
- 1 pound red beans, dried, soaked overnight and drained
- 1 bay leaf
- 2 tablespoons Cajun seasoning
- 1 celery stalk, chopped
- Salt and ground black pepper, to taste
- ½ green bell pepper, seeded and chopped
- 1 teaspoon dried parsley
- 5 cups water
- ¼ teaspoon cumin
- 1 garlic clove, peeled and chopped
- 1 small yellow onion, peeled and chopped

Directions:

In the Instant Pot, mix the beans with the sausage, bay leaf, Cajun seasoning, celery, salt, pepper, bell pepper, parsley, cumin, garlic, onion, and water, stir, cover, and cook on the Bean/Chili setting for 30 minutes. Release the pressure, uncover the Instant Pot, divide mix into bowls, and serve.

Nutrition:

- Calories: 248
- Fat: 5
- Fiber: 12.3
- Carbs: 40
- Protein: 15.4

Pork Sausages and Mashed Potatoes

Preparation time: 15 minutes
Cooking time: 15 minutes
Servings: 6
Ingredients:

For the potatoes:

- 4 potatoes, peeled and cut into cubes
- Salt and ground black pepper, to taste
- 1 teaspoon dry mustard
- 1 tablespoon butter
- 4 ounces milk, warmed
- 6 ounces water
- 1 tablespoon cheddar cheese, grated

For the sausages:

- 6 pork sausages
- 2 tablespoons extra virgin olive oil
- ½ cup onion jam
- 3 ounces red wine
- 3 ounces water
- Salt and ground black pepper, to taste
- 1 tablespoon cornstarch mixed with 1 tablespoon water

Directions:

Put potatoes into the Instant Pot, add 6 ounces water, salt and pepper, stir, cover, and cook on Steam mode for 5 minutes. Release the pressure, drain the potatoes and put them in a bowl. Add the milk, butter, mustard, and more salt and pepper, and mash well. Add the cheese, stir again and set the dish aside. Set the Instant Pot on Sauté mode, add the oil and heat it up. Add the sausages and brown them on all sides. Add the onion jam, wine, 3 ounces water, and salt and pepper. Cover the Instant Pot and cook on the Meat/Stew mode setting for 8 minutes. Release the pressure quickly and divide sausages among plates. Add the cornstarch mixture to the Instant Pot and stir well. Drizzle the sauce over sausages, and serve them with mashed potatoes.

Nutrition:

- Calories: 435
- Fat: 23
- Fiber: 5
- Carbs: 44.2
- Protein: 15

Meatloaf

Preparation time: 10 minutes
Cooking time: 40 minutes
Servings: 6

Ingredients:

- ⅓ cup milk
- ½ cup panko breadcrumbs
- 1 yellow onion, peeled and grated
- Salt and ground black pepper, to taste
- 2 eggs, whisked
- 2 pounds ground meat (beef, pork, veal)
- 2 cups water
- ¼ cup ketchup

Directions:

In a bowl, mix the breadcrumbs with the milk, stir and set aside for 5 minutes. Add the onion, salt, pepper, and eggs and stir. Add the ground meat and stir well. Place this on a greased aluminum foil and shape a loaf. Add the ketchup on top. Put the water into the Instant Pot, arrange meatloaf in the steamer basket of the Instant Pot, cover, and cook on the Meat/Stew setting for 35 minutes. Release the pressure for 10 minutes, uncover, take the meatloaf out, let it cool briefly for 5 minutes, slices, and serve it.

Nutrition:

- Calories: 300
- Fat: 18
- Fiber: 1
- Carbs: 10
- Protein: 24

Beef Meatloaf

Preparation time: 10 minutes
Cooking time: 25 minutes
Servings: 8

Ingredients:

- 2 pounds ground beef
- 3 bread slices
- ½ cup milk
- ¾ cup Parmesan cheese, grated
- Salt and ground black pepper, to taste
- 2 tablespoons dried parsley
- 2 cups water
- 8 bacon slices
- 3 eggs, whisked
- ½ cup barbecue sauce

Directions:

In a bowl, mix the bread slices with milk and set aside for 5 minutes. Add the meat, cheese, salt, pepper, eggs, and parsley and stir well. Shape into a loaf, place on aluminum foil, arrange bacon slices on top, tuck them underneath, and spread half of the barbecue sauce all over. Put the water in the Instant Pot, place the meatloaf in the steamer basket of the Instant Pot, cover and cook on Meat/Stew mode for 20 minutes. Release the pressure, uncover the Instant Pot, transfer meatloaf to a pan and spread the rest of the sauce over it. Introduce under a preheated broiler for 5 minutes, transfer to a platter, and slice.

Nutrition:

- Calories: 227
- Fat: 14.5
- Fiber: 1
- Carbs: 8.8
- Protein: 15

Meatball Delight

Preparation time: 10 minutes
Cooking time: 10 minutes
Servings: 8

Ingredients:

- 1½ pounds ground pork
- 2 tablespoons fresh parsley, chopped
- 1 egg
- 2 bread slices, soaked in water
- 2 garlic cloves, peeled and minced
- Salt and ground black pepper, to taste
- ¾ cup beef stock
- ½ teaspoon ground nutmeg
- ¼ cup flour
- 1 teaspoon Worcestershire sauce
- ½ teaspoon paprika
- 2 tablespoons extra virgin olive oil
- 2 carrots, peeled and chopped
- ¾ cup fresh peas
- 2 potatoes, cubed
- 1 bay leaf
- ¼ cup white wine

Directions:

In a bowl, mix the ground meat with the bread, egg, salt, pepper, parsley, paprika, garlic, and nutmeg, and stir well. Add 1 tablespoon of stock and Worcestershire sauce and stir again. Shape meatballs and dust them with flour. Set the Instant Pot on Sauté mode, add the oil and heat it up. Add the meatballs and brown them on all sides. Add the carrots, peas, potatoes, bay leaf, stock and wine, cover the Instant Pot and cook on the Meat/Stew setting for 6 minutes. Release the pressure, uncover the Instant Pot, discard the bay leaf, divide the meatballs into bowls, and serve.

Nutrition:

- Calories: 400
- Fat: 13
- Fiber: 7
- Carbs: 24
- Protein: 17

Meatballs and Tomato Sauce

Preparation time: 10 minutes
Cooking time: 10 minutes
Servings: 6

Ingredients:

- 1 onion, peeled and chopped
- ⅓ cup Parmesan cheese, grated
- ½ cup bread crumbs
- ½ teaspoon dried oregano
- Salt and ground black pepper, to taste
- ½ cup milk
- 1 pound ground meat
- 1 tablespoon extra virgin olive oil
- 1 egg, whisked
- 1 carrot, peeled and chopped
- ½ celery stalk, chopped
- 2¾ cups tomato puree
- 2 cups water

Directions:

In a bowl, mix the bread crumbs with cheese, half of the onion, oregano, salt, and pepper, and stir. Add the milk and meat and stir well. Add the egg and stir again. Set the Instant Pot on Sauté mode, add the oil, and heat it up. Add the onion, stir, and cook for 3 minutes. Add the celery and carrot, tomato puree, water, and salt and stir again. Shape the meatballs and add them to the Instant Pot, toss them to coat, cover, and cook on the Meat/Stew setting for 5 minutes. Release the pressure naturally for 10 minutes, and serve with your favorite spaghetti.

Nutrition:

- Calories: 150
- Fat: 3
- Fiber: 1
- Carbs: 4
- Protein: 8

Instant Pot Fish and Seafood Recipes

White Fish with Orange Sauce

Preparation time: 10 minutes
Cooking time: 7 minutes
Servings: 4

Ingredients:

- 4 white fish fillets
- 4 green onions, chopped
- Extra virgin olive oil
- 2 tablespoons ginger, chopped
- Salt and ground black pepper, to taste
- Juice from 1 orange
- Zest from 1 orange
- 1 cup fish stock

Directions:

Pat the fish fillets dry, season with salt and pepper and rub them with the olive oil. Put the stock, ginger, orange juice, orange zest, and onions into the Instant Pot. Put the fish fillets in the steamer basket, cover the Instant Pot and cook on the Steam setting for 7 minutes. Release the pressure, divide fish among plates, and drizzle the orange sauce on top.

Nutrition:

- Calories: 170
- Fat: 2
- Fiber: 0.4
- Carbs: 10
- Protein: 23

Steamed Fish

Preparation time: 10 minutes
Cooking time: 10 minutes
Servings: 4

Ingredients:

- 4 white fish fillets
- 1 cup olives, pitted and chopped
- 1 pound cherry tomatoes, cut into halves
- Thyme, dried
- 1 garlic clove, peeled and minced
- Olive oil
- Salt and ground black pepper, to taste
- 1 cup water

Directions:

Put the water into the Instant Pot. Put the fish fillets in the steamer basket of the Instant Pot. Add the tomatoes and olives on top. Add the garlic, thyme, oil, salt, and pepper. Cover the Instant Pot and cook on Steam mode for 10 minutes. Release the pressure, uncover the Instant Pot, divide fish, olives, and tomatoes mix among plates, and serve.

Nutrition:

- Calories: 157
- Fat: 3.2
- Fiber: 0
- Carbs: 0
- Protein: 29

Fish Curry

Preparation time: 10 minutes
Cooking time: 15 minutes
Servings: 6

Ingredients:
- 6 fish fillets, cut into medium pieces
- 1 tomato, chopped
- 14 ounces coconut milk
- 2 onions, sliced
- 2 bell peppers, cored and cut into strips
- 2 garlic cloves, peeled and minced
- 2 tablespoons curry powder
- 1 tablespoons coriander
- 1 tablespoon ginger, grated
- ½ teaspoon turmeric
- 2 teaspoons cumin
- Salt and ground black pepper, to taste
- ½ teaspoon fenugreek
- 1 teaspoon red pepper flakes
- 2 tablespoons lemon juice

Directions:
Set the Instant Pot on Sauté mode, add the oil and curry powder, and fry for 1 minute. Add the ginger, onion, and garlic, stir, and cook for 2 minutes. Add the coriander, turmeric, cumin, fenugreek, and red pepper flakes, stir, and cook 2 minutes. Add the coconut milk, tomatoes, fish, and bell peppers, stir, cover, and cook on Steam mode for 5 minutes. Release the pressure naturally, add the salt and pepper, stir, and divide into bowls. Serve with lemon juice on top.

Nutrition:
- Calories: 230
- Fat: 10
- Fiber: 3
- Carbs: 12
- Protein: 23

Mediterranean Fish

Preparation time: 10 minutes
Cooking time: 10 minutes
Servings: 4

Ingredients:
- 4 cod fillets
- 17 ounces tomatoes, cored and cut into halves
- 1 garlic clove, peeled and crushed
- 1 cup olives, pitted and chopped
- 2 tablespoons capers, drained and chopped
- Salt and ground black pepper, to taste
- 1 tablespoon fresh parsley, chopped
- 1 tablespoon extra virgin olive oil

Directions:
Put the tomatoes on the bottom of a heat-proof bowl. Add the parsley, salt, and pepper and toss to coat. Place the fish fillets on top, add the olive oil, salt, pepper, garlic, olives, and capers. Place the bowl in the steamer basket of the Instant Pot, cover and cook on the Steam setting for 5 minutes. Release the pressure naturally, divide among plates, and serve.

Nutrition:
- Calories: 170
- Fat: 9
- Fiber: 1
- Carbs: 4
- Protein: 23

Cod and Peas

Preparation time: 15 minutes
Cooking time: 5
Servings: 4

Ingredients:

- 16 ounces cod fillets
- 1 tablespoon fresh parsley, chopped
- 10 ounces peas
- 9 ounces wine
- ½ teaspoon dried oregano
- ½ teaspoon paprika
- 2 garlic cloves, peeled and chopped
- Salt and ground black pepper, to taste

Directions:

In a food processor, mix the garlic with the parsley, oregano and paprika and blend well. Add the wine, blend again and set the dish aside. Place the fish fillets in the steamer basket of the Instant Pot, add salt and pepper, cover and cook on the Steam setting for 2 minutes. Release the pressure and divide fish among plates. Add the peas to the steamer basket, cover the Instant Pot again and cook for 2 minutes. Release the pressure again and arrange peas next to fish fillets and serve.

Nutrition:

- Calories: 200
- Fat: 2
- Fiber: 2
- Carbs: 10
- Protein: 20

Poached Salmon

Preparation time: 10 minutes
Cooking time: 5 minutes
Servings: 4

Ingredients:

- 16 ounces salmon fillet, skin on
- Zest from 1 lemon
- 4 scallions, chopped
- 3 black peppercorns
- ½ teaspoon fennel seeds
- 1 bay leaf
- 1 teaspoon white wine vinegar
- 2 cups chicken stock
- ½ cup dry white wine
- ¼ cup fresh dill, chopped
- Salt and ground black pepper, to taste

Directions:

Put the salmon in the steamer basket of the Instant Pot and season with salt and pepper. Add the stock, scallions, lemon zest, peppercorns, fennel, vinegar, bay leaf, wine, stock, and dill to the Instant Pot. Cover and cook on the Steam setting for 5 minutes. Release the pressure, uncover the Instant Pot, and divide the salmon among plates. Set the Instant Pot on Manual mode and cook the liquid for a few minutes. Drizzle over the salmon, and serve.

Nutrition:

- Calories: 140
- Fat: 4
- Fiber: 0
- Carbs: 2
- Protein: 23

Crispy Salmon Fillet

Preparation time: 5 minutes
Cooking time: 10 minutes
Servings: 2

Ingredients:

- 2 salmon fillets
- 1 cup water
- Salt and ground black pepper, to taste
- 2 tablespoons extra virgin olive oil

Directions:

Put the water into the Instant Pot. Place the salmon in the steamer basket, cover and cook on Steam mode for 3 minutes. Release pressure, transfer the salmon to paper towels, and pat dry them. Heat up a pan with the oil over medium-high heat, add the salmon fillets skin side down, season with salt and pepper to taste, and cook for 2 minutes. Divide among plates, and serve.

Nutrition:

- Calories: 230
- Fat: 12
- Fiber: 1
- Carbs: 0
- Protein: 29

Salmon and Rice

Preparation time: 5 minutes
Cooking time: 5 minutes
Servings: 2

Ingredients:

- 2 salmon fillets
- Salt and ground black pepper, to taste
- ½ cup jasmine rice
- 1 cup chicken stock
- ¼ cup vegetable soup mix, dried
- 1 tablespoon butter
- Saffron

Directions:

In the Instant Pot, mix the stock with rice, soup mix, butter, and saffron and stir. Season the salmon with salt and pepper, place the fish in the steamer basket of the Instant Pot, cover, and cook on Steam mode for 5 minutes. Release the pressure, divide the salmon among plates, add the rice mix on the side, and serve.

Nutrition:

- Calories: 300
- Fat: 8
- Fiber: 0.5
- Carbs: 30
- Protein: 25

Salmon and Vegetables

Preparation time: 10 minutes
Cooking time: 10 minutes
Servings: 2

Ingredients:

- 2 salmon fillets, skin on
- 1 bay leaf
- 1 cup water
- 1 cinnamon stick
- 3 cloves
- 1 tablespoon canola oil
- 1 cup baby carrots
- 2 cups broccoli florets
- Salt and ground black pepper, to taste
- Lime wedges. for serving

Directions:

Put the water into the Instant Pot. Add the bay leaf, cinnamon stick, and cloves. Place the salmon fillets in the steamer basket of the Instant Pot after brushing them with canola oil. Season with salt and pepper, add the broccoli and carrots, cover the Instant Pot, and cook on the Steam setting for 6 minutes. Release the pressure for 4 minutes, uncover the Instant Pot, and divide the salmon and vegetables among plates. Drizzle with the sauce from the Instant Pot after discarding the cinnamon, cloves, and bay leaf, and serve with lime wedges on the side.

Nutrition:

- Calories: 170
- Fat: 4.5
- Fiber: 3.7
- Carbs: 13
- Protein: 17

Spicy Salmon

Preparation time: 10 minutes
Cooking time: 5 minutes
Servings: 4

Ingredients:

- 4 salmon fillets
- 2 tablespoons chili pepper, diced
- Juice of 1 lemon
- 1 lemon, sliced
- 1 cup water
- Salt and ground black pepper, to taste

Directions:

Place the salmon fillets in the steamer basket of the Instant Pot, add the salt, pepper, lemon juice, lemon slices, and chili pepper. Add 1 cup water to the Instant Pot, cover, and cook on the Steam setting for 5 minutes. Release the pressure, divide the salmon and lemon slices among plates, and serve.

Nutrition:

- Calories: 120
- Fat: 2
- Fiber: 0.5
- Carbs: 13
- Protein: 5

Salmon with Tomatoes

Preparation time: 10 minutes
Cooking time: 15 minutes
Servings: 4

Ingredients:

- 4 salmon fillets
- 1 lemon, sliced
- 1 white onion, peeled and chopped
- 3 tomatoes, cored and sliced
- 4 thyme sprigs
- Fresh parsley, chopped
- 3 tablespoons extra virgin olive oil
- Salt and ground black pepper, to taste
- 2 cups water

Directions:

Drizzle the oil on a parchment paper. Add a layer of tomatoes, salt and pepper. Drizzle some oil again, add the fish and season them with salt and pepper. Drizzle some more oil, add the thyme and parsley, onions, lemon slices, salt, and pepper. Fold and wrap packet, place in the steamer basket of the Instant Pot. Add the cups water to the Instant Pot, cover, and cook on Steam for 15 minutes. Release the pressure, uncover the Instant Pot, open the packet, divide the fish among plates, and serve.

Nutrition:

- Calories: 180
- Fat: 5
- Fiber: 1
- Carbs: 0
- Protein: 31

Salmon Burger

Preparation time: 10 minutes
Cooking time: 10 minutes
Servings: 4

Ingredients:

- 1 teaspoon extra virgin olive oil
- ½ cup panko bread crumbs
- 1 pound salmon meat, minced
- 2 tablespoons lemon zest
- Salt and ground black pepper, to taste
- Mustard, for serving
- Tomatoes slices, for serving
- Arugula leaves, for serving
- Sandwich buns

Directions:

Put the salmon into a food processor and blend it. Transfer to a bowl, add the bread crumbs, salt, pepper, and lemon zest, and stir well. Shape 4 patties and place them on a working surface. Set the Instant Pot on Sauté mode, add the oil, and heat it up. Add the patties, cook for 3 minutes on each side and place them on buns. Serve with tomatoes, arugula, and mustard.

Nutrition:

- Calories: 170
- Fat: 9
- Fiber: 0
- Carbs: 1
- Protein: 22

Creamy Fish Stew

Preparation time: 10 minutes
Cooking time: 25 minutes
Servings: 6

Ingredients:

- 17 ounces white fish, cut into medium chunks
- 1 yellow onion, peeled and chopped
- 13 ounces potatoes, peeled and cut into chunks
- 13 ounces milk
- Salt and ground black pepper, to taste
- 14 ounces chicken stock
- 14 ounces water
- 14 ounces half and half

Directions:

In the Instant Pot mix the fish with the onion, potatoes, water, milk, and stock. Cover and cook on the Meat/Stew setting for 10 minutes. Release the pressure, uncover, and set the Instant Pot on Manual mode. Add the salt, pepper, and half and half, stir, and cook for 10 minutes. Divide among bowls, and serve.

Nutrition:

- Calories: 194
- Fat: 4.4
- Fiber: 2
- Carbs: 21
- Protein: 17

Salmon and Raspberry Sauce

Preparation time: 2 hours
Cooking time: 5 minutes
Servings: 6

Ingredients:

- 6 salmon steaks
- 2 tablespoons extra virgin olive oil
- 4 leeks, sliced
- 2 garlic cloves, peeled and minced
- 2 tablespoons fresh parsley, chopped
- 1 cup clam juice
- 2 tablespoons lemon juice
- Salt and white pepper to the taste
- 1 teaspoon sherry
- ⅓ cup dill, diced
- Raspberries, for serving

For the raspberry vinegar:
- 2 pints red raspberries
- 1 pint cider vinegar

Directions:

Mix the red raspberries with vinegar and stir well. Add the salmon steaks and set aside in the refrigerator for 2 hours. Set the Instant Pot on Sauté mode, add the oil, and heat it up. Add the parsley, leeks, and garlic, stir, and cook for 2 minutes. Add the clam and lemon juice, sherry, salt, pepper, and dill and stir. Add the salmon steaks, cover, and cook on the Manual setting for 3 minutes. Release the pressure, uncover the Instant Pot, divide the salmon among plates, and serve with leeks and fresh raspberries.

Nutrition:

- Calories: 670
- Fat: 46
- Fiber: 1
- Carbs: 18
- Protein: 81

Fish Pudding

Preparation time: 10 minutes
Cooking time: 20 minutes
Servings: 4

Ingredients:

- 1 pound cod fillets, cut into medium pieces
- 2 tablespoons fresh parsley, chopped
- 4 ounces bread crumbs
- 2 teaspoons lemon juice
- 2 eggs, whisked
- 2 ounces butter
- ½ pint milk
- ½ pint shrimp sauce
- Salt and ground black pepper, to taste
- ½ pint water

Directions:

In a bowl, mix the fish with the bread crumbs, lemon juice, parsley, salt, and pepper and stir. Heat up a pan with the butter over medium-high heat. Put the milk in a pot and bring to a boil over medium-high heat. Pour the butter and milk over the egg and stir well. Add this to the fish and set aside for 3 minutes. Pour everything into a greased pudding dish and place in the steamer basket of the Instant Pot. Add the pint water to the Instant Pot, cover and cook on the Manual setting for 15 minutes. Release the pressure, uncover, divide among plates, and serve with shrimp sauce.

Nutrition:

- Calories: 200
- Fat: 3
- Fiber: 1
- Carbs: 8
- Protein: 9

Jambalaya

Preparation time: 10 minutes
Cooking time: 4 minutes
Servings: 8

Ingredients:

- 1 pound chicken breast, boneless, skinless, and chopped
- 1 pound shrimp, peeled and deveined
- 2 tablespoons extra virgin olive oil
- 1 pound sausage, already cooked and chopped
- 2 cups onions, chopped
- 1½ cups rice
- 2 tablespoons garlic, chopped
- 2 cups green, yellow and red bell peppers, chopped
- 3½ cups chicken stock
- 1 tablespoon Creole seasoning
- 1 tablespoon Worcestershire sauce
- 1 cup tomatoes, crushed

Directions:

Set the Instant Pot on Sauté mode, add the chicken and Creole seasoning, stir, brown on all sides, and transfer to a bowl. Add the oil and heat it up. Add the peppers, onions, and garlic, stir, and cook for 2 minutes. Add the rice, stir, and cook for 2 minutes. Add the tomato puree, stock, and Worcestershire sauce and return the chicken to the Instant Pot. Stir everything, cover, and cook for 10 minutes. Release the pressure, add the sausage and shrimp, stir, cover and cook on the Manual setting for 2 minutes. Release the pressure, uncover, divide among plates, and serve.

Nutrition:

- Calories: 250
- Fat: 13
- Fiber: 1
- Carbs: 22
- Protein: 27

Tuna and Noodle Casserole

Preparation time: 10 minutes
Cooking time: 15 minutes
Servings: 4

Ingredients:

- 8 ounces egg noodles
- ½ cup red onion, chopped
- 1 tablespoon extra virgin olive oil
- 1¼ cups water
- 14 ounces canned tomatoes, chopped and mixed with oregano, basil and garlic
- Salt and ground black pepper, to taste
- 14 ounces canned tuna, drained
- 8 ounces artichoke hearts, drained and chopped
- 1 tablespoon fresh parsley, chopped
- Crumbled feta cheese

Directions:

Set the Instant Pot on Sauté mode, add the oil and heat it up. Add the onion, stir, and cook for 2 minutes. Add the tomatoes, noodles, salt, pepper, and water, set the Instant Pot on Manual mode and cook for 10 minutes. Add the tuna and artichokes, stir, cover and cook for 5 minutes. Release the pressure, divide the casserole among plates, sprinkle the cheese and parsley on top, and serve.

Nutrition:

- Calories: 300
- Fat: 4
- Fiber: 9
- Carbs: 23
- Protein: 29

Cheesy Tuna

Preparation time: 5 minutes
Cooking time: 5 minutes
Servings: 4

Ingredients:

- 14 ounces canned tuna, drained
- 16 ounces egg noodles
- 28 ounces cream of mushroom soup
- 1 cup peas, frozen
- 3 cups water
- 4 ounces cheddar cheese, grated
- ¼ cup breadcrumbs

Directions:

Add the noodles, water, tuna, peas, and soup to the Instant Pot, stir, cover, cook on the Manual setting for 4 minutes, and release the pressure. Add the cheese and stir. Transfer everything to a baking dish, spread breadcrumbs all over and place under a preheated broiler for 3 minutes. Divide among plates, and serve.

Nutrition:

- Calories: 270
- Fat: 12
- Fiber: 0.5
- Carbs: 20
- Protein: 15

Roasted Mackerel

Preparation time: 10 minutes
Cooking time: 6 minutes
Servings: 4

Ingredients:

- 18 ounces mackerel, cut into pieces
- 3 garlic cloves, peeled and minced
- 8 shallots, peeled and chopped
- 1 teaspoon dried shrimp powder
- 1 teaspoon turmeric
- 1 tablespoon chili paste
- 2 lemongrass sticks, cut into halves
- 1 small piece of ginger, chopped
- 2 tablespoons cilantro
- 3½ ounces water
- 5 tablespoons vegetable oil
- 1 ⅓ tablespoons tamarind paste mixed with 3½ ounces water
- Salt, to taste
- 1 tablespoon sugar

Directions:

In your blender, mix the garlic with the shallots, chili paste, turmeric, and shrimp powder and blend well. Set the Instant Pot on Sauté mode, add the oil, and heat it up. Add the fish pieces; chili paste, ginger, lemongrass, and cilantro and cook for 1 minute. Add the tamarind mix, water, salt, and sugar, stir, cover and cook on the Manual setting for 5 minutes. Release the pressure, uncover the Instant Pot, divide among plates, and serve.

Nutrition:

- Calories: 189
- Fat: 11
- Fiber: 0
- Carbs: 1
- Protein: 20

Miso Mackerel

Preparation time: 10 minutes
Cooking time: 50 minutes
Servings: 4

Ingredients:

- 2 pounds mackerel, cut into big pieces
- 1 cup water
- 1 garlic clove, peeled and crushed
- 1 shallot, peeled and sliced
- 1-inch ginger piece, chopped
- ⅓ cup sake
- ⅓ cup mirin
- ¼ cup miso
- 1 onion, peeled and sliced thin
- 2 celery stalks, sliced
- 1 tablespoon rice vinegar
- 1 teaspoon spicy mustard
- Salt, to taste
- 1 teaspoon sugar

Directions:

Set the Instant Pot on Sauté mode, add the mirin, sake, ginger, garlic, and shallot, stir, and boil for 2 minutes. Add the miso and water and stir. Add the mackerel, cover the Instant Pot and cook on the Steam setting for 45 minutes. Put the onion and celery in a bowl and cover with ice water. In another bowl, mix the vinegar with salt, sugar, and mustard and stir well. Release the pressure from the Instant Pot naturally for 10 minutes and divide mackerel among plates. Drain the onion and celery well and mix with mustard dressing. Add to the mackerel, and serve.

Nutrition:

- Calories: 290
- Fat: 13
- Fiber: 0
- Carbs: 15
- Protein: 24

Mackerel with Lemon

Preparation time: 10 minutes
Cooking time: 10 minutes
Servings: 4

Ingredients:

- 4 mackerel fillets
- 3 ounces breadcrumbs
- Juice and zest of 1 lemon
- 1 tablespoon chives, diced
- Salt and ground black pepper, to taste
- 1 egg, whisked
- 3 tablespoons butter
- 1 tablespoon vegetable oil
- 10 ounces water
- 1 lemon, cut into wedges

Directions:

In a bowl, mix the breadcrumbs with the lemon juice, lemon zest, salt, pepper, egg, and chives and stir very well. Coat the mackerel with this mixture. Set the Instant Pot on Sauté mode, add the oil and 1 tablespoon butter and heat up. Add the fish, brown on all sides and transfer to a plate. Clean the Instant Pot and add the water. Grease a heat proof dish with the remaining butter and place in the Instant Pot. Add the fish, cover the Instant Pot and cook on the Steam setting for 6 minutes. Release the pressure, divide the mackerel among plates, and serve with lemon wedges.

Nutrition:

- Calories: 140
- Fat: 7.8
- Fiber: 0
- Carbs: 1
- Protein: 13

Steamed Mussels

Preparation time: 10 minutes
Cooking time: 5 minutes
Servings: 4

Ingredients:

- 2 pounds mussels, cleaned and scrubbed
- 1 radicchio, cut into thin strips
- 1 white onion, peeled and chopped
- 1 pound baby spinach
- ½ cup dry white wine
- 1 garlic clove, peeled and crushed
- ½ cup water
- Extra virgin olive oil

Directions:

Arrange the baby spinach and radicchio on appetizer plates. Set the Instant Pot on Sauté mode, add the oil and heat it up. Add the garlic and onion, stir, and cook for 4 minutes. Add the wine, stir, and cook for 1 minute. Place the mussels in the steamer basket of the Instant Pot , cover, and cook on Manual for 1 minute. Release the pressure and divide the mussels on top of the spinach and radicchio. Add the cooking liquid all over, and serve.

Nutrition:

- Calories: 50
- Fat: 1
- Fiber: 1
- Carbs: 0.3
- Protein: 1.1

Spicy Mussels

Preparation time: 10 minutes
Cooking time: 5 minutes
Servings: 3

Ingredients:

- 28 ounces canned crushed tomatoes
- ½ cup white onion, peeled and chopped
- 2 jalapeño peppers, chopped
- ¼ cup dry white wine
- ¼ cup extra virgin olive oil
- ¼ cup balsamic vinegar
- 2 pounds mussels, cleaned and scrubbed
- 2 tablespoons red pepper flakes
- 2 garlic cloves, peeled and minced
- Salt, to taste
- ½ cup fresh basil, chopped
- Lemon wedges, for serving

Directions:

Set the Instant Pot on Sauté mode, add the tomatoes, onion, jalapeños, wine, oil, vinegar, garlic, and pepper flakes, stir, and bring to a boil. Add the mussels, stir, cover, and cook on Manual for 4 minutes. Release the pressure, uncover, discard any unopened mussels, add the salt and basil, stir, divide among bowls, and serve with lemon wedges.

Nutrition:

- Calories: 50
- Fat: 0.2
- Fiber: 0.2
- Carbs: 1
- Protein: 1.5

Mussels and Spicy Sauce

Preparation time: 10 minutes
Cooking time: 4 minutes
Servings: 4

Ingredients:

- 2 pounds mussels, scrubbed and debearded
- 2 tablespoons extra virgin olive oil
- 1 yellow onion, peeled and chopped
- ½ teaspoon red pepper flakes
- 14 ounces tomatoes, cored and chopped
- 2 teaspoons garlic, minced
- ½ cup chicken stock
- 2 teaspoons dried oregano

Directions:

Set the Instant Pot on Sauté mode, add the oil, and heat it up. Add the onions, stir, and cook for 3 minutes. Add the pepper flakes and garlic, stir, and cook for 1 minute. Add the stock, oregano, and tomatoes and stir well. Add the mussels, stir, cover and cook on Manual mode for 2 minutes. Release the pressure, discard and unopened mussels, divide among bowls, and serve.

Nutrition:

- Calories: 60
- Fat: 0.2
- Fiber: 0.2
- Carbs: 1
- Protein: 1.3

Mussels with Sausage

Preparation time: 5 minutes
Cooking time: 5 minutes
Servings: 4

Ingredients:

- 2 pounds mussels, scrubbed and debearded
- 12 ounces amber beer
- 1 tablespoon extra virgin olive oil
- 1 yellow onion, chopped
- 8 ounces spicy sausage
- 1 tablespoon paprika

Directions:

Set the Instant Pot on Sauté mode, add the oil, and heat it up. Add the onion, stir, and cook for 2 minutes. Add the sausages and cook for 4 minutes. Add the paprika, beer, and mussels, stir, cover, and cook on Manual for 2 minutes. Release the pressure, uncover, discard any unopened mussels, transfer to bowls, and serve.

Nutrition:

- Calories: 100
- Fat: 4
- Fiber: 1
- Carbs: 3
- Protein: 14

Cioppino

Preparation time: 10 minutes
Cooking time: 15 minutes
Servings: 4

Ingredients:

- 12 littleneck clams
- 12 mussels
- 1½ pounds shrimp, peeled and deveined
- 1½ pounds fish fillets, cut into medium pieces
- 1 cup butter
- 2 yellow onions, peeled and chopped
- 3 garlic cloves, peeled and minced
- ½ cup fresh parsley, chopped
- 20 ounces canned diced tomatoes
- 8 ounces clam juice
- 1½ cups white wine
- 2 bay leaves
- ½ teaspoon dried marjoram
- 1 tablespoon dried basil
- Salt and ground black pepper, to taste

Directions:

Set the Instant Pot on Sauté mode, add the butter and melt it. Add the onion and garlic, stir, and cook for 2 minutes. Add the clam juice, tomatoes, wine, parsley, basil, bay leaves, marjoram, salt, and pepper, stir, cover and cook on the Manual setting for 10 minutes. Release the pressure and switch the Instant Pot to Sauté mode. Add the clams and mussels, stir, and cook for 8 minutes. Discard any unopened mussels and clams, add the fish and shrimp, stir, and cook for 4 minutes. Divide among bowls, and serve.

Nutrition:

- Calories: 300
- Fat: 12
- Fiber: 12
- Carbs: 10
- Protein: 20

Clams and Chorizo

Preparation time: 10 minutes
Cooking time: 15 minutes
Servings: 4

Ingredients:
- 15 littleneck clams
- 30 mussels, scrubbed and debearded
- 2 chorizo sausages, sliced
- 1 pound baby red potatoes
- 1 yellow onion, peeled and chopped
- 10 ounces beer
- 2 tablespoons fresh parsley, chopped
- 1 teaspoon extra virgin olive oil
- Lemon wedges, for serving

Directions:

Set the Instant Pot on Sauté mode, add the oil and heat it up. Add the chorizo and onions, stir, and cook for 4 minutes. Add the clams, mussels, potatoes and beer, stir, cover, and cook on the Steam setting for 10 minutes. Release the pressure, uncover, add the parsley, stir, divide among bowls, and serve with lemon wedges on the side.

Nutrition:
- Calories: 203
- Fat: 3
- Fiber: 8
- Carbs: 10
- Protein: 20

Parmesan Clams

Preparation time: 10 minutes
Cooking time: 5 minutes
Servings: 4

Ingredients:
- 24 clams, shucked
- 3 garlic cloves, peeled and minced
- 4 tablespoons butter
- ¼ cup fresh parsley, chopped
- ¼ cup Parmesan cheese, grated
- 1 teaspoon dried oregano
- 1 cup breadcrumbs
- 2 cups water
- Lemon wedges, for serving

Directions:

In a bowl, mix the breadcrumbs with the cheese, oregano, parsley, butter, and garlic and stir. Place 1 tablespoon of this mix in the clams. Place the clams in the steamer basket of the Instant Pot , add the water to the Instant Pot, cover, and cook on the Manual setting for 4 minutes. Release the pressure, uncover, divide among plates, and serve with lemon wedges.

Nutrition:
- Calories: 80
- Fat: 5
- Fiber: 0
- Carbs: 6
- Protein: 3

King Crab Legs

Preparation time: 5 minutes
Cooking time: 3 minutes
Servings: 4

Ingredients:
- 4 pounds king crab legs, broken in half
- 3 lemon wedges
- ¼ cup butter
- 1 cup water

Directions:
Put the crab legs in the steamer basket of the Instant Pot . Add the water to the Instant Pot, cover and cook on the Steam setting for 3 minutes. Release the pressure, uncover, transfer the crab legs to a bowl with the butter, and serve with lemon wedges on the side.

Nutrition:
- Calories: 50
- Fat: 0.2
- Fiber: 0.2
- Carbs: 0
- Protein: 7

Spicy Shrimp Delight

Preparation time: 10 minutes
Cooking time: 5 minutes
Servings: 4

Ingredients:
- 1½ pounds shrimp, peeled and deveined
- 2 tablespoons extra virgin olive oil
- 1 cup yellow onion, peeled and chopped
- 2 tablespoons fresh parsley, chopped
- 4 garlic cloves, peeled and minced
- 2 teaspoons hot paprika
- ½ cup fish stock
- ¼ cup dry white wine
- 1 cup tomato sauce
- Saffron
- White sugar
- 1 teaspoon red pepper flakes
- ¼ teaspoon dried thyme
- 1 bay leaf
- Salt and ground black pepper, to taste

Directions:
Set the Instant Pot on the Sauté mode, add the oil, and heat up. Add the shrimp, cook for 1 minute, and transfer to a platter. Add the onion, stir, and cook for 2 minutes. Add the parsley, garlic, paprika, and wine, stir, and cook for 2 minutes. Add the stock, tomato sauce, red pepper flakes, sugar, saffron, thyme, bay leaf, salt, and pepper. Cover and cook on the Manual setting for 4 minutes. Release the pressure, uncover, add the shrimp, cover again and cook on the Steam setting for 2 minutes. Release the pressure, uncover the Instant Pot, divide the shrimp mixture among plates, and serve.

Nutrition:
- Calories: 566
- Fat: 20
- Fiber: 8
- Carbs: 30
- Protein: 40

Shrimp Paella

Preparation time: 10 minutes
Cooking time: 5 minutes
Servings: 4

Ingredients:
- 20 shrimp, deveined
- 1 cup jasmine rice
- ¼ cup butter
- Salt and ground black pepper, to taste
- ¼ cup fresh parsley, chopped
- Red pepper flakes
- Saffron
- Juice of 1 lemon
- 1½ cups water
- 4 garlic cloves, peeled and minced
- Melted butter, for serving
- Hard cheese, grated, for serving
- Parsley, chopped, for serving

Directions:
Put the shrimp into the Instant Pot. Add the rice, butter, salt, pepper, parsley, lemon juice, water, garlic, and a pinch of red pepper flakes and saffron. Stir, cover, and cook on the Steam setting for 5 minutes. Release the pressure, uncover the Instant Pot, remove the shrimp and peel them. Return them to the Instant Pot, stir well, and divide into bowls. Add the melted butter, cheese, and parsley on top, and serve.

Nutrition:
- Calories: 320
- Fat: 4
- Fiber: 1.4
- Carbs: 12
- Protein: 22

Shrimp Boil

Preparation time: 10 minutes
Cooking time: 5 minutes
Servings: 4

Ingredients:
- 1½ pounds shrimp, heads removed
- 12 ounces Andouille sausage, already cooked and chopped
- 4 ears of corn, each cut into 3 pieces
- 1 tablespoon Old Bay seasoning
- 16 ounces beer
- Salt and ground black pepper, to taste
- 1 teaspoon red pepper flakes
- 2 sweet onions, peeled and cut into wedges
- 1 pound potatoes, cut into medium chunks
- 8 garlic cloves, peeled and crushed
- French baguettes, for serving

Directions:
In the Instant Pot, mix the beer with the Old Bay seasoning, red pepper flakes, salt, pepper, onions, garlic, potatoes, corn, sausage, and shrimp. Cover the Instant Pot and cook on the Steam setting for 5 minutes. Release the pressure, uncover the Instant Pot, divide the shrimp and other ingredients into bowls, and serve with French baguettes.

Nutrition:
- Calories: 360
- Fat: 10
- Fiber: 9
- Carbs: 41
- Protein: 30

Spicy Shrimp Curry

Preparation time: 10 minutes
Cooking time: 30 minutes
Servings: 4

Ingredients:

- 1 pound shrimp, peeled and deveined
- ⅓ cup butter
- 2 bay leaves
- 1 cinnamon stick
- 10 cloves
- 3 cardamom pods
- 2 red onions, peeled and chopped
- 14 red chilies, dried
- 3 green chilies, chopped
- ½ cup cashews
- 1 tablespoon garlic, crushed
- 1 tablespoon ginger, crushed
- 4 tomatoes, cored and chopped
- Salt, to taste
- 1 teaspoon sugar
- 1 teaspoon coriander
- ½ cup heavy cream

Directions:

Set the Instant Pot on Sauté mode, add the butter and melt it. Add the bay leaves, cardamom, cinnamon stick, and onion, stir, and cook for 3 minutes. Add the red chilies, green chilies, cashews, tomatoes, garlic, and ginger and stir. Add the salt, stir, cover and cook on the Manual setting for 15 minutes. Release the pressure, transfer everything to a blender and pulse several times. Strain into a pan and heat it up over medium-high heat. Add the shrimp, stir, cover, and cook for 12 minutes. Add coriander, cream and sugar, stir, cook for 2 minutes, take off heat, and divide among plates.

Nutrition:

- Calories: 299
- Fat: 9
- Fiber: 3
- Carbs: 26
- Protein: 27

Shrimp Curry

Preparation time: 10 minutes
Cooking time: 6 minutes
Servings: 4

Ingredients:

- 1 pound shrimp, peeled and deveined
- 1 cup bouillon
- 4 lemon slices
- Salt and ground black pepper, to taste
- ½ teaspoon curry powder
- ¼ cup mushrooms, sliced
- ¼ cup yellow onion, chopped
- 2 tablespoons shortening
- ½ cup raisins
- 3 tablespoons flour
- 1 cup milk

Directions:

Set the Instant Pot on Sauté mode, add the shortening, and heat up. Add the onion and mushroom, stir, and cook for 2 minutes. Add the salt, pepper, curry powder, lemon, bouillon, raisins, and shrimp. Stir, cover, and cook on the Steam setting for 2 minutes. In a bowl, mix the flour with milk and whisk well. Release the pressure from the Instant Pot, uncover, add the flour and milk mix, stir well, and cook until curry thickens on Manual mode. Divide among bowls, and serve.

Nutrition:

- Calories: 300
- Fat: 7
- Fiber: 2.5
- Carbs: 34
- Protein: 29

Shrimp and Dill Sauce

Preparation time: 10 minutes
Cooking time: 10 minutes
Servings: 4

Ingredients:

- 1 pound shrimp, peeled and deveined
- 2 tablespoons shortening
- 1 tablespoon yellow onion, chopped
- 1 cup white wine
- 2 tablespoons cornstarch
- ¾ cup milk
- 1 teaspoon fresh dill, chopped

Directions:

Set the Instant Pot on Sauté mode, add the shortening, and heat it up. Add the onion, stir, and cook for 2 minutes. Add the shrimp and wine, stir, cover and cook on the Manual setting for 2 minutes. Release the pressure, uncover the Instant Pot, and set it on Manual mode. In a bowl, mix the cornstarch with milk and stir. Add this to the shrimp and stir until it thickens. Add the dill, stir, simmer for 5 minutes, divide among bowls, and serve.

Nutrition:

- Calories: 300
- Fat: 10
- Fiber: 0
- Carbs: 7
- Protein: 10

Shrimp and Potatoes

Preparation time: 10 minutes
Cooking time: 15 minutes
Servings: 4

Ingredients:

- 2 pounds shrimp, peeled and deveined
- 1 pound tomatoes, cored, peeled, and chopped
- 8 potatoes, cut into quarters
- Salt, to taste
- 4 tablespoons extra virgin olive oil
- 4 onions, peeled and chopped
- 1 teaspoon coriander
- 1 teaspoon curry powder
- Juice of 1 lemon
- 1 tablespoon watercress, chopped

Directions:

Put potatoes in the steamer basket of the Instant Pot , add some water, cover and cook on the Steam setting for 10 minutes. Release the pressure, transfer the potatoes to a bowl, and wipe out the Instant Pot. Set the Instant Pot on Sauté mode, add the oil, and heat it up. Add the onions, stir, and cook for 5 minutes. Add the salt, coriander, and curry powder, stir, and cook for 5 minutes. Add the tomatoes, shrimp, lemon juice, and potatoes. Stir, cover, and cook on the Manual setting for 3 minutes. Release the pressure again, divide among bowls, and serve with watercress on top.

Nutrition:

- Calories: 140
- Fat: 2
- Fiber: 0
- Carbs: 5
- Protein: 19

Shrimp Creole

Preparation time: 10 minutes
Cooking time: 5 minutes
Servings: 4

Ingredients:
- 1 cup shrimp, already cooked
- 1½ cups rice, already cooked
- ½ teaspoon sugar
- 2 teaspoons vinegar
- 1 cup tomato juice
- Salt, to taste
- 1 teaspoons chili powder
- 1 yellow onion, peeled and chopped
- 1 cup celery, chopped
- 2 tablespoons shortening

Directions:
Set the Instant Pot on Sauté mode, add the shortening and heat it up. Add the onion and celery, stir, and cook for 2 minutes. Add the salt, chili powder, tomato juice, vinegar, sugar, and shrimp, and rice. Stir, cover and cook on the Manual setting for 3 minutes. Release the pressure, uncover the Instant Pot, divide among plates, and serve.

Nutrition:
- Calories: 294
- Fat: 9
- Fiber: 1.5
- Carbs: 27
- Protein: 24

Shrimp Teriyaki

Preparation time: 10 minutes
Cooking time: 4 minutes
Servings: 4

Ingredients:
- 1 pounds shrimp, peeled and deveined
- 2 tablespoons soy sauce
- ½ pound pea pods
- 3 tablespoons vinegar
- ¾ cup pineapple juice
- 1 cup chicken stock
- 3 tablespoons sugar

Directions:
Put the shrimp and pea pods into the Instant Pot. In a bowl, mix the soy sauce with vinegar, pineapple juice, stock, and sugar and stir well. Pour this into the Instant Pot, stir, cover, and cook on the Manual setting for 3 minutes. Release the pressure, uncover, divide among plates, and serve.

Nutrition:
- Calories: 200
- Fat: 4.2
- Fiber: 0.7
- Carbs: 13
- Protein: 38

Spicy Shrimp and Rice

Preparation time: 20 minutes
Cooking time: 10 minutes
Servings: 4

Ingredients:

- 18 ounces shrimp, peeled and deveined
- Salt, to taste
- ½ tablespoon mustard seeds
- ¼ cup vegetable oil
- 2 teaspoons dry mustard
- 1 teaspoon turmeric
- 2 green chilies, cut into halves lengthwise
- 2 onions, diced
- 4 ounces curd, beaten
- 1-inch piece of ginger, peeled and chopped
- Rice, already cooked, for serving

Directions:

Put the mustard seeds in a bowl, add enough water to cover, set aside for 10 minutes, drain and grind very well. Put the shrimp in a bowl, add oil, dry mustard, turmeric, mustard paste, salt, onions, chilies, curd, and ginger, toss to coat and set aside for 10 minutes. Transfer everything to the Instant Pot, cover and cook on Steam mode for 10 minutes. Release the pressure, divide among plates, and serve with boiled rice.

Nutrition:

- Calories: 200
- Fat: 2
- Fiber: 1
- Carbs: 7
- Protein: 11

Shrimp Scampi

Preparation time: 10 minutes
Cooking time: 4 minutes
Servings: 4

Ingredients:

- 1 pound shrimp, cooked, peeled and deveined
- 2 tablespoons extra virgin olive oil
- 1 garlic clove, peeled and minced
- 10 ounces canned diced tomatoes
- ⅓ cup tomato paste
- ¼ teaspoon dried oregano
- 1 tablespoon fresh parsley, diced
- ⅓ cup water
- 1 cup Parmesan cheese, grated
- Spaghetti noodles, already cooked, for serving

Directions:

Set the Instant Pot on Sauté mode, add the oil and heat up. Add the garlic, stir, and cook for 2 minutes. Add the shrimp, tomato paste, tomatoes, water, oregano and parsley, stir, cover, and cook on the Manual setting for 3 minutes. Release pressure, divide among plates, add spaghetti noodles, sprinkle with cheese, and serve.

Nutrition:

- Calories: 288
- Fat: 20
- Fiber: 0
- Carbs: 0.01
- Protein: 23

Fish and Shrimp

Preparation time: 10 minutes
Cooking time: 10 minutes
Servings: 4

Ingredients:

- 2 pounds flounder
- ½ cup water
- ½ pound shrimp, cooked, peeled and deveined
- 2 tablespoons butter
- Salt and ground black pepper, to taste
- 4 lemon wedges

Directions:

Season the fish with salt and pepper and place in the steamer basket of the Instant Pot. Add water to the Instant Pot, cover, and cook on the Steam setting for 10 minutes. Release the pressure, uncover the Instant Pot, transfer the fish to plates and set aside. Discard the water, wipe the Instant Pot clean, and set on Sauté mode. Add the butter and melt it. Add the shrimp, salt and pepper, stir and divide among plates on top of fish, and serve with lemon wedges on the side.

Nutrition:

- Calories: 200
- Fat: 0.2
- Fiber: 0.2
- Carbs: 1
- Protein: 12

Shrimp with Risotto and Herbs

Preparation time: 10 minutes
Cooking time: 20 minutes
Servings: 4

Ingredients:

- 4 tablespoons butter
- 2 garlic cloves, peeled and minced
- 1 yellow onion, peeled and chopped
- 1½ cups Arborio rice
- 2 tablespoons dry white wine
- ⅛ cup fresh parsley, chopped
- 4½ cups chicken stock
- Salt and ground black pepper, to taste
- 1 pound shrimp, peeled and deveined
- ¾ cup Parmesan cheese, grated
- ⅛ cup fresh tarragon, chopped

Directions:

Set the Instant Pot on Sauté mode, add 2 tablespoons butter, and melt. Add the garlic and onion, stir, and cook for 4 minutes. Add the rice, stir, and cook for 1 minute. Add the wine, stir, and cook 30 seconds. Add 3 cups stock, salt, and pepper, stir, cover and cook on the Rice setting for 9 minutes. Release the pressure, uncover the Instant Pot, add the shrimp, the rest of the stock, set the Instant Pot on Sauté mode, and cook for 5 minutes, stirring occasionally. Add the cheese, the rest of the butter, tarragon, and parsley, stir, divide among plates, and serve.

Nutrition:

- Calories: 400
- Fat: 8
- Fiber: 4
- Carbs: 15
- Protein: 29

Octopus and Potatoes

Preparation time: 10 minutes
Cooking time: 35 minutes
Servings: 6

Ingredients:

- 2 pounds octopus, cleaned, head removed, emptied, tentacles separated
- 2 pounds potatoes
- Water
- 3 garlic cloves, peeled and crushed
- ½ teaspoon peppercorns
- 1 bay leaf
- 2 tablespoons parsley, diced
- 5 tablespoons vinegar
- Salt and ground black pepper, to taste
- 2 tablespoons extra virgin olive oil

Directions:

Put potatoes into the Instant Pot, add water to cover them, salt and pepper, cover the Instant Pot and cook on the Manual setting for 15 minutes. Release the pressure, transfer potatoes to a bowl, peeled and chopped. Put octopus into the Instant Pot, add more water, bay leaf, 1 garlic clove, peppercorns and more salt. Stir, cover and cook on the Manual setting for 20 minutes. Release the pressure, drain octopus, chop it and add to potatoes. In a bowl, mix olive oil with vinegar, 2 garlic cloves, salt and pepper and stir very well. Add this to octopus salad, also add parsley, toss to coat, and serve.

Nutrition:

- Calories: 300
- Fat: 12
- Fiber: 2
- Carbs: 14
- Protein: 20

Seafood Gumbo

Preparation time: 10 minutes
Cooking time: 25 minutes
Servings: 10

Ingredients:

- ¾ cup vegetable oil
- 1¼ cups flour
- 1 cup white onions, chopped
- ½ cup celery, chopped
- 1 cup green bell pepper, chopped
- 4 garlic cloves, chopped
- 2 tablespoons peanut oil
- 6 plum tomatoes, cored and chopped
- Cayenne pepper
- 3 bay leaves
- ½ teaspoon onion powder
- ½ teaspoon garlic powder
- 1 teaspoon dried thyme
- 1 teaspoon celery seeds
- 1 teaspoon sweet paprika
- 1 pound smoked sausage, sliced
- 2 quarts chicken stock
- 24 shrimp, peeled and deveined
- 24 crawfish tails
- 24 oysters
- ½ pound crab meat
- Salt and ground black pepper, to taste
- Rice, already cooked, for serving

Directions:

Heat up a pan with the vegetable oil over medium heat, add the flour and stir for 3-4 minutes. Set the Instant Pot on Sauté mode, add the peanut oil and heat it up. Add the celery, peppers, onions and garlic, stir, and cook for 10 minutes. Add the sausage, tomatoes, stock, bay leaves, cayenne, onion powder, and garlic powder, thyme, paprika, and celery seeds, stir, and cook for 3 minutes. Add the flour mixture and stir until combined. Add the shrimp, crawfish, crab, oysters, salt and pepper, stir, cover, and cook on the Meat/Stew setting for 15 minutes. Release the pressure, uncover, divide the gumbo among bowls with rice, and serve.

Nutrition:

- Calories: 800
- Fat: 58
- Fiber: 3
- Carbs: 35
- Protein: 36

Octopus Stew

Preparation time: 1 day
Cooking time: 8 minutes
Servings: 4

Ingredients:
- 1 octopus, cleaned, head removed, emptied, tentacles separated
- 1 cup red wine
- 1 cup white wine
- 1 cup water
- ½ cup vegetable oil
- ½ cup extra virgin olive oil
- 2 tablespoons hot sauce
- 1 tablespoon paprika
- 1 tablespoon tomato paste
- Salt and ground black pepper, to taste
- ½ bunch fresh parsley, chopped
- 2 garlic cloves, peeled and minced
- 1 yellow onion, peeled and chopped
- 4 potatoes, cut into quarters.

Directions:

Put the octopus in a bowl and add the white wine, red wine, water, vegetable oil, hot sauce, paprika, tomato paste, salt, pepper, and parsley. Toss to coat, cover, and keep in refrigerated for 1 day. Set the Instant Pot on Sauté mode, add the olive oil and heat it up. Add the onions and potatoes, stir and cook for 3 minutes. Add the garlic, octopus, and marinade, stir, cover, and cook on the Meat/Stew setting for 8 minutes. Release the pressure, uncover the Instant Pot, divide stew among bowls, and serve.

Nutrition:
- Calories: 210
- Fat: 9
- Fiber: 0
- Carbs: 4
- Protein: 32

Greek Octopus

Preparation time: 10 minutes
Cooking time: 16 minutes
Servings: 6
Ingredients:
- 1 octopus, cleaned, head removed, emptied, tentacles separated
- 2 rosemary sprigs
- 2 teaspoons dried oregano
- ½ yellow onion, peeled and roughly chopped
- 4 thyme sprigs
- ½ lemon
- 1 teaspoon black peppercorns
- 3 tablespoons extra virgin olive oil

For the marinade:
- ¼ cup extra virgin olive oil
- Juice of ½ lemon
- 4 garlic cloves, peeled and minced
- 2 thyme sprigs
- 1 rosemary sprig
- Salt and ground black pepper, to taste

Directions:

Put the octopus into the Instant Pot. Add the oregano, 2 rosemary sprigs, 4 thyme sprigs, onion, lemon, 3 tablespoons olive oil, peppercorns and salt. Stir, cover, and cook on Manual mode for 10 minutes. Release the pressure, uncover the Instant Pot, transfer octopus on a cutting board, cut tentacles and place them in a bowl. Add ¼ cup olive oil, lemon juice, garlic, 1 rosemary sprig, 2 thyme sprigs, salt and pepper, toss to coat and set aside for 1 hour. Heat up your grill on medium heat, add the octopus, grill for 3 minutes on each side, and divide among plates. Drizzle the marinade over octopus, and serve.

Nutrition:
- Calories: 161
- Fat: 1
- Fiber: 0
- Carbs: 1
- Protein: 9

Stuffed Squid

Preparation time: 10 minutes
Cooking time: 20 minutes
Servings: 4

Ingredients:
- 4 squid
- 1 cup sticky rice
- 14 ounces vegetable stock
- 2 tablespoons sake
- 4 tablespoons soy sauce
- 1 tablespoon mirin
- 2 tablespoons sugar

Directions:

Chop the tentacles from 1 squid and mix with the rice. Fill each squid with rice and seal ends with toothpicks. Place squid into the Instant Pot, add the stock, soy sauce, sake, sugar, and mirin. Cover and cook on the Steam setting for 15 minutes. Release the pressure, uncover the Instant Pot, divide stuffed squid among plates, and serve.

Nutrition:
- Calories: 148
- Fat: 2.4
- Fiber: 1.1
- Carbs: 7
- Protein: 11

Squid Masala

Preparation time: 10 minutes
Cooking time: 15 minutes
Servings: 4

Ingredients:
- 17 ounces squid, cleaned and cut
- 1½ tablespoons chili powder
- Salt and ground black pepper, to taste
- ¼ teaspoon turmeric
- 2 cups water
- 5 pieces coconut
- 4 garlic cloves, peeled and minced
- ½ teaspoons cumin seeds
- 3 tablespoons extra virgin olive oil
- ¼ teaspoon mustard seeds
- 1-inch ginger piece, peeled and chopped

Directions:

Put the squid into the Instant Pot. Add the chili powder, turmeric, salt, pepper, and water, stir, cover, and cook on Manual for 15 minutes. In a blender, mix the coconut with the ginger, garlic, and cumin seeds and blend well. Heat up a pan with oil over medium high heat, add the mustard seeds and toast for 2-3 minutes. Release the pressure from the Instant Pot and transfer the squid and water to the pan. Stir and mix with the coconut blend. Cook until everything thickens, divide among plates, and serve.

Nutrition:
- Calories: 255
- Fat: 0
- Fiber: 1
- Carbs: 7
- Protein: 9

Braised Squid

Preparation time: 10 minutes
Cooking time: 20 minutes
Servings: 4

Ingredients:
- 1 pound squid, cleaned and cut
- 1 pound fresh peas
- ½ pounds canned crushed tomatoes
- 1 yellow onion, peeled and chopped
- White wine
- Olive oil
- Salt and ground black pepper, to taste

Directions:
Set the Instant Pot on Sauté mode, add some oil and heat it up. Add the onion, stir, and cook for 3 minutes. Add the squid, stir, and cook for 3 more minutes. Add the wine, tomatoes and peas, stir, cover, and cook for 20 minutes. Release the pressure, uncover the Instant Pot, add salt and pepper, stir, divide among plates, and serve.

Nutrition:
- Calories: 145
- Fat: 1
- Fiber: 0
- Carbs: 7
- Protein: 12

Squid Roast

Preparation time: 10 minutes
Cooking time: 25 minutes
Servings: 4

Ingredients:
- 1 pound squid, cleaned and cut into small pieces
- 10 garlic cloves, peeled and minced
- 2-inch ginger piece, peeled and grated
- 2 green chilies, chopped
- 2 yellow onions, peeled and chopped
- 1 bay leaf
- ½ tablespoon lemon juice
- ¼ cup coconut, sliced
- 1 tablespoon coriander
- ¾ tablespoon chili powder
- 1 teaspoon garam masala
- Salt and ground black pepper, to taste
- Turmeric
- 1 teaspoon mustard seeds
- ¾ cup water
- 3 tablespoons vegetable oil

Directions:
Set the Instant Pot on Sauté mode, add the oil and heat it up. Add the mustard seeds and fry for 1 minute. Add the coconut and cook 2 minutes. Add the ginger, onions, garlic, and chilies, stir, and cook 30 seconds. Add the salt, pepper, bay leaf, coriander, chili powder, garam masala, turmeric, water, lemon juice, and squid. Stir, cover and cook on Steam mode for 25 minutes. Release pressure, uncover, divide among plates, and serve.

Nutrition:
- Calories: 209
- Fat: 10
- Fiber: 0.5
- Carbs: 9.3
- Protein: 20

Instant Pot Vegetable Recipes

Artichokes with Lemon Sauce

Preparation time: 10 minutes
Cooking time: 20 minutes
Servings: 4

Ingredients:
- 4 artichokes
- 1 tablespoon tarragon, chopped
- 2 cups chicken stock
- 2 lemons
- 1 celery stalk, chopped
- ½ cup extra virgin olive oil
- Salt, to taste

Directions:

Discard the stems and petal tips from artichokes. Zest the lemons, cut into 4 slices and place them into the Instant Pot. Place an artichoke on each lemon slices, add the stock, cover the Instant Pot and cook on the Steam setting for 20 minutes. Release the pressure, uncover the Instant Pot and transfer artichokes to a platter. In a food processor, mix the tarragon with the lemon zest, the pulp from the second lemon, celery, salt, and olive oil and pulse well. Drizzle this over artichokes, and serve.

Nutrition:
- Calories: 200
- Fat: 12
- Fiber: 9
- Carbs: 20
- Protein: 6

Artichoke Hearts

Preparation time: 10 minutes
Cooking time: 40 minutes
Servings: 4

Ingredients:
- 4 artichokes, washed, stems and petal tips cut off
- Salt and ground black pepper, to taste
- 2 tablespoons lemon juice
- ¼ cup extra virgin olive oil
- 2 teaspoons balsamic vinegar
- 1 teaspoon dried oregano
- 2 cups water
- 2 garlic cloves, peeled and minced

Directions:

Put the artichokes in the steamer basket of the Instant Pot. Add the water to the Instant Pot, cover and cook them on Steam mode for 8 minutes. In a bowl, mix lemon juice with vinegar, oil, salt, pepper, garlic, and oregano, and stir very well. Release the pressure from the Instant Pot, transfer artichokes to a plate, cut them into halves, take out the hearts and arrange them on a platter. Drizzle the vinaigrette over artichokes and let them marinate for 30 minutes. Heat up a grill over medium heat, add the artichokes, and cook for 3 minutes on each side. Serve them warm.

Nutrition:
- Calories: 120
- Fat: 2
- Fiber: 1
- Carbs: 1
- Protein: 4

Artichokes and Spinach Dip

Preparation time: 10 minutes
Cooking time: 5 minutes
Servings: 6

Ingredients:
- 14 ounces canned artichoke hearts
- 8 ounces cream cheese
- 16 ounces Parmesan cheese, grated
- 10 ounces spinach
- ½ cup chicken stock
- 8 ounces mozzarella cheese, shredded
- ½ cup sour cream
- 3 garlic cloves, peeled and minced
- ½ cup mayonnaise
- 1 teaspoon onion powder

Directions:

In the Instant Pot, mix the artichokes with the stock, garlic, spinach, cream cheese, sour cream, onion powder and mayonnaise, stir, cover and cook on the Manual setting for 5 minutes. Release the pressure, uncover the Instant Pot, add the cheeses, stir well, transfer to a bowl and serve with chips or crackers.

Nutrition:
- Calories: 288
- Fat: 20
- Fiber: 0
- Carbs: 8
- Protein: 15

Savory Artichoke Dip

Preparation time: 10 minutes
Cooking time: 22 minutes
Servings: 2

Ingredients:
- 2 artichokes, washed, stems and petal tips cut off
- 1 bay leaf
- 1 cup water
- 2 garlic cloves, chopped
- 1 lemon cut into halves

For the sauce:
- ¼ cup coconut oil
- ¼ cup extra virgin olive oil
- 3 anchovy fillets
- 3 garlic cloves

Directions:

Put the artichokes in the steamer basket of the Instant Pot, add the water to the Instant Pot, lemon halves, 2 garlic cloves, and bay leaf, cover, and cook on the Manual setting for 20 minutes. Release the pressure naturally for 10 minutes, uncover the Instant Pot and divide the artichokes among plates. In a food processor, mix the coconut oil with the anchovies, garlic, and olive oil and blend well. Pour this into a bowl, and serve.

Nutrition:
- Calories: 300
- Fat: 14
- Fiber: 9
- Carbs: 45
- Protein: 15

Wrapped Asparagus Spears

Preparation time: 5 minutes
Cooking time: 4 minutes
Servings: 4

Ingredients:

- 1 pound asparagus, trimmed
- 8 ounces prosciutto slices
- 2 cups water
- Salt

Directions:

Wrap the asparagus spears in prosciutto slices and place them on the bottom of the steamer basket into the Instant Pot. Add the water to the Instant Pot, add a pinch of salt, cover and cook on the Steam setting for 4 minutes. Release the pressure naturally, uncover, transfer the asparagus spears on a platter, and serve at room temperature.

Nutrition:

- Calories: 60
- Fat: 3
- Fiber: 1
- Carbs: 3
- Protein: 4

Asparagus and Shrimp

Preparation time: 4 minutes
Cooking time: 3 minutes
Servings: 4

Ingredients:

- 1 cup water
- 1 pound shrimp, peeled and deveined
- 1 teaspoon extra virgin olive oil
- 1 bunch asparagus, trimmed
- ½ tablespoon Cajun seasoning

Directions:

Put the water into the Instant Pot. Put the asparagus in the steamer basket of the Instant Pot and add the shrimp on top. Drizzle with olive oil, sprinkle with Cajun seasoning, stir, cover and cook on Steam mode for 2 minutes. Release the pressure naturally, transfer the asparagus and shrimp to plates, and serve.

Nutrition:

- Calories: 150
- Fat: 1.4
- Fiber: 4
- Carbs: 15
- Protein: 23

Beet Salad

Preparation time: 10 minutes
Cooking time: 30 minutes
Servings: 4

Ingredients:

- 4 beets
- 1 cup water
- 2 tablespoons balsamic vinegar
- A bunch of fresh parsley, chopped
- Salt and ground black pepper, to taste
- 1 tablespoon extra virgin olive oil
- 1 garlic clove, peeled and chopped
- 2 tablespoons capers

Directions:

Put the beets in the steamer basket of the Instant Pot, add the water to the Instant Pot, cover, and cook for 20 minutes on the Steam mode. In a bowl, mix the parsley with garlic, salt, pepper, olive oil, and capers and stir well. Release the pressure from the Instant Pot, uncover, transfer the beets to a cutting board, let them cool briefly, peel and slice them, and arrange them on a platter. Add the vinegar over them and drizzle the parsley dressing at the end.

Nutrition:

- Calories: 44
- Fat: 2.4
- Fiber: 1
- Carbs: 0
- Protein: 1

Beets with Blue Cheese

Preparation time: 10 minutes
Cooking time: 20 minutes
Servings: 6

Ingredients:

- 6 beets
- Salt and ground black pepper, to taste
- ¼ cup blue cheese, crumbled
- 1 cup water

Directions:

Put the beets in the steamer basket of the Instant Pot, add the water to the Instant Pot, cover, and cook on the Manual setting for 20 minutes. Release the pressure naturally, uncover the Instant Pot, transfer the beets to a cutting board, set aside to cool down, peel them, and cut them into quarters. Put beets in a bowl, add the blue cheese, salt and pepper, stir, and serve.

Nutrition:

- Calories: 160
- Fat: 1
- Fiber: 5
- Carbs: 10
- Protein: 7

Beet and Orange Salad

Preparation time: 10 minutes
Cooking time: 10 minutes
Servings: 4

Ingredients:

- 1½ pounds beets
- 2 teaspoons orange zest, grated
- 3 strips orange peel
- 2 tablespoons cider vinegar
- ½ cup orange juice
- 2 tablespoons brown sugar
- 2 scallions, chopped
- 2 teaspoons mustard
- 1 cup arugula
- 1 cup mustard greens

Directions:

Scrub the beets well, cut them in half, and put them in a bowl. In the Instant Pot, mix the orange peel with the vinegar and orange juice and stir. Add the beets, cover the Instant Pot, cook on the Steam setting for 7 minutes, and release the pressure naturally. Uncover the Instant Pot, take the beets, and transfer them to a bowl. Discard the peel strips from the Instant Pot, add the mustard and sugar and stir well. Add the scallions and grated orange zest to the beets and toss them. Add the liquid from the Instant Pot over the beets, toss to coat, and serve on plates on top of mixed salad greens.

Nutrition:

- Calories: 140
- Fat: 6
- Fiber: 3.1
- Carbs: 11
- Protein: 4

Beet and Tomato Salad

Preparation time: 30 minutes
Cooking time: 30 minutes
Servings: 8

Ingredients:

- 1½ cups water
- 8 small beets, trimmed
- 1 red onion, peeled and sliced
- 4 ounces goat cheese
- 1 cup apple cider vinegar
- 1 cup water
- 2 teaspoons pickling juice
- Salt and ground black pepper, to taste
- 2 tablespoons sugar
- 1 pint mixed cherry tomatoes, cut into halves
- 2 ounces pecans
- 2 tablespoons extra virgin olive oil

Directions:

Put the beets in the steamer basket of the Instant Pot, add 1½ cups water, cover, and cook on the Steam setting for 20 minutes. Release the pressure, uncover the Instant Pot, transfer the beets to a cutting board, let them cool down, peel them, chop them, and put them in a bowl. Clean the Instant Pot, add the water, vinegar, sugar, pickling juice, and salt, stir, cover, and cook on the Manual setting for 2 minutes. Release the pressure, strain the liquid into a bowl, add the onions, stir, and set aside for 10 minutes. Add the tomatoes to beets and onions and stir. In a bowl, mix 4 tablespoons of liquid from the onions with 2 tablespoons olive oil, salt, and pepper and stir. Add this to beet salad and stir. Add goat cheese and pecans, toss to coat, and serve.

Nutrition:

- Calories: 163
- Fat: 8
- Fiber: 4
- Carbs: 12
- Protein: 4.5

Turkey-stuffed Bell Peppers

Preparation time: 15 minutes
Cooking time: 15 minutes
Servings: 4
Ingredients:

- 1 pound turkey meat, ground
- 1 cup water
- 2 green onions, chopped
- 5 ounces canned green chilies, chopped
- 1 jalapeño pepper, chopped
- 2 teaspoons chili powder
- ½ cup panko bread crumbs
- 1 teaspoon garlic powder
- 1 teaspoon cumin
- Salt, to taste
- 4 bell peppers, tops, and seeds discarded
- 4 pepper jack cheese slices
- 1 avocado, pitted, peeled, and chopped
- Crushed tortilla chips
- Pico de gallo

For the chipotle sauce:
- Zest from 1 lime
- Juice from 1 lime
- ½ cup sour cream
- 2 tablespoons chipotle in adobo sauce
- 1/8 teaspoon garlic powder

Directions:

In a bowl, mix the sour cream with chipotle in adobo sauce, lime zest, lime juice, and garlic powder, stir well, and keep in the refrigerator until you are ready to serve. In a bowl, mix the turkey with green onions, green chilies, bread crumbs, jalapeño, cumin, salt, chili powder, and garlic powder, stir well, and stuff the peppers with this mixture. Add the water to the Instant Pot, add the peppers in the steamer basket, cover, and cook on the Manual setting for 15 minutes. Release the pressure naturally for 10 minutes, transfer the bell peppers to a pan, add cheese on top, place under a preheated broiler and broil until cheese is browned. Divide the bell peppers on plates, top with the chipotle sauce, and serve.

Nutrition:

- Calories: 177
- Fat: 5
- Fiber: 3.3
- Carbs: 22
- Protein: 13

Stuffed Bell Peppers

Preparation time: 10 minutes
Cooking time: 15 minutes
Servings: 4

Ingredients:

- 4 bell peppers, tops and seeds removed
- Salt and ground black pepper, to taste
- 16 ounces ground beef
- 1 cup white rice, already cooked
- 1 egg
- ½ cup milk
- 2 onions, peeled and chopped
- 8 ounces water
- 10 ounces canned tomato soup

Directions:

Put some water in a pot, bring to a boil over medium heat, add the bell peppers, blanch them for 3 minutes, drain, and transfer them to a working surface. In a bowl, mix the beef with rice, salt, pepper, egg, milk, and onions and stir well. Stuff the bell peppers with this mixture and place them into the Instant Pot. Add the tomato soup mixed with the water, cover the Instant Pot and cook on the Manual setting for 12 minutes. Release the pressure, divide the bell peppers among plates, drizzle tomato sauce on top, and serve.

Nutrition:

- Calories: 200
- Fat: 12
- Fiber: 1.5
- Carbs: 13
- Proteins 12

Broccoli and Garlic

Preparation time: 10 minutes
Cooking time: 12 minutes
Servings: 4

Ingredients:
- 1 broccoli head, cut into 4 pieces
- ½ cup water
- 1 tablespoon peanut oil
- 6 garlic cloves, peeled and minced
- 1 tablespoon Chinese rice wine
- Salt, to taste

Directions:
Put the broccoli in the steamer basket of you Instant Pot, add the water to the Instant Pot, cover, and cook on Steam mode for 12 minutes. Release the pressure, transfer the broccoli to a bowl filled with cold water, drain, and place it in a bowl. Heat up a pan with the oil over medium high heat, add the garlic, stir, and cook for 3 minutes. Add the broccoli and rice wine, stir, and cook for 1 minute. Add the salt, stir, and cook 30 seconds. Transfer to plates, and serve.

Nutrition:
- Calories: 100
- Fat: 1
- Fiber: 0
- Carbs: 3
- Protein: 6

Brussels Sprouts with Pomegranate

Preparation time: 5 minutes
Cooking time: 10 minutes
Servings: 4

Ingredients:
- 1 pound Brussels sprouts
- Salt and ground black pepper, to taste
- 1 pomegranate, seeds separated
- ¼ cup pine nuts, toasted
- Extra virgin olive oil
- 1 cup water

Directions:
Put the Brussels sprouts in the pressure cooker of the Instant Pot, add 1 cup water to the Instant Pot, cover and cook on the Manual setting for 4 minutes. Release the pressure, uncover the Instant Pot, and transfer sprouts to a bowl. Add the salt, pepper, pomegranate seeds, and pine nuts and stir. Add the olive oil, toss to coat, and serve.

Nutrition:
- Calories: 100
- Fat: 1
- Fiber: 4
- Carbs: 11
- Protein: 4

Brussels Sprouts and Bacon

Preparation time: 4 minutes
Cooking time: 6 minutes
Servings: 4

Ingredients:

- 1 pound Brussels sprouts, trimmed and cut into halves
- Salt and ground black pepper, to taste
- ½ cup bacon, chopped
- 1 tablespoon mustard
- 1 cup chicken stock
- 1 tablespoon butter
- 2 tablespoons fresh dill, diced

Directions:

Set the Instant Pot on Sauté mode, add the bacon and cook until crispy. Add the Brussels sprouts, stir, and cook for 2 minutes. Add the stock, mustard, salt, and pepper, stir, cover, and cook on the Steam setting for 4 minutes. Release the pressure, uncover the Instant Pot, add the butter and dill, set the Instant Pot on Sauté mode, stir, and divide among serving plates.

Nutrition:

- Calories: 175
- Fat: 11
- Fiber: 5.6
- Carbs: 14
- Protein: 6.6

Brussels Sprouts with Parmesan Cheese

Preparation time: 10 minutes
Cooking time: 6 minutes
Servings: 4

Ingredients:

- 1 pound Brussels sprouts, washed
- Juice of 1 lemon
- Salt and ground black pepper, to taste
- 2 tablespoons butter
- 1 cup water
- 3 tablespoons Parmesan cheese, grated

Directions:

Put the Brussels sprouts into the Instant Pot, add salt, pepper, and the water, stir, cover, and cook on the Steam setting for 3 minutes. Release the pressure, transfer the Brussels sprouts to a bowl, discard the water, and wipe the Instant Pot clean. Set the Instant Pot on Sauté mode, add the butter, and melt it. Add the lemon juice and stir well. Add the Brussels sprouts, stir, and transfer to plates. Add more salt and pepper, if needed and the Parmesan cheese on top.

Nutrition:

- Calories: 160
- Fat: 2
- Fiber: 1
- Carbs: 7
- Protein: 12

Brussels Sprouts and Potatoes

Preparation time: 10 minutes
Cooking time: 5 minutes
Servings: 4

Ingredients:

- 1½ pounds Brussels sprouts, washed and trimmed
- 1 cup new potatoes, chopped
- 1½ tablespoons bread crumbs
- ½ cup beef stock
- Salt and ground black pepper, to taste
- 1½ tablespoons butter

Directions:

Put the Brussels sprouts and potatoes into the Instant Pot. Add the stock, salt, and pepper, cover, and cook on the Steam setting for 5 minutes. Release the pressure, uncover the Instant Pot, set on Sauté mode, add the butter and bread crumbs, toss to coat well, divide among plates, and serve.

Nutrition:

- Calories: 100
- Fat: 2.5
- Fiber: 4.6
- Carbs: 18
- Protein: 4

Savoy Cabbage and Cream

Preparation time: 10 minutes
Cooking time: 9 minutes
Servings: 4

Ingredients:

- 1 cup bacon, chopped
- 1 medium Savoy cabbage head, chopped
- 1 yellow onion, peeled and chopped
- 2 cups vegetable stock
- ¼ teaspoon nutmeg
- Salt and ground black pepper, to taste
- 1 bay leaf
- 1 cup coconut milk
- 2 tablespoons dried parsley

Directions:

Set the Instant Pot on Sauté mode, add the bacon and onion, stir, and cook until bacon is crispy. Add the stock, cabbage, bay leaf, salt, pepper, and nutmeg, stir, cover, and cook on Steam mode for 5 minutes. Release the pressure, uncover the Instant Pot, and set it on Sauté mode again. Add the milk, more salt and pepper, if needed, and parsley, stir, and cook for 4 minutes. Divide among plates and serve.

Nutrition:

- Calories: 160
- Fat: 10
- Fiber: 2.2
- Carbs: 13
- Protein: 5

Cabbage with Bacon

Preparation time: 10 minutes
Cooking time: 8 minutes
Servings: 8

Ingredients:
- 1 green cabbage head, chopped
- ¼ cup butter
- 2 cups chicken stock
- 3 bacon slices, chopped
- Salt and ground black pepper, to taste

Directions:

Set the Instant Pot on Sauté mode, add the bacon, stir, and cook for 4 minutes. Add the butter and stir until it melts. Add the cabbage, stock, salt, and pepper, stir, cover, and cook on the Steam setting for 3 minutes. Release the pressure, uncover the Instant Pot, transfer the cabbage to plates, and serve.

Nutrition:
- Calories: 100
- Fat: 4
- Fiber: 3
- Carbs: 7
- Protein: 2

Cabbage and Sausages

Preparation time: 10 minutes
Cooking time: 5 minutes
Servings: 4

Ingredients:
- 3 tablespoons butter
- 1 green cabbage head, chopped
- Salt and ground black pepper, to taste
- 1 pound sausage links, sliced
- 15 ounces canned diced tomatoes
- ½ cup yellow onion, chopped
- 2 teaspoons turmeric

Directions:

Set the Instant Pot on Sauté mode, add the sausage, stir, and cook until they are brown. Drain the excess grease, add the butter, cabbage, tomatoes salt, pepper, onion, and turmeric, stir, cover, and cook on the Manual setting for 2 minutes. Release the pressure, uncover, divide cabbage, and sausages among plates, and serve.

Nutrition:
- Calories: 140
- Fat: 6
- Fiber: 4
- Carbs: 11
- Protein: 10

Sweet and Spicy Cabbage

Preparation time: 10 minutes
Cooking time: 8 minutes
Servings: 4

Ingredients:
- 1 cabbage, cut into 8 wedges
- 1 tablespoon sesame seed oil
- 1 carrots, peeled and grated
- ¼ cup apple cider vinegar
- 1½ cups water
- 1 teaspoon sugar
- ½ teaspoon cayenne pepper
- ½ teaspoon red pepper flakes
- 2 teaspoons cornstarch

Directions:

Set the Instant Pot on Sauté mode, add the oil and heat it up. Add the cabbage, stir, and cook for 3 minutes. Add the carrots, 1¼ cups water, sugar, vinegar, cayenne pepper, and pepper flakes, stir, cover, and cook on the Steam setting for 5 minutes. Release the pressure, uncover the Instant Pot, and divide cabbage and carrots among plates. Add the cornstarch mixed with the remaining water to the Instant Pot, set it on Manual mode, stir well, and bring to a boil. Drizzle over the cabbage and carrots, and serve.

Nutrition:
- Calories: 90
- Fat: 4.5
- Fiber: 2.1
- Carbs: 11
- Protein: 1

Sweet Carrots

Preparation time: 10 minutes
Cooking time: 15 minutes
Servings: 4

Ingredients:
- 2 cups baby carrots
- A pinch of salt
- 1 tablespoon brown sugar
- ½ tablespoon butter
- ½ cup water

Directions:

In the Instant Pot, mix the butter with the water, salt, and sugar and stir well. Set the Instant Pot on Sauté mode and cook for 30 seconds. Add the carrots, stir, cover, and cook on the Steam setting for 15 minutes. Release the pressure, uncover the Instant Pot, set it on Sauté mode, and cook for 1 minute. Serve hot.

Nutrition:
- Calories: 60
- Fat: 0.1
- Fiber: 1
- Carbs: 4
- Protein: 1

Maple-glazed Carrots

Preparation time: 10 minutes
Cooking time: 4 minutes
Servings: 4

Ingredients:
- 2 pounds carrots, peeled and sliced diagonally
- 1 tablespoon maple syrup
- Ground black pepper, to taste
- 1 tablespoon butter
- 1 cup water
- ¼ cup raisins

Directions:
Put the carrots into the Instant Pot. Add the water and raisins, cover, and cook on the Steam setting for 4 minutes. Release the pressure, uncover, add the butter and maple syrup, stir, divide the carrots among plates, and sprinkle with black pepper before serving them.

Nutrition:
- Calories: 60
- Fat: 1.1
- Fiber: 2.6
- Carbs: 12
- Protein: 1

Carrots with Molasses

Preparation time: 10 minutes
Cooking time: 2 minutes
Servings: 4

Ingredients:
- 16 ounces baby carrots
- Salt and ground black pepper, to taste
- 2 tablespoons butter
- 4 ounces molasses
- 2 ounces water
- 2 tablespoon dill, chopped

Directions:
Put the carrots, water, salt, pepper, and molasses into the Instant Pot, stir, cover, and cook on the Manual setting for 3 minutes. Release the pressure, uncover the Instant Pot, add the butter and dill, stir, divide among plates, and serve.

Nutrition:
- Calories: 60
- Fat: 1
- Fiber: 2
- Carbs: 4
- Protein: 3

Cauliflower with Pasta

Preparation time: 10 minutes
Cooking time: 10 minutes
Servings: 4

Ingredients:
- 2 tablespoons butter
- 8 cups cauliflower florets
- 2 garlic cloves, peeled and minced
- 1 cup chicken stock
- Salt, to taste
- 2 cups spinach, chopped
- 1 pound fettuccine noodles
- 2 green onions, chopped
- 1 tablespoon gorgonzola cheese, grated
- 3 sundried tomatoes, chopped
- Balsamic vinegar

Directions:
Set the Instant Pot on Sauté mode, add the butter, and melt it. Add the garlic, stir, and cook for 2 minutes. Add the stock, salt, and cauliflower, stir, cover, and cook on the Manual setting for 6 minutes. Release the pressure for 10 minutes, transfer the cauliflower to a blender, and pulse well. Add the spinach and green onions and stir. Heat up a pot with some water and a pinch of salt over medium-high heat, bring to a boil, add the pasta, cook according to instructions, drain, and divide among plates. Add the cauliflower sauce, cheese, tomatoes, and a splash of vinegar on top, toss to coat, and serve.

Nutrition:
- Calories: 160
- Fat: 5
- Fiber: 3
- Carbs: 23
- Protein: 13

Collard Greens and Bacon

Preparation time: 10 minutes
Cooking time: 26 minutes
Servings: 6

Ingredients:
- 1 pound collard greens, trimmed
- ¼ pound bacon, chopped
- Salt and ground black pepper, to taste
- ½ cup water

Directions:
Set the Instant Pot on Sauté mode, add the bacon, stir, and cook for 5 minutes. Add the collard greens, salt, pepper, and water, stir, cover and cook on the Steam setting for 20 minutes. Release the pressure, uncover, divide the mixture among plates, and serve.

Nutrition:
- Calories: 130
- Fat: 8
- Fiber: 2
- Carbs: 4
- Protein: 6

Savory Collard Greens

Preparation time: 10 minutes
Cooking time: 20 minutes
Servings: 4

Ingredients:

- 1 bunch collard greens, trimmed
- 2 tablespoons extra virgin olive oil
- ½ cup chicken stock
- 2 tablespoons tomato puree
- 1 yellow onion, peeled and chopped
- 3 garlic cloves, peeled and minced
- Salt and ground black pepper, to taste
- 1 tablespoon balsamic vinegar
- 1 teaspoon sugar

Directions:

In the Instant Pot, mix the stock with the oil, garlic, vinegar, onion, and tomato puree and stir well. Roll the collard greens into cigar-shaped bundles to the Instant Pot. Add the salt, pepper, and sugar, cover, and cook on the Steam setting for 20 minutes. Release the pressure, uncover the Instant Pot, divide the collard greens among plates, and serve.

Nutrition:

- Calories: 130
- Fat: 7
- Fiber: 4.5
- Carbs: 12
- Protein: 4
- Sugar: 4

Classic Collard Greens

Preparation time: 10 minutes
Cooking time: 25 minutes
Servings: 8

Ingredients:

- 1 onion, peeled and chopped
- 2 tablespoons extra virgin olive oil
- 3 garlic cloves, peeled and crushed
- 2½ pounds collard greens, chopped
- Salt and ground black pepper, to taste
- 2 cups chicken stock
- 2 tablespoons apple cider vinegar
- 1 tablespoon brown sugar
- ½ teaspoon crushed red pepper
- 2 smoked turkey wings

Directions:

Set the Instant Pot on Sauté mode, add the oil and heat it up. Add the onions, stir, and cook for 2 minutes. Add the garlic, stir, and cook for 1 minute. Add the stock, greens, vinegar, salt, pepper, crushed red pepper, and sugar and stir. Add the turkey, cover, and cook on the Steam setting for 20 minutes. Release the pressure fast, uncover the Instant Pot, divide greens and turkey among plates, and serve.

Nutrition:

- Calories: 100
- Fat: 1.4
- Fiber: 1.7
- Carbs: 4
- Protein: 6

Braised Endive

Preparation time: 10 minutes
Cooking time: 7 minutes
Servings: 4

Ingredients:
- 4 endives, trimmed and cut into halves
- Salt and ground black pepper, to taste
- 1 tablespoon lemon juice
- 1 tablespoon butter

Directions:

Set the Instant Pot on Sauté mode. Add the butter and melt it. Arrange the endives in the Instant Pot, add the salt, pepper, and lemon juice, cover, and cook on the Steam setting for 7 minutes. Release the pressure naturally, arrange the endives on a platter, add the cooking liquid all over them, and serve.

Nutrition:
- Calories: 80
- Fat: 3.1
- Fiber: 0.5
- Carbs: 12
- Protein: 1.2

Endive with Ham

Preparation time: 10 minutes
Cooking time: 20 minutes
Servings: 4

Ingredients:
- 4 endives, trimmed
- Salt and ground black pepper, to taste
- 1 tablespoon white flour
- 4 slices ham
- 2 tablespoons butter
- ½ teaspoon nutmeg
- 14 ounces milk

Directions:

Put the endives in the steamer basket of the Instant Pot, add some water to the Instant Pot, cover and cook on the Steam setting for 10 minutes. Heat up a pan with the butter over medium heat, stir, and melt it. Add the flour, stir well, and cook for 3 minutes. Add the milk, salt, pepper, and nutmeg, stir well, reduce the heat to low, and cook for 10 minutes. Release the pressure from the Instant Pot, uncover it, transfer them to a cutting board, and roll each in a slice of ham. Arrange the endives in a pan, add the milk mixture over them, place under a preheated broiler and broil for 10 minutes. Slice, arrange on plates, and serve.

Nutrition:
- Calories: 120
- Fat: 1
- Fiber: 2
- Carbs: 6
- Protein: 23

Sautéed Endive

Preparation time: 10 minutes
Cooking time: 15 minutes
Servings: 4

Ingredients:
- 8 endives, trimmed
- Salt and ground black pepper, to taste
- 4 tablespoon butter
- Juice of ½ lemon
- ½ cup water
- 1 teaspoon sugar
- 2 tablespoons fresh parsley, chopped

Directions:

Put the endives into the Instant Pot, add 1 tablespoon butter, lemon juice, ½ cup water, sugar, salt, and pepper, stir, cover, and cook on the Steam setting for 10 minutes. Release the pressure, uncover the Instant Pot, and transfer the endives to a plate. Heat up a pan with the remaining tablespoons butter over medium-high heat, add the endives, more salt and pepper, if needed, and parsley. Stir and cook for 5 minutes. Transfer the endives to plates, and serve.

Nutrition:
- Calories: 90
- Fat: 1
- Fiber: 4
- Carbs: 4
- Protein: 2

Endive Risotto

Preparation time: 10 minutes
Cooking time: 20 minutes
Servings: 2

Ingredients:
- ¾ cup rice
- 2 Belgian endives, trimmed, cut into halves lengthwise, and roughly chopped
- ½ yellow onion, peeled and chopped
- 2 tablespoons extra virgin olive oil
- ½ cup white wine
- 2 cups vegetable stock
- 2 ounces Parmesan cheese, grated
- 3 tablespoons heavy cream
- Salt and ground black pepper, to taste

Directions:

Set the Instant Pot on Sauté mode, add the oil, and heat it up. Add the onion, stir, and sauté for 4 minutes. Add the endives, stir, and cook for 4 minutes. Add the rice, wine, salt, pepper, stock, stir, cover, and cook on the Steam setting for 10 minutes. Release the pressure fast, uncover the Instant Pot, and set it on Sauté mode. Add the cheese and heavy cream, stir, cook for 1 minute, transfer to plates, and serve.

Nutrition:
- Calories: 260
- Fat: 5
- Fiber: 5
- Carbs: 13
- Protein: 16

Eggplant Ratatouille

Preparation time: 15 minutes
Cooking time: 8 minutes
Servings: 6

Ingredients:
- 1 eggplant, peeled and thinly sliced
- 2 garlic cloves, peeled and minced
- 3 tablespoons extra virgin olive oil
- Salt and ground black pepper, to taste
- 1 cup onion, peeled and chopped
- 1 green bell pepper, seeded and chopped
- 1 red bell pepper, seeded and chopped
- ½ cup water
- 1 teaspoon dried thyme
- 14 ounces canned diced tomatoes
- Sugar
- 1 cup fresh basil, chopped

Directions:
Set the Instant Pot on Sauté mode, add the oil, and heat it up. Add the bell peppers, onion, and garlic, stir, and cook for 3 minutes. Add the eggplant, water, salt, pepper, thyme, sugar, and tomatoes, cover the Instant Pot and cook on the Steam setting for 4 minutes. Release the pressure fast, uncover the Instant Pot, add the basil, stir gently, divide among plates, and serve.

Nutrition:
- Calories: 109
- Fat: 5
- Fiber: 3
- Carbs: 14
- Protein: 2

Eggplant Marinara

Preparation time: 10 minutes
Cooking time: 8 minutes
Servings: 2

Ingredients:
- 4 cups eggplant, cubed
- 1 tablespoon extra virgin olive oil
- 3 garlic cloves, peeled and minced
- 1 tablespoon onion powder
- Salt and ground black pepper, to taste
- 1 cup marinara sauce
- ½ cup water
- Spaghetti noodles, already cooked

Directions:
Set the Instant Pot on Sauté mode, add the oil, and heat it up. Add the garlic, stir, and cook for 2 minutes. Add the eggplant, salt, pepper, onion powder, marinara sauce, and water, stir gently, cover and cook on the Steam setting for 8 minutes. Release the pressure, uncover the Instant Pot, and serve with spaghetti.

Nutrition:
- Calories: 130
- Fat: 3
- Fiber: 2
- Carbs: 3
- Protein: 3

Babaganoush

Preparation time: 10 minutes
Cooking time: 4 minutes
Servings: 6

Ingredients:
- 2 pounds eggplant, peeled and cut into medium chunks
- Salt and ground black pepper, to taste
- ⅓ cup extra virgin olive oil
- ½ cup water
- 4 garlic cloves, peeled
- ¼ cup lemon juice
- 1 bunch thyme, chopped
- 1 tablespoon tahini
- 3 olives, pitted and sliced

Directions:
Put the eggplant pieces into the Instant Pot, add ¼ cup oil, set the Instant Pot on Sauté mode, and heat up. Add the garlic, water, salt, and pepper, stir, cover, and cook on the Steam setting for 3 minutes. Release the pressure, uncover the Instant Pot, transfer the eggplant pieces and garlic to a blender, add the lemon juice and tahini and pulse well. Add the thyme and blend again. Transfer eggplant spread to a bowl, top with olive slices and a drizzle of oil, and serve.

Nutrition:
- Calories: 70
- Fat: 2
- Fiber: 2
- Carbs: 7
- Protein: 1

Eggplant Surprise

Preparation time: 10 minutes
Cooking time: 7 minutes
Servings: 4

Ingredients:
- 1 eggplant, roughly chopped
- 3 zucchini, roughly chopped
- 3 tomatoes, cored and sliced
- 2 tablespoons lemon juice
- Salt and ground black pepper, to taste
- 1 teaspoon dried thyme
- 1 teaspoon dried oregano
- 3 tablespoons extra virgin olive oil

Directions:
Put the eggplant pieces into the Instant Pot. Add the zucchini and tomatoes. In a bowl, mix the lemon juice with salt, pepper, thyme, oregano, and oil and stir well. Pour this over the vegetables, toss to coat, cover the Instant Pot and cook on the Steam setting for 7 minutes. Release the pressure, uncover the Instant Pot, divide among plates, and serve.

Nutrition:
- Calories: 140
- Fat: 3.4
- Fiber: 7
- Carbs: 20
- Protein: 5

Braised Fennel

Preparation time: 10 minutes
Cooking time: 12 minutes
Servings: 4

Ingredients:

- 2 fennel bulbs, trimmed and cut into quarters
- 3 tablespoons extra virgin olive oil
- Salt and ground black pepper, to taste
- 1 garlic clove, peeled and chopped
- 1 dried red pepper
- ¾ cup vegetable stock
- Juice of ½ lemon
- ¼ cup white wine
- ¼ cup Parmesan cheese, grated

Directions:

Set the Instant Pot on Sauté mode, add the oil, and heat it up. Add the garlic and red pepper, stir, cook for 2 minutes, and discard the garlic. Add the fennel, stir, and brown it for 8 minutes. Add the salt, pepper, stock, wine, cover, and cook on the Steam setting for 4 minutes. Release the pressure, uncover the Instant Pot, add the lemon juice, more salt and pepper, if needed, and cheese. Toss to coat, divide among plates, and serve.

Nutrition:

- Calories: 70
- Fat: 1
- Fiber: 2
- Carbs: 2
- Protein: 1

Fennel Risotto

Preparation time: 10 minutes
Cooking time: 10 minutes
Servings: 2

Ingredients:

- 1½ cups Arborio rice
- 1 yellow onion, peeled and chopped
- 3 cups chicken stock
- 1 fennel bulb, trimmed and chopped
- 2 tablespoons butter
- 1 tablespoon extra virgin olive oil
- ¼ cup white wine
- Salt and ground black pepper, to taste
- ½ teaspoon thyme, dried
- 3 tablespoons tomato paste
- ⅓ cup Parmesan cheese, grated

Directions:

Set the Instant Pot on Sauté mode, add the butter and melt it. Add the fennel and onion, stir, sauté for 4 minutes, and transfer to a bowl. Add the oil to the Instant Pot and heat it up. Add the rice, stir, and cook for 3 minutes. Add the tomato paste, stock, fennel, onions, wine, salt, pepper, and thyme, stir, cover, and cook on the Manual setting for 8 minutes. Release the pressure, uncover, add cheese, stir, divide among plates, and serve.

Nutrition:

- Calories: 200
- Fat: 10
- Fiber: 2
- Carbs: 20
- Protein: 12

Kale with Garlic and Lemon

Preparation time: 10 minutes
Cooking time: 5 minutes
Servings: 4

Ingredients:
- 3 garlic cloves, peeled and chopped
- 1 tablespoon extra virgin olive oil
- 1 pound kale, trimmed
- Salt and ground black pepper, to taste
- ½ cup water
- Juice of ½ lemon

Directions:
Set the Instant Pot on Sauté mode, add the oil, and heat it up. Add the garlic, stir, and cook for 2 minutes. Add the kale and water, cover, and cook on the Steam setting for 5 minutes. Release the pressure, uncover the Instant Pot, add the salt, pepper, and lemon juice, stir, divide among plates, and serve.

Nutrition:
- Calories: 60
- Fat: 3
- Fiber: 1
- Carbs: 2.4
- Protein: 0.7

Braised Kale

Preparation time: 10 minutes
Cooking time: 10 minutes
Servings: 2

Ingredients:
- 10 ounces kale, chopped
- 1 yellow onion, peeled and sliced thin
- 1 tablespoon kale
- 3 carrots, peeled and sliced
- ½ cup chicken stock
- 1 tablespoon butter
- 5 garlic cloves, peeled and chopped
- Salt and ground black pepper, to taste
- Balsamic vinegar
- ¼ teaspoon red pepper flakes

Directions:
Set the Instant Pot on Sauté mode, add the butter, and melt it. Add the carrots and onion, stir, and sauté for 2 minutes. Add the garlic, stir, and cook for 1 minute. Add the kale, stock, salt, and pepper, stir, cover, and cook on the Manual setting for 7 minutes. Release the pressure, uncover the Instant Pot, add the vinegar and pepper flakes, toss to coat, divide among plates, and serve.

Nutrition:
- Calories: 60
- Fat: 2
- Fiber: 2
- Carbs: 4
- Protein: 1

Kale and Bacon

Preparation time: 10 minutes
Cooking time: 10 minute
Servings: 4

Ingredients:

- 6 bacon slices, chopped
- 1 tablespoon vegetable oil
- 1 onion, peeled and sliced thin
- 6 garlic cloves, peeled and chopped
- 1½ cups chicken stock
- 1 tablespoon brown sugar
- 2 tablespoons apple cider vinegar
- 10 ounces kale leaves, chopped
- 1 teaspoon red chili peppers
- 1 teaspoon liquid smoke
- Salt and ground black pepper, to taste

Directions:

Set the Instant Pot on Sauté mode, add the oil, and heat it up. Add the bacon, stir, and cook for 1-2 minutes. Add the onion, stir, and cook for 3 minutes. Add the garlic, stir, and cook for 1 minute. Add the vinegar, stock, sugar, liquid smoke, red chilies, salt, pepper, kale, stir, cover, and cook on the Manual setting for 5 minutes. Release the pressure fast, uncover, divide among plates, and serve.

Nutrition:

- Calories: 140
- Fat: 7
- Fiber: 1
- Carbs: 7
- Protein: 2

Okra Pilaf

Preparation time: 10 minutes
Cooking time: 25 minutes
Servings: 4

Ingredients:

- 2 cups okra, sliced
- 4 bacon slices, chopped
- 2 teaspoons paprika
- 1 cup brown rice
- 1 cup tomatoes, cored and chopped
- 2¼ cups water
- Salt and ground black pepper, to taste

Directions:

Set the Instant Pot on Sauté mode, add the bacon, and brown it for 2 minutes. Add the okra, stir, and cook for 5 minutes. Add the paprika and rice, stir, and cook for 2 minutes. Add the salt, pepper, water, and tomatoes, stir, cover, and cook for 16 minutes. Release the pressure, uncover the Instant Pot, divide pilaf among plates, and serve.

Nutrition:

- Calories: 300
- Fat: 11
- Fiber: 4.2
- Carbs: 41
- Protein: 7.8

Okra and Corn

Preparation time: 10 minutes
Cooking time: 17 minutes
Servings: 6

Ingredients:
- 1 pound okra, trimmed
- 6 scallions, chopped
- 3 green bell peppers, seeded and chopped
- Salt and ground black pepper, to taste
- 2 tablespoons vegetable oil
- 1 teaspoon sugar
- 28 ounces canned diced tomatoes
- 1 cup corn kernels

Directions:

Set the Instant Pot on Sauté mode, add the oil, and heat it up. Add the scallions and bell peppers, stir, and cook for 5 minutes. Add the okra, salt, pepper, sugar, and tomatoes, stir, cover, and cook on the Manual setting for 10 minutes. Release the pressure fast, uncover, add the corn, cover the Instant Pot again and cook on the Manual setting for 2 minutes. Release the pressure, transfer the okra mixture on plates, and serve.

Nutrition:
- Calories: 140
- Fat: 5
- Fiber: 6
- Carbs: 22
- Protein: 4
- Sugar: 9

Steamed Leeks

Preparation time: 10 minutes
Cooking time: 10 minutes
Servings: 4

Ingredients:
- 4 leeks, washed, roots and ends cut off
- Salt and ground black pepper, to taste
- ⅓ cup water
- 1 tablespoon butter

Directions:

Put the leeks into the Instant Pot, add the water, butter, salt, and pepper, stir, cover, and cook on the Steam setting for 5 minutes. Release the pressure, uncover the Instant Pot, set it on Sauté mode, and cook the leeks for 5 minutes. Divide among plates, and serve.

Nutrition:
- Calories: 70
- Fat: 4
- Fiber: 1.4
- Carbs: 10
- Protein: 1.2

Crispy Potatoes

Preparation time: 10 minutes
Cooking time: 7 minutes
Servings: 4

Ingredients:

- ½ cup water
- 1 pound Yukon gold potatoes, cubed
- Salt and ground black pepper, to taste
- 2 tablespoons butter
- Juice of ½ lemon
- ¼ cup parsley leaves, chopped

Directions:

Put the water into the Instant Pot, add the potatoes in the steamer basket, cover, and cook on the Steam setting for 5 minutes. Release the pressure naturally, uncover the Instant Pot, and set it on Sauté mode. Add the butter, lemon juice, parsley, salt, and pepper, stir, and cook for 2 minutes. Transfer to plates, and serve.

Nutrition:

- Calories: 132
- Fat: 1
- Fiber: 0
- Carbs: 23
- Protein: 3

Roasted Potatoes

Preparation time: 10 minutes
Cooking time: 17 minutes
Servings: 4

Ingredients:

- 2 pounds baby potatoes
- 5 tablespoons vegetable oil
- Salt and ground black pepper, to taste
- 1 rosemary sprig
- 5 garlic cloves
- ½ cup stock

Directions:

Set the Instant Pot on Sauté mode, add the oil, and heat it up. Add the potatoes, rosemary, and garlic, stir, and brown them for 10 minutes. Prick each potato with a fork, add the stock, salt, and pepper, to the Instant Pot, cover, and cook on the Manual setting for 7 minutes. Release the pressure, uncover the Instant Pot, divide the potatoes among plates, and serve.

Nutrition:

- Calories: 50
- Fat: 1.4
- Fiber: 1
- Carbs: 7.4
- Protein: 1

Zucchinis and Tomatoes

Preparation time: 10 minutes
Cooking time: 12 minutes
Servings: 4

Ingredients:

- 6 zucchini, roughly chopped
- 2 yellow onions, chopped
- 1 tablespoon vegetable oil
- 1 cup tomato puree
- 1 pound cherry tomatoes, cut into halves
- A drizzle of olive oil
- Salt and ground black pepper, to taste
- 2 garlic cloves, minced
- 1 bunch basil, chopped

Directions:

Set the Instant Pot on Sauté mode, add the vegetable oil, and heat it up. Add the onion, stir, and cook for 5 minutes. Add the tomatoes, tomato puree, zucchini, salt, and pepper, stir, cover, and cook on the Steam setting for 5 minutes. Release the pressure, uncover the Instant Pot, add the garlic and basil, stir, and divide among plates. Drizzle some olive oil at the end, and serve.

Nutrition:

- Calories: 155
- Fat: 2
- Fiber: 4
- Carbs: 12
- Protein: 22

Turnips and Carrots

Preparation time: 5 minutes
Cooking time: 9 minutes
Servings: 4

Ingredients:

- 2 turnips, peeled and sliced
- 3 carrots, peeled and sliced
- 1 small onion, peeled and chopped
- 1 teaspoon cumin
- 1 tablespoon extra virgin olive oil
- 1 cup water
- Salt and ground black pepper, to taste
- 1 teaspoon lemon juice

Directions:

Set the Instant Pot on Sauté mode, add the oil, and heat it up. Add the onion, stir, and sauté for 2 minutes. Add the turnips, carrots, cumin, and lemon juice, stir, and cook for 1 minute. Add the salt, pepper, and water, stir, cover, and cook on the Steam setting for 6 minutes. Release the pressure, uncover the Instant Pot, divide the turnips and carrots among plates, and serve.

Nutrition:

- Calories: 70
- Fat: 0
- Fiber: 1
- Carbs: 0.4
- Protein: 2

Spicy Turnips

Preparation time: 10 minutes
Cooking time: 22 minutes
Servings: 4

Ingredients:

- 20 ounces turnips, peeled and chopped
- 1 teaspoon garlic, peeled and minced
- 1 teaspoon ginger, grated
- 2 yellow onions, peeled and chopped
- 2 tomatoes, cored and chopped
- 1 teaspoon sugar
- 1 teaspoon cumin
- 1 teaspoon coriander
- 2 green chilies, chopped
- ½ teaspoon turmeric
- 1 cup water
- 2 tablespoons butter
- Salt, to taste
- ½ cup fresh cilantro, chopped

Directions:

Set the Instant Pot on Sauté mode, add the butter, and melt it. Add the green chilies, garlic, and ginger, stir, and cook for 1 minute. Add the onions, stir, and cook 3 minutes. Add the salt, tomatoes, turmeric, cumin, and coriander, stir, and cook 3 minutes. Add the turnips and water, stir, cover, and cook on Steam mode for 15 minutes. Release the pressure, uncover the Instant Pot, add the sugar, and coriander, stir, divide among plates, and serve.

Nutrition:

- Calories: 80
- Fat: 2.4
- Fiber: 4
- Carbs: 12
- Protein: 3

Stuffed Tomatoes

Preparation time: 10 minutes
Cooking time: 10 minutes
Servings: 4

Ingredients:

- 4 tomatoes, tops cut off and flesh removed
- Salt and ground black pepper, to taste
- 1 yellow onion, peeled and chopped
- 1 tablespoon butter
- 2 tablespoons celery, chopped
- ½ cup mushrooms, chopped
- 1 slice of bread, crumbled
- 1 cup cottage cheese
- ¼ teaspoon caraway seeds
- 1 tablespoon fresh parsley, chopped
- ½ cup water

Directions:

Chop the tomato flesh and put it in a bowl. Heat up a pan with the butter over medium-high heat, add the onion and celery, stir, and cook for 3 minutes. Add the tomato flesh, and mushrooms, stir, and cook for 1 minute. Add the salt, pepper, bread, cheese, caraway seeds, and parsley, stir, and cook for 4 minutes. Fill each tomato shell with this mix and arrange them in the steamer basket of the Instant Pot. Add the water to the Instant Pot, cover, and cook on the Manual setting for 2 minutes. Release the pressure fast, uncover the Instant Pot, transfer stuffed tomatoes to plates, and serve.

Nutrition:

- Calories: 140
- Fat: 3
- Fiber: 1.4
- Carbs: 10
- Protein: 4

Instant Pot Soups and Stews Recipes

Chicken Soup

Preparation time: 10 minutes
Cooking time: 17 minutes
Servings: 4

Ingredients:
- 4 chicken breasts, skinless and boneless
- 2 tablespoons extra virgin olive oil
- 1 onion, peeled and chopped
- 3 garlic cloves, peeled and minced
- 16 ounces chunky salsa
- 29 ounces canned diced tomatoes
- 29 ounces chicken stock
- Salt and ground black pepper, to taste
- 2 tablespoons dried parsley
- 1 teaspoon garlic powder
- 1 tablespoon onion powder
- 1 tablespoon chili powder
- 15 ounces frozen corn
- 32 ounces canned black beans, drained

Directions:
Set the Instant Pot on Sauté mode, add the oil, and heat it up. Add the onion, stir, and cook 5 minutes. Add the garlic, stir, and cook for 1 minute. Add the chicken breasts, salsa, tomatoes, stock, salt, pepper, parsley, garlic powder, onion powder, and chili powder, stir, cover, and cook on the Soup setting for 8 minutes. Release the pressure for 10 minutes, uncover the Instant Pot, transfer the chicken breasts to a cutting board, shred with 2 forks, and return to pot. Add the beans and corn, set the Instant Pot on Manual mode and cook for 2-3 minutes. Divide into soup bowls, and serve.

Nutrition:
- Calories: 210
- Fat: 4.4
- Fiber: 4.3
- Carbs: 18
- Protein: 26

Corn Soup

Preparation time: 10 minutes
Cooking time: 15 minutes
Servings: 4

Ingredients:
- 2 leeks, chopped
- 2 tablespoons butter
- 2 garlic cloves, peeled and minced
- 6 ears of corn, kernels cut off, cobs reserved
- 2 bay leaves
- 4 tarragon sprigs, chopped
- 1-quart chicken stock
- Salt and ground black pepper, to taste
- Extra virgin olive oil
- 1 tablespoon fresh chives, chopped

Directions:
Set the Instant Pot on Sauté mode, add the butter and melt it. Add the garlic and leeks, stir, and cook for 4 minutes. Add the corn, corn cobs, bay leaves, tarragon, and stock to cover everything, cover the Instant Pot and cook on the Soup setting for 15 minutes. Release the pressure, uncover the Instant Pot, discard the bay leaves and corn cobs, and transfer everything to a blender. Pulse well to obtain a smooth soup, add the rest of the stock and blend again. Add the salt and pepper, stir well, divide into soup bowls, and serve cold with chives and olive oil on top.

Nutrition:
- Calories: 300
- Fat: 8.3
- Fiber: 8
- Carbs: 50
- Protein: 13

Butternut Squash Soup

Preparation time: 10 minutes
Cooking time: 16 minutes
Servings: 6

Ingredients:

- 1½ pounds butternut squash, baked, peeled and cubed
- ½ cup green onions, chopped
- 3 tablespoons butter
- ½ cup carrots, peeled and chopped
- ½ cup celery, chopped
- 29 ounces chicken stock
- 1 garlic clove, peeled and minced
- ½ teaspoon Italian seasoning
- 15 ounces canned diced tomatoes
- Salt and ground black pepper, to taste
- 1/8 teaspoon red pepper flakes
- 1 cup orzo, already cooked
- 1/8 teaspoon nutmeg, grated
- 1½ cup half and half
- 1 cup chicken meat, already cooked and shredded
- Green onions, chopped, for serving

Directions:

Set the Instant Pot on Sauté mode, add the butter and melt it. Add the celery, carrots, and onions, stir, and cook for 3 minutes. Add the garlic, stir, and cook for 1 minute. Add the squash, tomatoes, stock, Italian seasoning, salt, pepper, pepper flakes, and nutmeg. Stir, cover the Instant Pot, and cook on the Soup setting for 10 minutes. Release the pressure, uncover, and puree everything with an immersion blender. Set the Instant Pot on Manual mode, add the half and half, orzo, and chicken, stir, and cook for 3 minutes. Divide the soup into bowls, sprinkle green onions on top, and serve.

Nutrition:

- Calories: 130
- Fat: 2.3
- Fiber: 0.4
- Carbs: 18
- Protein: 6

Potato and Cheese Soup

Preparation time: 10 minutes
Cooking time: 10 minutes
Servings: 6

Ingredients:

- 6 cups potatoes, cubed
- 2 tablespoons butter
- ½ cup yellow onion, chopped
- 28 ounces chicken stock
- Salt and ground black pepper, to taste
- 2 tablespoons dried parsley
- 1/8 teaspoon red pepper flakes
- 2 tablespoons cornstarch
- 2 tablespoons water
- 3 ounces cream cheese, cubed
- 2 cups half and half
- 1 cup cheddar cheese, shredded
- 1 cup corn
- 6 bacon slices, cooked and crumbled

Directions:

Set the Instant Pot on Sauté mode, add the butter and melt it. Add the onion, stir, and cook 5 minutes. Add half of the stock, salt, pepper, pepper flakes, and parsley and stir. Put the potatoes in the steamer basket, cover the Instant Pot and cook on the Steam setting for 4 minutes. Release the pressure fast, uncover the Instant Pot, and transfer the potatoes to a bowl. In another bowl, mix the cornstarch with water and stir well. Set the Instant Pot to Manual mode, add the cornstarch slurry, cream cheese, and shredded cheese and stir well. Add the rest of the stock, corn, bacon, potatoes, half and half. Stir, bring to a simmer, ladle into bowls, and serve.

Nutrition:

- Calories: 188
- Fat: 7.14
- Fiber: 1.5
- Carbs: 22
- Protein: 9

Split Pea Soup

Preparation time: 10 minutes
Cooking time: 20 minutes
Servings: 6
Ingredients:

- 2 tablespoons butter
- 1 pound chicken sausage, ground
- 1 yellow onion, peeled and chopped
- ½ cup carrots, peeled and chopped
- ½ cup celery, chopped
- 2 garlic cloves, peeled and minced
- 29 ounces chicken stock
- Salt and ground black pepper, to taste
- 2 cups water
- 16 ounces split peas, rinsed
- ½ cup half and half
- ¼ teaspoon red pepper flakes

Directions:

Set the Instant Pot on Sauté mode, add the sausage, brown it on all sides and transfer to a plate. Add the butter to the Instant Pot and melt it. Add the celery, onions, and carrots, stir, and cook 4 minutes. Add the garlic, stir and cook for 1 minute. Add the water, stock, peas and pepper flakes, stir, cover and cook on the Soup setting for 10 minutes. Release the pressure, puree the mix using an immersion blender and set the Instant Pot on Manual mode. Add the sausage, salt, pepper, and half and half, stir, bring to a simmer, and ladle into soup bowls.

Nutrition:

- Calories: 30
- Fat: 11
- Fiber: 12
- Carbs: 14
- Protein: 20

Beef and Rice Soup

Preparation time: 10 minutes
Cooking time: 15 minutes
Servings: 6

Ingredients:

- 1 pound ground beef
- 3 garlic cloves, peeled and minced
- 1 yellow onion, peeled and chopped
- 1 tablespoon vegetable oil
- 1 celery stalk, chopped
- 28 ounces beef stock
- 14 ounces canned crushed tomatoes
- ½ cup white rice
- 12 ounces spicy tomato juice
- 15 ounces canned garbanzo beans, rinsed
- 1 potato, cubed
- Salt and ground black pepper, to taste
- ½ cup frozen peas
- 2 carrots, peeled and sliced thin

Directions:

Set the Instant Pot on Sauté mode, add the beef, stir, cook until it browns, and transfer to a plate. Add the oil to the Instant Pot and heat it up. Add the celery and onion, stir, and cook for 5 minutes. Add the garlic, stir and cook for 1 minute. Add the tomato juice, stock, tomatoes, rice, beans, carrots, potatoes, beef, salt, and pepper, stir, cover and cook on the Manual setting for 5 minutes. Release the pressure, uncover the Instant Pot, and set it on Manual mode. Add more salt and pepper, if needed, and the peas, stir, bring to a simmer, transfer to bowls, and serve hot.

Nutrition:

- Calories: 230
- Fat: 7
- Fiber: 4
- Carbs: 10
- Protein: 3

Chicken Noodle Soup

Preparation time: 10 minutes
Cooking time: 12 minutes
Servings: 6

Ingredients:

- 1 yellow onion, peeled and chopped
- 1 tablespoon butter
- 1 celery stalk, chopped
- 4 carrots, peeled and sliced
- Salt and ground black pepper, to taste
- 6 cups chicken stock
- 2 cups chicken, already cooked and shredded
- Egg noodles, already cooked

Directions:

Set the Instant Pot on Sauté mode, add the butter and heat it up. Add the onion, stir, and cook 2 minutes. Add the celery and carrots, stir, and cook 5 minutes. Add the chicken and stock, stir, cover the Instant Pot and cook on the Soup setting for 5 minutes. Release the pressure, uncover the Instant Pot, add salt and pepper to taste, and stir. Divide the noodles into soup bowls, add the soup over them, and serve.

Nutrition:

- Calories: 100
- Fat: 1
- Fiber: 1
- Carbs: 4
- Protein: 7

Chicken and Wild Rice Soup

Preparation time: 10 minutes
Cooking time: 15 minutes
Servings: 6

Ingredients:
- 1 cup yellow onion, peeled and chopped
- 2 tablespoons butter
- 1 cup celery, chopped
- 1 cup carrots, chopped
- 28 ounces chicken stock
- 2 chicken breasts, skinless, boneless and chopped
- 6 ounces wild rice
- Red pepper flakes
- Salt and ground black pepper, to taste
- 1 tablespoon dried parsley
- 2 tablespoons cornstarch mixed with 2 tablespoons water
- 1 cup milk
- 1 cup half and half
- 4 ounces cream cheese, cubed

Directions:

Set the Instant Pot on Sauté mode, add the butter and melt it. Add the carrot, onion, and celery, stir and cook for 5 minutes. Add the rice, chicken, stock, parsley, salt, and pepper, stir, cover, and cook on the Soup setting for 5 minutes. Release the pressure, uncover, add the cornstarch mixed with water, stir, and set the Instant Pot on Manual mode. Add the cheese, milk, and half and half, stir, heat up, transfer to bowls, and serve.

Nutrition:
- Calories: 200
- Fat: 7
- Fiber: 1
- Carbs: 19
- Protein: 5

Creamy Tomato Soup

Preparation time: 10 minutes
Cooking time: 6 minutes
Servings: 8

Ingredients:
- 1 yellow onion, peeled and chopped
- 3 tablespoons butter
- 1 carrot, peeled and chopped
- 2 celery stalks, chopped
- 2 garlic cloves, peeled and minced
- 29 ounces chicken stock
- Salt and ground black pepper, to taste
- ¼ cup fresh basil, chopped
- 3 pounds tomatoes, peeled, cored, and cut into quarters
- 1 tablespoon tomato paste
- 1 cup half and half
- ½ cup Parmesan cheese, shredded

Directions:

Set the Instant Pot on Sauté mode, add the butter and melt it. Add the onion, carrots, and celery, stir, and cook for 3 minutes. Add the garlic, stir, and cook for 1 minute. Add the tomatoes, tomato paste, stock, basil, salt, and pepper, stir, cover, and cook on the Soup setting for 5 minutes. Release the pressure, uncover the Instant Pot and puree the soup using and immersion blender. Add the half and half and cheese, stir, set the Instant Pot on Manual mode and heat everything up. Divide the soup into soup bowls, and serve.

Nutrition:
- Calories: 280
- Fat: 8
- Fiber: 4
- Carbs: 32
- Protein: 24

Zuppa Toscana

Preparation time: 10 minutes
Cooking time: 17 minutes
Servings: 8

Ingredients:

- 1 pound chicken sausage, ground
- 6 bacon slices, chopped
- 3 garlic cloves, peeled and minced
- 1 cup yellow onion, peeled and chopped
- 1 tablespoon butter
- 40 ounces chicken stock
- Salt and ground black pepper, to taste
- Red pepper flakes
- 3 potatoes, cubed
- 3 tablespoons cornstarch
- 12 ounces evaporated milk
- 1 cup Parmesan, shredded
- 2 cup spinach, chopped

Directions:

Set the Instant Pot on Sauté mode, add the bacon, stir, cook until it's crispy, and transfer to a plate. Add the sausage to the Instant Pot, stir, cook until it browns on all sides, and also transfer to a plate. Add the butter to the Instant Pot and melt it. Add the onion, stir, and cook for 5 minutes. Add the garlic, stir, and cook for 1 minute. Add ⅓ of the stock, salt, pepper, and pepper flakes and stir. Place the potatoes in the steamer basket of the Instant Pot, cover and cook on the Steam setting for 4 minutes. Release the pressure, uncover the Instant Pot, and transfer the potatoes to a bowl. Add the rest of the stock to the Instant Pot with the cornstarch mixed with the evaporated milk, stir, and set the Instant Pot on Manual mode. Add the cheese, sausage, bacon, potatoes, spinach, more salt and pepper, if needed, stir, divide into bowls, and serve.

Nutrition:

- Calories: 170
- Fat: 4
- Fiber: 2
- Carbs: 24
- Protein: 10

Minestrone Soup

Preparation time: 10 minutes
Cooking time: 15 minutes
Servings: 8
Ingredients:

- 1 tablespoon extra virgin olive oil
- 1 celery stalk, chopped
- 2 carrots, peeled and chopped
- 1 onion, peeled and chopped
- 1 cup corn kernels
- 1 zucchini, chopped
- 3 pounds tomatoes, cored, peeled, and chopped
- 4 garlic cloves, peeled and minced
- 29 ounces chicken stock
- 1 cup uncooked pasta
- Salt and ground black pepper, to taste
- 1 teaspoon Italian seasoning
- 2 cups baby spinach
- 15 ounces canned kidney beans
- 1 cup Asiago cheese, grated
- 2 tablespoons fresh basil, chopped

Directions:

Set the Instant Pot on Sauté mode, add the oil and heat it up. Add the onion, stir, and cook for 5 minutes. Add the carrots, garlic, celery, corn, and zucchini, stir, and cook 5 minutes. Add the tomatoes, stock, Italian seasoning, pasta, salt, and pepper, stir, cover, and cook on the Soup setting for 4 minutes. Release the pressure fast, uncover, add the beans, basil, and spinach. Add more salt and pepper, if needed, divide into bowls, add the cheese on top, and serve.

Nutrition:

- Calories: 110
- Fat: 2
- Fiber: 4
- Carbs: 18
- Protein: 5

Tomato Soup

Preparation time: 10 minutes
Cooking time: 45 minutes
Servings: 6

Ingredients:

For the roasted tomatoes:
- 14 garlic cloves, peeled and crushed
- 3 pounds cherry tomatoes, cut into halves
- Salt and ground black pepper, to taste
- 2 tablespoons extra virgin olive oil
- ½ teaspoon red pepper flakes

For the soup:
- 1 yellow onion, peeled and chopped
- 2 tablespoons olive oil
- 1 red bell pepper, seeded and chopped
- 3 tablespoons tomato paste
- 2 celery ribs, chopped

- 2 cups chicken stock
- 1 teaspoon garlic powder
- 1 teaspoon onion powder
- ½ tablespoon dried basil
- ½ teaspoon red pepper flakes
- Salt and ground black pepper, to taste
- 1 cup heavy cream

For serving:
- Fresh basil leaves, chopped
- ½ cup Parmesan cheese, grated

Directions:

Place the tomatoes and garlic in a baking tray, drizzle 2 tablespoons oil, season with salt, pepper and a ½ teaspoon of red pepper flakes, toss to coat, introduce in the oven at 425°F, and roast for 25 minutes. Take the tomatoes out of the oven and set aside. Set the Instant Pot on Sauté mode, add the oil, and heat it up. Add the onion, bell pepper, celery, salt, pepper, garlic powder, onion powder, basil, the remaining red pepper flakes, stir, and cook for 3 minutes. Add the tomato paste, roasted tomatoes, and garlic and stir. Add the stock, cover the Instant Pot, and cook on the Manual setting for 10 minutes. Release the pressure, uncover the Instant Pot and set it on Sauté mode. Add the heavy cream and blend everything using an immersion blender. Divide in bowls, add basil and cheese on top, and serve.

Nutrition:

- Calories: 150
- Fat: 1
- Fiber: 3
- Carbs: 3
- Protein: 4

Carrot Soup

Preparation time: 10 minutes
Cooking time: 16 minutes
Servings: 4

Ingredients:
- 1 tablespoon vegetable oil
- 1 onion, peeled and chopped
- 1 tablespoon butter
- 1 garlic clove, peeled and minced
- 1 pound carrots, peeled and chopped
- 1 small ginger piece, peeled and grated
- Salt and ground black pepper, to taste
- ¼ teaspoon brown sugar
- 2 cups chicken stock
- 1 tablespoon Sriracha
- 14 ounces canned coconut milk
- Cilantro leaves, chopped, for serving

Directions:
Set the Instant Pot on Sauté mode, add the butter and oil, and heat them up. Add the onion, stir and cook for 3 minutes. Add the ginger and garlic, stir, and cook for 1 minute. Add the sugar, carrots, salt, and pepper, stir, and cook 2 minutes. Add the sriracha, coconut milk, stock, stir, cover, and cook on the Soup setting for 6 minutes. Release the pressure for 10 minutes, uncover the Instant Pot, blend the soup with an immersion blender, add more salt and pepper, if needed, and divide into soup bowls. Add the cilantro on top, and serve.

Nutrition:
- Calories: 60
- Fat: 1
- Fiber: 3.1
- Carbs: 12
- Protein: 2

Ham and White Bean Soup

Preparation time: 10 minutes
Cooking time: 15 minutes
Servings: 8

Ingredients:
- 1 pound white beans, soaked for 1 hour and drained
- 1 carrot, peeled and chopped
- 1 tablespoon extra virgin olive oil
- 1 yellow onion, peeled and chopped
- 3 garlic cloves, peeled and minced
- 1 tomato, cored, peeled and chopped
- 1 pound ham, chopped
- Salt and ground black pepper, to taste
- 4 cups water
- 4 cups vegetable stock
- 1 teaspoon dried mint
- 1 teaspoon paprika
- 1 teaspoon dried thyme

Directions:
Set the Instant Pot on Sauté mode, add the oil, and heat it up. Add the carrot, onion, garlic, tomato, stir, and cook for 5 minutes. Add the beans, ham, salt, pepper, water, stock, mint, paprika, and thyme, stir, cover, and cook on the Bean/Chili setting for 15 minutes. Release the pressure for 10 minutes, uncover the Instant Pot, divide into soup bowls, and serve.

Nutrition:
- Calories: 177
- Fat: 2
- Fiber: 1
- Carbs: 26
- Protein: 14

Lentil Soup

Preparation time: 10 minutes
Cooking time: 30 minutes
Servings: 4

Ingredients:

- 2 celery stalks, chopped
- 1 tablespoon olive oil
- 1 small onion, peeled and chopped
- 2 carrots, peeled and chopped
- ½ pound chicken sausage, ground
- 3½ cups beef stock
- 2 teaspoons garlic, peeled and minced
- 1 cup lentils
- 15 ounces canned diced tomatoes
- Salt and ground black pepper, to taste
- 2 cups spinach

Directions:

Set the Instant Pot on Sauté mode, add the oil, and heat it up. Add the celery, onion, carrots, stir, and cook for 4 minutes. Add the chicken sausage, stir, and cook 5 minutes. Add the stock, garlic, lentils, tomatoes, salt, pepper, and spinach, stir, cover and cook on the Soup setting for 25 minutes. Release the pressure, uncover the Instant Pot, divide into soup bowls, and serve.

Nutrition:

- Calories: 175
- Fat: 1
- Fiber: 1
- Carbs: 2
- Protein: 2

Cabbage Soup

Preparation time: 10 minutes
Cooking time: 10 minutes
Servings: 4

Ingredients:

- 1 cabbage head, chopped
- 12 ounces baby carrots
- 3 celery stalks, chopped
- ½ onion, peeled and chopped
- 1 packet vegetable soup mix
- 2 tablespoons olive oil
- 12 ounces soy burger
- 3 teaspoons garlic, peeled and minced
- ¼ cup cilantro, chopped
- 4 cups chicken stock
- Salt and ground black pepper, to taste

Directions:

In the Instant Pot, mix the cabbage with the celery, carrots, onion, soup mix, soy burger, stock, olive oil, and garlic, stir, cover, and cook on Soup mode for 5 minutes. Release the pressure, uncover the Instant Pot, add the salt, pepper, and cilantro, stir again well, divide into soup bowls, and serve.

Nutrition:

- Calories: 100
- Fat: 1
- Fiber: 2
- Carbs: 10
- Protein: 10

Cream of Asparagus

Preparation time: 10 minutes
Cooking time: 25 minutes
Servings: 4

Ingredients:

- 2 pounds green asparagus, trimmed, tips cut off and cut into medium pieces
- 3 tablespoons butter
- 1 yellow onion, peeled and chopped
- 6 cups chicken stock
- ¼ teaspoon lemon juice
- ½ cup crème fraiche
- Salt and ground white pepper, to taste

Directions:

Set the Instant Pot on Sauté mode, add the butter and melt it. Add the asparagus, salt, and pepper, stir, and cook for 5 minutes. Add 5 cups of the stock, cover the Instant Pot, and cook on Soup mode for 15 minutes. Release the pressure, uncover the Instant Pot and transfer soup to a blender. Pulse several times and return to the Instant Pot. Set the Instant Pot on Manual mode, add the crème fraiche, the rest of the stock, salt, pepper, and lemon juice, bring to a boil, divide into soup bowls, and serve.

Nutrition:

- Calories: 80
- Fat: 8
- Fiber: 1
- Carbs: 16
- Protein: 6.3

Artichoke Soup

Preparation time: 10 minutes
Cooking time: 20 minutes
Servings: 4

Ingredients:

- 5 artichoke hearts, washed and trimmed
- 1 leek, sliced
- 5 tablespoons butter
- 6 garlic cloves, peeled and minced
- ½ cup shallots, chopped
- 8 ounces Yukon gold potatoes, chopped
- 12 cups chicken stock
- 1 bay leaf
- Fresh parsley, chopped
- 2 thyme sprigs
- ¼ teaspoon black peppercorns, crushed
- Salt, to taste
- ¼ cup cream

Directions:

Set the Instant Pot on Sauté mode, add the butter and melt it. Add the artichoke hearts, shallots, leek, and garlic, stir, and brown for 3-4 minutes. Add the potatoes, stock, bay leaf, thyme, parsley, peppercorns, and salt, stir, cover, and cook on the Soup setting for 15 minutes. Release the pressure, uncover the Instant Pot, discard the herbs, blend well using an immersion blender, add salt to taste and the cream, stir well, divide into bowls, and serve.

Nutrition:

- Calories: 95
- Fat: 2
- Fiber: 4
- Carbs: 15
- Protein: 4

Beet Soup

Preparation time: 10 minutes
Cooking time: 10 minutes
Servings: 4

Ingredients:
- 1 tablespoon sesame oil
- 1 cup red lentils
- 1 red onion, peeled and chopped
- 2 carrots, peeled and chopped
- 3 beets, peeled and chopped
- 3 bay leaves
- 6 cups vegetable stock
- ½ teaspoon fresh thyme
- 3 tablespoons dark miso
- 1½ tablespoons fresh parsley, chopped
- Salt and ground black pepper, to taste

Directions:

Set the Instant Pot on Sauté mode, add the oil and heat it up. Add the onion, stir, and cook for 5 minutes. Add the lentils, carrots, beets, thyme, bay leaves, stock, salt, and pepper, stir, cover, and cook on the Soup setting for 5 minutes. Release the pressure, uncover the Instant Pot, discard the bay leaves, and puree the soup using an immersion blender. Add the miso mixed with some water, more salt and pepper, if needed, and parsley, stir, divide into soup bowls, and serve.

Nutrition:
- Calories: 100
- Fat: 4
- Fiber: 2
- Carbs: 8
- Protein: 3

Cream of Broccoli

Preparation time: 10 minutes
Cooking time: 10 minutes
Servings: 4

Ingredients:
- 1 yellow onion, peeled and chopped
- 3 carrots, peeled and chopped
- 1 potato, chopped
- 1 broccoli head, separated into florets and chopped
- 1 tablespoons olive oil
- 2 cups chicken stock
- 5 garlic cloves, peeled and minced
- Salt and ground black pepper, to taste
- 2 tablespoons cream
- Cheddar cheese, grated, for serving
- 1 tablespoon fresh chives, chopped

Directions:

Set the Instant Pot on Sauté mode, add the oil and heat it up. Add the onion and garlic, stir, and cook for 2 minutes. Add the broccoli, carrots, potato, stock, salt, pepper, stir, cover, and cook on the Soup setting for 5 minutes. Release the pressure, uncover the Instant Pot, set it on Manual mode, add the cream, cheese, and chives, stir, heat up for 2 minutes, divide into bowls, and serve.

Nutrition:
- Calories: 180
- Fat: 11
- Fiber: 3
- Carbs: 14
- Protein: 6

Celery Soup

Preparation time: 10 minutes
Cooking time: 17 minutes
Servings: 2

Ingredients:

- 1 yellow onion, peeled and chopped
- 7 celery stalks, chopped
- 3 potatoes, chopped
- 1 teaspoon extra virgin olive oil
- Salt and ground black pepper, to taste
- 4 cups vegetable stock
- 1 tablespoon curry powder
- 1 teaspoon celery seeds
- ½ cup parsley, chopped, for serving

Directions:

Set the Instant Pot on Sauté mode, add the oil and heat it up. Add the onion, celery seeds, and curry powder, stir, and cook for 1 minute. Add the celery and potatoes, stir, and cook for 5 minutes. Add the stock, salt, pepper stir, cover, and cook on the Manual setting for 10 minutes. Release the pressure, uncover the Instant Pot, blend well using an immersion blender, add the parsley, stir, divide into soup bowls, and serve.

Nutrition:

- Calories: 90
- Fat: 4
- Fiber: 4
- Carbs: 8.5
- Protein: 2

Chestnut Soup

Preparation time: 10 minutes
Cooking time: 25 minutes
Servings: 4

Ingredients:

- 1 pound canned chestnuts, drained and rinsed
- 1 celery stalk, chopped
- 4 tablespoons butter
- 1 yellow onion, peeled and chopped
- 1 sage leaf, chopped
- Salt and ground white pepper, to taste
- 1 bay leaf
- 1 potato, chopped
- 4 cups chicken stock
- 2 tablespoons rum
- Nutmeg
- Heavy cream, for serving
- Sage leaves, chopped, for serving

Directions:

Set the Instant Pot on Sauté mode, add the butter and melt it. Add the onion, sage, celery, salt, and pepper, stir, and cook for 5 minutes. Add the chestnuts, potato, bay leaf, and stock, stir, cover, and cook on Soup mode for 20 minutes. Release the pressure, uncover the Instant Pot, add the nutmeg and rum, discard the bay leaf and blend the soup using an immersion blender. Divide the soup into bowls, add the cream and sage leaves on top, and serve.

Nutrition:

- Calories: 230
- Fat: 13
- Fiber: 2
- Carbs: 22
- Protein: 2.1

Fennel Soup

Preparation time: 10 minutes
Cooking time: 15 minutes
Servings: 3

Ingredients:

- 1 fennel bulb, chopped
- 1 bay leaf
- 1 leek, chopped
- 2 cups water
- 1 tablespoon extra virgin olive oil
- ½ cube vegetable bouillon
- Salt and ground black pepper, to taste
- 2 teaspoons Parmesan cheese, grated

Directions:

In the Instant Pot, mix the fennel with the leek, bay leaf, vegetable bouillon, and water. Stir, cover, and cook on the Soup setting for 15 minutes. Release the pressure, uncover the Instant Pot, add the cheese, oil, salt, and pepper, stir, divide into bowls, and serve.

Nutrition:

- Calories: 100
- Fat: 2.2
- Fiber: 4
- Carbs: 15
- Protein: 5

Cauliflower Soup

Preparation time: 10 minutes
Cooking time: 10 minutes
Servings: 6

Ingredients:

- 1 small onion, peeled and chopped
- 1 cauliflower head, separated into florets and chopped
- 2 tablespoons butter
- 3 cups chicken stock
- Salt and ground black pepper, to taste
- 1 teaspoon garlic powder
- 4 ounces cream cheese, cubed
- 1 cup cheddar cheese, grated
- ½ cup half and half

Directions:

Set the Instant Pot on Sauté mode, add the butter and melt it. Add the onion, stir, and cook for 3 minutes. Add the cauliflower, stock, salt, pepper, and garlic powder, stir, cover, and cook on the Soup setting for 5 minutes. Release the pressure, uncover the Instant Pot, blend everything using an immersion blender, add more salt and pepper, if needed, cream cheese, grated cheese, and half and half. Stir, set the Instant Pot on Manual mode, heat up for 2 minutes, divide into soup bowls, and serve.

Nutrition:

- Calories: 78
- Fat: 1.2
- Fiber: 1
- Carbs: 10
- Protein: 3

Turkey and Sweet Potato Soup

Preparation time: 10 minutes
Cooking time: 12 minutes
Servings: 4

Ingredients:

- 1 pound Italian turkey sausage, chopped
- 1 yellow onion, peeled and chopped
- 2 celery stalks, chopped
- 2 carrots, peeled and chopped
- 1 big sweet potato, cubed
- 5 cups turkey stock
- 2 garlic cloves, peeled and minced
- 1 teaspoon red pepper flakes
- 1 teaspoon dried basil
- 1 teaspoon dried oregano
- Salt and ground black pepper, to taste
- 1 teaspoon dried thyme
- 5 ounces spinach, chopped
- 2 bay leaves

Directions:

Set the Instant Pot on Sauté mode, add the sausage, brown it, and transfer to a plate. Add the onion, celery and carrots, stir, and cook for 2 minutes. Add the potato, stir, and cook 2 minutes. Add the stock, garlic, red pepper flakes, salt, pepper, basil, oregano, thyme, spinach, and bay leaves. Stir, cover and cook on the Soup setting for 4 minutes. Release the pressure, uncover the Instant Pot, discard bay leaves, divide soup into bowls, and serve.

Nutrition:

- Calories: 190
- Fat: 12
- Fiber: 1
- Carbs: 2
- Protein: 5

Chicken Meatball Soup

Preparation time: 10 minutes
Cooking time: 20 minutes
Servings: 6

Ingredients:

- 1½ pounds chicken breast, ground
- Salt and ground black pepper, to taste
- 2 tablespoons arrowroot powder
- 1 teaspoon garlic powder
- ½ teaspoon crushed red pepper
- 1 teaspoon onion powder
- ½ tablespoon dried basil
- ½ tablespoon dried oregano
- 2 tablespoons nutritional yeast

For the soup:

- 6 cups chicken stock
- 4 celery stalks, chopped
- 3 carrots, dried chopped
- 2 yellow onions, dried chopped
- 1 bunch kale, chopped
- 2 teaspoons dried thyme
- 2 garlic cloves, dried minced
- ½ teaspoon red pepper flakes
- 2 eggs, whisked
- 2 tablespoons extra virgin olive oil

Directions:

Set the Instant Pot on Sauté mode, add the oil and heat it up. Add the onions, celery, and carrots, stir, and cook for 3 minutes. Add the garlic, salt, pepper, kale, stock, 2 teaspoons thyme½ teaspoon red pepper, stir, and cook for 10 minutes. In a bowl, mix the chicken with arrowroot, salt, pepper, ½ teaspoon red pepper, garlic powder, onion powder, oregano, basil, and yeast and stir well. Shape the meatballs using your hands and drop them gently into the soup. Cover the Instant Pot and cook on the Soup setting for 15 minutes. Release the pressure, uncover the Instant Pot, and set it on Sauté mode. Add the eggs slowly, stir, and cook for 2 minutes. Divide into soup bowls, and serve hot.

Nutrition:

- Calories: 190
- Fat: 2.8
- Fiber: 2.3
- Carbs: 10
- Protein: 29

Vegetable Soup

Preparation time: 10 minutes
Cooking time: 15 minutes
Servings: 4

Ingredients:

- 1 onion, peeled and chopped
- 1 tablespoon coconut oil
- Salt and ground black pepper, to taste
- ½ red chili, chopped
- 2 carrots, peeled and chopped
- 2 celery sticks, chopped
- 6 mushrooms, sliced
- 4 garlic cloves, peeled and minced
- ½ cup dried porcini mushrooms
- 3.5 ounces kale leaves, chopped
- 1 cup tomatoes, chopped
- 1 zucchini, chopped
- 4 cups vegetable stock
- 1 bay leaf
- 1 teaspoon lemon zest
- ½ cup fresh parsley, chopped

Directions:

Set the Instant Pot on Sauté mode, add the oil and heat it up. Add the onion, celery, carrots, salt, and pepper, stir, and cook for 1 minute. Add the chili pepper, mushrooms, garlic, stir, and cook for 2 minutes. Add the kale leaves, zucchini, tomatoes, bay leaf, and stock, stir, cover, and cook on the Soup setting for 10 minutes. Release the pressure naturally, uncover the Instant Pot, divide the soup into bowls, add the lemon zest and parsley on top, and serve.

Nutrition:

- Calories: 80
- Fat: 1
- Fiber: 2
- Carbs: 14
- Protein: 2

Chicken Chili Soup

Preparation time: 10 minutes
Cooking time: 30 minutes
Servings: 4

Ingredients:

- 1 white onion, peeled and chopped
- 2 tablespoons olive oil
- 1 jalapeño pepper, chopped
- 4 garlic cloves, peeled and minced
- 2 teaspoons dried oregano
- 1 teaspoon cumin
- ½ teaspoon red pepper flakes
- 3 cups chicken stock
- 1 pound chicken breast, skinless and boneless
- 30 ounces canned cannellini beans, drained
- Salt and ground black pepper, to taste
- Fresh cilantro, chopped, for serving
- Tortilla chips, for serving
- Lime wedges, for serving

Directions:

Set the Instant Pot on Sauté mode, add the oil and heat it up. Add jalapeño and onion, stir, and cook for 3 minutes. Add the garlic, stir, and cook for 1 minute. Add the oregano, cumin, pepper flakes, stock, chicken, beans, salt, and pepper, stir, cover, and cook on Soup for 30 minutes. Release the pressure, uncover the Instant Pot, shred the meat with 2 forks, add more salt and pepper, stir, and divide into soup bowls. Serve with cilantro on top and with tortilla chips and lime wedges on the side.

Nutrition:

- Calories: 200
- Fat: 8
- Fiber: 6
- Carbs: 17
- Protein: 19

Broccoli and Bacon Soup

Preparation time: 10 minutes
Cooking time: 10 minutes
Servings: 6

Ingredients:

- 4 bacon slices, chopped
- 1 teaspoon olive oil
- 2 small broccoli heads, chopped
- 1 leek, chopped
- 1 celery rib, chopped
- 2 cups spinach, chopped
- 4 tablespoons basmati rice
- 1 tablespoon Parmesan cheese, grated
- 1 quart vegetable stock
- Salt and ground black pepper, to taste

Directions:

Set the Instant Pot on Sauté mode, add the oil and bacon, cook until crispy, transfer to a plate, and set aside. Add the broccoli, leek, celery, spinach, rice, salt, pepper, and stock, stir, cover and cook on the Soup setting for 6 minutes. Release the pressure, uncover, add more salt and pepper if needed, add the bacon, divide into soup bowls, and serve with cheese on top.

Nutrition:

- Calories: 151
- Fat: 2.2
- Fiber: 7
- Carbs: 26
- Protein: 10

Chorizo, Chicken, and Kale Soup

Preparation time: 10 minutes
Cooking time: 10 minutes
Servings: 8

Ingredients:

- 9 ounces chorizo, casings removed
- 2 tablespoons olive oil
- 4 chicken thighs, chopped
- Salt and ground black pepper, to taste
- 4 garlic cloves, peeled and minced
- 2 yellow onions, peeled and chopped
- 4 cups chicken stock
- 15 ounces canned diced tomatoes
- 3 potatoes, chopped
- 2 bay leaves
- 5 ounces baby kale
- 14 ounces garbanzo beans, drained

Directions:

Set the Instant Pot on Sauté mode, add the oil and heat it up. Add the chorizo, chicken, and onion, stir, and cook 5 minutes. Add the garlic, stir, and cook for 1 minute. Add the stock, tomatoes, and bay leaves and stir again. Add the kale, potatoes, salt and pepper, stir, cover, and cook on the Soup setting for 4 minutes. Release the pressure, uncover the Instant Pot, add the beans, more salt and pepper, if needed, stir, divide into bowls, and serve.

Nutrition:

- Calories: 200
- Fat: 9
- Fiber: 2
- Carbs: 19
- Protein: 11

Endive Soup

Preparation time: 10 minutes
Cooking time: 25 minutes
Servings: 4

Ingredients:
- 1 tablespoon canola oil
- 2 teaspoons sesame oil
- 2 scallions, chopped
- 3 garlic cloves peeled and chopped
- 1 tablespoon ginger, grated
- 1 teaspoon chili sauce
- ½ cup uncooked rice
- 6 cups vegetable stock
- 1½ tablespoons soy sauce
- 3 endives, trimmed and chopped
- Salt and ground white pepper, to taste

Directions:
Set the Instant Pot on Sauté mode, add the canola oil and sesame oil, and heat it up. Add the scallions and garlic, stir, and cook for 4 minutes. Add the chili sauce and ginger, stir, and cook for 1 minute. Add the stock and soy sauce, stir, and cook for 2 minutes. Add the rice, stir, cover and cook on the Steam setting for 15 minutes. Release the pressure, uncover the Instant Pot, add the salt, pepper and endives, stir, cover again and cook on the Manual setting for 5 minutes. Release the pressure again, uncover the Instant Pot, stir, divide into bowls, and serve.

Nutrition:
- Calories: 207
- Fat: 9
- Fiber: 12
- Carbs: 12
- Protein: 11.5

Chicken Enchilada Soup

Preparation time: 10 minutes
Cooking time: 30 minutes
Servings: 4

Ingredients:
- 2 chicken breasts, boneless and skinless and chopped
- 1¼ cups red enchilada sauce
- 3 cups chicken stock
- 14 ounces canned diced tomatoes
- 28 ounces canned black beans, drained
- 15 ounces canned corn, drained
- Salt and ground black pepper, to taste
- 4 ounces canned green chilies, chopped
- 2 garlic cloves, peeled and minced
- 1 cup white onion, peeled and chopped
- ½ cup quinoa
- 1 teaspoon cumin
- 1 teaspoon dried oregano

For serving:
- Fresh, cilantro, chopped
- Avocado, pitted, peeled, and chopped
- Red onion, peeled and diced
- Cheddar cheese, shredded

Directions:
In the Instant Pot, mix the chicken with enchilada sauce, stock, tomatoes, black beans, corn, green chilies, salt, pepper, garlic, onion, quinoa, cumin, and oregano, stir, cover, and cook on Soup mode for 25 minutes. Release the pressure, uncover the Instant Pot, divide the soup into bowls, and serve with cilantro, avocado, and red onion on top and with shredded cheese sprinkled all over.

Nutrition:
- Calories: 400
- Fat: 23
- Fiber: 3
- Carbs: 23
- Protein: 27

Beef and Barley Soup

Preparation time: 10 minutes
Cooking time: 25 minutes
Servings: 4

Ingredients:

- 1½ pounds beef stew meat, chopped
- 2 tablespoons vegetable oil
- Salt and ground black pepper, to taste
- 10 cremini mushrooms, cut into quarters
- 1 cup celery, diced
- 1 cup carrots, diced
- 1 cup onion, diced
- 8 garlic cloves, peeled and minced
- 6 cups beef stock
- 2 bay leaves
- 1 cup water
- ½ teaspoon dried thyme
- 1 potato, chopped
- ⅔ cup barley

Directions:

Set the Instant Pot on Sauté mode, add the oil and heat it up. Add the meat, salt, and pepper, stir, cook for 3 minutes, and transfer to a plate. Add the mushrooms, stir, brown them for 2 minutes, and transfer to a plate. Add the onion, celery, and carrots to the Instant Pot, stir, and cook for 4 minutes. Return the meat, mushrooms to the Instant Pot and stir. Add the bay leaves, thyme, water, stock, salt, and pepper, stir, cover, and cook on the Manual setting for 16 minutes. Release the pressure, uncover the Instant Pot, add the potatoes and barley, stir, cover, and cook on Manual for 1 hour. Release the pressure again, stir the soup, divide it into bowls, and serve.

Nutrition:

- Calories: 120
- Fat: 3
- Fiber: 2
- Carbs: 11
- Protein: 5

Beef Stew

Preparation time: 10 minutes
Cooking time: 30 minutes
Servings: 8

Ingredients:

- 1 tablespoon vegetable oil
- 2 pounds beef stew, cubed
- 1 yellow onion, peeled and chopped
- 5 carrots, peeled and chopped
- 8 potatoes, cubed
- Salt and ground black pepper, to taste
- 2 teaspoons cornstarch
- 2 beef bouillon cubes
- 2 cups water

Directions:

Set the Instant Pot on Sauté mode, add the oil and heat it up. Add the beef and onion, stir, and cook until it browns on all sides. Add the carrots, water, and bouillon, stir, cover, and cook on Soup mode for 20 minutes. Put some water in a stockpot, add some salt, bring to a boil over medium-high heat, add the potatoes, cook for 10 minutes, and drain them. Release the pressure, uncover the Instant Pot and set it on manual mode. Add the cornstarch mixed with some water, salt, pepper, and potatoes, stir, bring to a boil, take off heat, and divide stew among plates.

Nutrition:

- Calories: 300
- Fat: 12
- Fiber: 5
- Carbs: 1
- Protein: 25

Pork Stew

Preparation time: 10 minutes
Cooking time: 30 minutes
Servings: 4

Ingredients:
- 1½ pounds pork shoulder, cubed
- 1 yellow onion, peeled and chopped
- 3 tablespoons extra virgin olive oil
- 1 red bell pepper, seeded and chopped
- 2 garlic cloves, peeled and chopped
- 1 rutabaga, cubed
- Salt and ground black pepper, to taste
- 8 baby potatoes
- 4 carrots, peeled and cut into big chunks
- ½ cup chicken stock
- 14 ounces canned diced tomatoes

Directions:
Set the Instant Pot on Sauté mode, add 2 tablespoons of the oil and heat it up. Add the pork, salt and pepper, brown on all sides, and transfer to a bowl. Add the onions, garlic, bell pepper, and the rest of the oil to the Instant Pot, stir, and cook for 3 minutes. Return the pork to pot, add the carrots, potatoes, rutabaga, salt, pepper, tomatoes, and stock, stir, cover, and cook on Meat/Stew for 20 minutes. Release the pressure, uncover the Instant Pot, stir the stew, divide into bowls, and serve.

Nutrition:
- Calories: 272
- Fat: 6
- Fiber: 3
- Carbs: 27
- Protein: 24

Chicken Stew

Preparation time: 10 minutes
Cooking time: 1 hour and 15 minutes
Servings: 6

Ingredients:
- 6 chicken thighs
- 1 teaspoon vegetable oil
- Salt and ground black pepper, to taste
- 1 yellow onion, peeled and chopped
- 1 celery stalk, chopped
- ½ teaspoon dried thyme
- 2 tablespoons tomato paste
- ½ cup white wine
- 2 cups chicken stock
- 15 ounces canned diced tomatoes,
- ¾ pound baby carrots
- 1½ pounds new potatoes

Directions:
Set the Instant Pot on Sauté mode, add the oil and heat it up. Add the chicken, salt, and pepper, brown for 4 minutes on each side and transfer to a plate. Add the celery, onion, tomato paste, carrots, thyme, salt, and pepper, stir, and cook for 5 minutes. Add the wine, stir, bring to a boil, and simmer for 3 minutes. Add the stock, chicken, tomatoes, and potatoes in the steamer basket of the Instant Pot. Cover Instant Pot and cook on the Manual setting for 30 minutes. Release the pressure, uncover the Instant Pot, take potatoes out of the Instant Pot and put them in a bowl. Transfer the chicken pieces to a cutting board, set aside to cool down for a few minutes, discard the bones, shred meat, and return it to the stew. Add more salt and pepper, if needed, stir, divide into bowls, and serve hot.

Nutrition:
- Calories: 271
- Fat: 2
- Fiber: 4
- Carbs: 18
- Protein: 15

Simple Fish Chowder

Preparation time: 10 minutes
Cooking time: 10 minutes
Servings: 4

Ingredients:
- 1 yellow onion, peeled and chopped
- 2 celery ribs, chopped
- ¾ cup bacon, chopped
- 1 carrot, peeled and chopped
- 2 garlic cloves, peeled and chopped
- 3 cups potatoes, cubed
- 4 cups chicken stock
- 1 pound haddock fillets
- 2 tablespoons butter
- 1 cup frozen corn
- Salt and ground white pepper, to taste
- 1 tablespoon potato starch
- 2 cups heavy cream

Directions:

Set the Instant Pot on Sauté mode, add the butter and melt it. Add the bacon, stir, and cook until crispy. Add the garlic, celery and onion, stir, and cook for 3 minutes. Add the salt, pepper, fish, potatoes, corn, and stock, stir, cover, and cook on the Manual setting for 5 minutes. Release the pressure naturally, uncover the Instant Pot, add the heavy cream mixed with potato starch, stir well, set the Instant Pot on Soup mode, and cook for 3 minutes. Divide into bowls, and serve.

Nutrition:
- Calories: 195
- Fat: 4.4
- Fiber: 2
- Carbs: 21
- Protein: 17

Fast Bean Stew

Preparation time: 10 minutes
Cooking time: 25 minutes
Servings: 4

Ingredients:
- 1 yellow onion, peeled and chopped
- 2 carrots, peeled and chopped
- 1 garlic head, halved
- 1 pound chickpeas, drained
- 22 ounces canned diced tomatoes
- 22 ounces water
- 1 teaspoon dried oregano
- 3 bay leaves
- 2 tablespoons olive oil
- Salt and ground black pepper, to taste
- ½ teaspoon red pepper flakes
- Olive oil, for serving
- 2 tablespoons Parmesan cheese, grated

Directions:

Put the onion, carrots, garlic, chickpeas, tomatoes, water, oregano, bay leaves, 2 tablespoons olive oil, salt, and pepper into the Instant Pot. Cover, cook on the Meat/Stew setting for 25 minutes, and release pressure. Ladle into bowls, add the cheese, pepper flakes and a drizzle of oil on top, and serve.

Nutrition:
- Calories: 164
- Fat: 2
- Fiber: 9
- Carbs: 28
- Protein: 8.2

Sweet Potato Stew

Preparation time: 10 minutes
Cooking time: 20 minutes
Servings: 4

Ingredients:
- 1 onion, peeled and chopped
- 1 sweet potato, cubed
- 3 garlic cloves, peeled and chopped
- 1 celery stalk, chopped
- 2 carrots, peeled and chopped
- 1 cup green lentils
- ½ cup red lentils
- 2 cups vegetable stock
- ¼ cup raisins
- 14 ounces canned diced tomatoes
- Salt and ground black pepper, to taste

For the spice blend:
- 1 teaspoon cumin
- 1 teaspoon turmeric
- ½ teaspoon ground cinnamon
- 1 teaspoon paprika
- 2 teaspoons coriander
- ¼ teaspoon ginger, grated
- Cloves
- Red chili flakes

Directions:
Set the Instant Pot on Sauté mode, add the onions and brown them for 2 minutes, adding some of the stock from time to time. Add the garlic, stir, and cook for 1 minute. Add the carrots, raisins, celery, and sweet potatoes, stir, and cook for 1 minute. Add the lentils, stock, tomatoes, salt, pepper, turmeric, cinnamon, paprika, cumin, coriander, ginger, cloves, and chili flakes, stir, cover, and cook on the Meat/Stew setting for 15 minutes. Release the pressure, uncover the Instant Pot, stir the stew, add more salt and pepper, if needed, ladle into bowls, and serve.

Nutrition:
- Calories: 150
- Fat: 9
- Fiber: 3
- Protein: 4
- Carbs: 25

Spinach Stew

Preparation time: 10 minutes
Cooking time: 30 minutes
Servings: 4

Ingredients:
- 1 small yellow onion, chopped
- 2 teaspoons olive oil
- 1 celery stalk, chopped
- 2 carrots, chopped
- 4 garlic cloves, minced
- 1 teaspoon turmeric
- 2 teaspoons cumin
- 1 teaspoon thyme
- Salt and ground black pepper, to taste
- 1 cup brown lentils, rinsed
- 6 cups baby spinach
- 4 cups veggie stock

Directions:
Set the Instant Pot on Sauté mode, add the oil and heat it up. Add the onions, celery, and carrots, stir, and cook for 5 minutes. Add the garlic, turmeric, cumin, thyme, salt, and pepper, stir, and cook for 1 minute. Add the stock and lentils, stir, cover, and cook on the Manual setting for 12 minutes. Release the pressure for 10 minutes, uncover the Instant Pot, add the spinach, more salt and pepper, stir, divide into bowls, and serve.

Nutrition:
- Calories: 100
- Fat: 2
- Fiber: 5
- Carbs: 16
- Protein: 7

Cabbage Stew

Preparation time: 10 minutes
Cooking time: 25 minutes
Servings: 4

Ingredients:
- 2 tablespoons extra virgin olive oil
- 2 pounds ground pork
- Salt and ground black pepper, to taste
- 1 small yellow onion, peeled and chopped
- 1 red chili pepper, chopped
- 1 cabbage head, shredded
- 2 tablespoons butter
- 2 tablespoons water

Directions:

Set the Instant Pot on Sauté mode, add the oil and heat it up. Add the pork, salt and pepper, stir, and brown on all side for 6 minutes. Add the cabbage, onion, and chili pepper and stir. Add the butter and water, stir, cover and cook on the Meat/Stew setting for 13 minutes. Release pressure, uncover the Instant Pot, divide into bowls, and serve.

Nutrition:
- Calories: 140
- Fat: 1
- Fiber: 2
- Carbs: 30
- Protein: 3

Simple Turkey Stew

Preparation time: 10 minutes
Cooking time: 35 minutes
Servings: 4

Ingredients:
- 1 tablespoon avocado oil
- 1 yellow onion, peeled and chopped
- 3 celery stalks, chopped
- 2 carrots, peeled and chopped
- Salt and ground black pepper, to taste
- 2 cups potatoes, chopped
- 3 cups turkey meat, already cooked and shredded
- 15 ounces canned tomatoes, chopped
- 5 cups turkey stock
- 1 tablespoon cranberry sauce
- 1 teaspoon garlic, minced

Directions:

Set the Instant Pot on Sauté mode, add the oil and heat it up. Add the carrots, celery, and onions, stir and cook for 3 minutes. Add the potatoes, tomatoes, stock, garlic, meat, and cranberry sauce, stir, cover, and cook on Meat/Stew for 30 minutes. Release the pressure, uncover the Instant Pot, add salt and pepper, stir, divide into bowls, and serve.

Nutrition:
- Calories: 210
- Fat: 4
- Fiber: 0
- Carbs: 15
- Protein: 28

Mushroom and Beef Stew

Preparation time: 10 minutes
Cooking time: 25 minutes
Servings: 6

Ingredients:
- 1 tablespoon olive oil
- 1 red onion, peeled and chopped
- 2 pounds beef chuck, cubed
- 1 teaspoon fresh rosemary, chopped
- 1 celery stalk, chopped
- ½ cup red wine
- 1 cup beef stock
- Salt and ground black pepper, to taste
- 1 ounce dried porcini mushrooms, chopped
- 2 carrots, peeled and chopped
- 2 tablespoons flour
- 2 tablespoons butter

Directions:
Set the Instant Pot on Sauté mode, add the oil and beef, stir, and brown for 5 minutes. Add the onion, celery, rosemary, salt, pepper, wine, and stock and stir. Add the carrots and mushrooms, cover the Instant Pot and cook on the Meat/Stew setting for 15 minutes. Release the pressure, uncover the Instant Pot and set it on Manual mode. Meanwhile, heat up a pan over medium-high heat, add the butter, and melt it. Add the flour and 6 tablespoons of cooking liquid from the stew and stir well. Pour this over the stew, stir, cook for 5 minutes, divide into bowls, and serve.

Nutrition:
- Calories: 322
- Fat: 18
- Fiber: 3
- Carbs: 12
- Protein: 24

Oxtail Stew

Preparation time: 10 minutes
Cooking time: 40 minutes
Servings: 4

Ingredients:
- 5 pounds oxtails
- 1 yellow onion, peeled and chopped
- Salt and ground black pepper, to taste
- 3 carrots, peeled and chopped
- 3 celery stalks, chopped
- 1 garlic clove, peeled and chopped
- 1 bunch parsley, chopped
- 2 cups red wine, chopped
- 1 cup tomatoes, cored and chopped
- 1 cup water
- Sugar: to the taste

Directions:
In the Instant Pot, mix the oxtails with salt, pepper, onion, carrots, celery, garlic, tomatoes, red wine, parsley, water and sugar, stir, cover, and cook on Meat/Stew for 40 minutes. Release the pressure, uncover the Instant Pot, divide the oxtail stew into bowls, and serve.

Nutrition:
- Calories: 312
- Fat: 12
- Fiber: 14
- Carbs: 15
- Protein: 14
- Sugar: 1

Lamb Stew

Preparation time: 10 minutes
Cooking time: 30 minutes
Servings: 4

Ingredients:

- 2 pounds lamb shoulder, cubed
- ¼ cup red wine vinegar
- 1 tablespoon garlic, peeled and minced
- 14 ounces canned diced tomatoes
- 2 yellow onions, peeled and chopped
- 1 tablespoon olive oil
- 2 tablespoons tomato paste
- 1 teaspoon dried oregano
- 1 teaspoon dried basil
- Salt and ground black pepper, to taste
- 2 bay leaves
- 1 red bell pepper, seeded and chopped
- 1 green bell pepper, seeded and chopped
- ⅓ cup fresh parsley, chopped

Directions:

Set the Instant Pot on Sauté mode, add the oil and heat it up. Add the onions and garlic, stir, and cook for 2 minutes. Add the vinegar, stir, and cook for 2 minutes. Add the lamb, tomatoes, tomato paste, oregano, basil, salt, pepper, and bay leaves, stir, cover the Instant Pot and cook on the Meat/Stew setting for 12 minutes. Release the pressure for 10 minutes, uncover the Instant Pot, discard the bay leaves, add the bell peppers, more salt and pepper, if needed, stir, cover, and cook on Manual for 8 more minutes. Release the pressure again, uncover, add the parsley, stir and divide into bowls.

Nutrition:

- Calories: 700
- Fat: 52
- Fiber: 4.4
- Carbs: 17
- Protein: 40

Drunken Lamb Stew

Preparation time: 10 minutes
Cooking time: 15 minutes
Servings: 6

Ingredients:

- 2 onions, peeled and chopped
- 3 pounds lamb shoulder, cut into medium chunks
- 2 potatoes, roughly chopped
- Salt and ground black pepper, to taste
- 2 thyme sprigs, chopped
- 6 ounces dark beer
- 2 cups water
- 2 carrots, seeded and chopped
- ¼ cup fresh parsley, minced

Directions:

Put the onions and lamb into the Instant Pot. Add the salt, pepper, potatoes, thyme, water, beer, and carrots, stir, cover and cook on the Meat/Stew setting for 15 minutes. Release the pressure, uncover the Instant Pot, add the parsley, more salt and pepper, if needed, stir, divide into bowls, and serve.

Nutrition:

- Calories: 236
- Fat: 8
- Fiber: 2.5
- Carbs: 22
- Protein: 19

German Stew

Preparation time: 10 minutes
Cooking time: 10 minutes
Servings: 4

Ingredients:
- 1 pound kielbasa, cut into medium pieces
- 14 ounces canned diced tomatoes
- 2 potatoes, cut into quarters
- 1 small jar sauerkraut
- 1 onion, peeled and cut into medium chunks

Directions:

In the Instant Pot, add the kielbasa, tomatoes, potatoes, sauerkraut, and onion, stir, cover, and cook on the Manual setting for 10 minutes. Release the pressure, uncover the Instant Pot, divide stew into bowls, and serve.

Nutrition:
- Calories: 140
- Fat: 4
- Fiber: 2
- Carbs: 11
- Protein: 12

Beef and Root Vegetables Stew

Preparation time: 10 minutes
Cooking time: 32 minutes
Servings: 4

Ingredients:
- 1 pound beef chuck, cubed
- 2 tablespoons olive oil
- 2 bacon slices, cooked and crumbled
- ½ cup white flour
- Salt and ground black pepper, to taste
- 1 rutabaga, diced
- 1 cup cipollini onions, peeled
- 4 carrots, peeled and chopped
- 4 garlic cloves, peeled and minced
- 2 cups beef stock
- 1 tablespoon tomato paste
- ½ cup bourbon
- A bunch of thyme, chopped
- A bunch of rosemary, chopped
- 1 cup peas
- 2 bay leaves

Directions:

Mix the flour with salt and pepper and place on a plate. Dredge the meat in flour mix and set aside. Set the Instant Pot on Sauté mode, add the oil and heat up. Add the meat, brown on all sides, and transfer to a bowl. Add the garlic, bourbon, stock, thyme, rutabaga, carrots, tomato paste, rosemary, and onions, stir, and cook for 2 minutes. Return the beef to the Instant Pot, cover, and cook on the Manual setting for 10 minutes. Release the pressure, uncover the Instant Pot, add the bay leaves, bacon, peas, more salt and pepper, stir, and cook on Meat/Stew for 12 minutes. Release the pressure again, uncover the Instant Pot, stir, discard the bay leaves, divide into bowls, and serve.

Nutrition:
- Calories: 302
- Fat: 9
- Fiber: 6
- Carbs: 33
- Protein: 18

Italian Sausage Stew

Preparation time: 10 minutes
Cooking time: 20 minutes
Servings: 6

Ingredients:

- 1 pound Italian sausage, crumbled
- ½ pound cherry tomatoes, cut into halves
- 1 sweet onion, peeled and chopped
- 1½ pounds Yukon gold potatoes, cubed
- ¾ pound collard greens, sliced thin
- 1 cup chicken stock
- Salt and ground black pepper, to taste
- Juice of ½ lemon

Directions:

Set the Instant Pot on Sauté mode, add the sausage, stir, and cook for 8 minutes. Add the onions and tomatoes, stir, and cook 4 minutes. Add the potatoes, stock, salt, pepper, and collard greens, stir, cover the Instant Pot and cook on the Meat/Stew setting for 10 minutes. Release the pressure, uncover the Instant Pot, add more salt and pepper and lemon juice, stir, divide into bowls, and serve.

Nutrition:

- Calories: 230
- Fat: 10
- Fiber: 1
- Carbs: 24
- Protein: 28

Okra Stew

Preparation time: 10 minutes
Cooking time: 20 minutes
Servings: 4

Ingredients:

- 1 yellow onion, peeled and chopped
- 1 garlic clove, peeled and minced
- 1 pound beef chuck, cubed
- 1 cardamom pod
- 2 cups chicken stock
- 14 ounces frozen okra, sliced
- 12 ounces tomato sauce
- Salt and ground black pepper, to taste
- ½ cup parsley, chopped
- Olive oil
- Juice of ½ lemon

For the marinade:
- ½ teaspoon onion powder
- ½ teaspoon garlic powder
- Salt
- 1 tablespoon 7-spice mix

Directions:

In a bowl, mix the meat with 7-spice mix, a pinch of salt, onion garlic, and garlic powder, toss to coat and set the dish aside. Set the Instant Pot on Sauté mode, add some olive oil, and heat it up. Add the onion, stir, and cook 2 minutes. Add the garlic and cardamom, stir, and cook for 1 minute. Add the meat, stir, and brown meat for 2 minutes. Add the stock, tomato sauce, okra, salt, and pepper, stir, cover, and cook on Meat/Stew for 20 minutes. Release the pressure, uncover the Instant Pot, add more salt and pepper, if needed, lemon juice, and parsley, stir, divide into bowls, and serve.

Nutrition:

- Calories: 230
- Fat: 10
- Fiber: 8
- Carbs: 15
- Protein: 20

Instant Pot Beans and Grains Recipes

Barley and Mushroom Risotto

Preparation time: 10 minutes
Cooking time: 30 minutes
Servings: 4

Ingredients:
- 2 cups yellow onions, peeled and chopped
- 1 tablespoon olive oil
- 1 cup pearl barley
- 1 teaspoon fennel seeds
- 2 tablespoons black barley
- 3 cups chicken stock
- ⅓ cup dry sherry
- 1½ cups water
- 1.5 ounce dried mushrooms
- Salt and ground black pepper, to taste
- ¼ cup Parmesan cheese, grated

Directions:
Set the Instant Pot on Sauté mode, add the oil, and heat it up. Add the fennel and onions, stir, and cook for 4 minutes. Add the barley, sherry, mushrooms, stock, water, salt, and pepper and stir well. Cover the Instant Pot, cook on the Rice setting for 18 minutes, release the pressure, uncover the Instant Pot, and set it on Manual mode. Add more salt and pepper, if needed, stir and cook for 5 minutes. Divide into bowls, add the cheese on top, and serve.

Nutrition:
- Calories: 200
- Fat: 5
- Fiber: 6.1
- Carbs: 31
- Protein: 7.6

Barley with Vegetables

Preparation time: 10 minutes
Cooking time: 25 minutes
Servings: 4

Ingredients:
- 1 tablespoon extra virgin olive oil
- 1 tablespoon butter
- 1 white onion, peeled and chopped
- 1 garlic clove, peeled and minced
- 1½ cups pearl barley, rinsed
- 1 celery stalk, chopped
- ⅓ cup mushrooms, chopped
- 4 cups vegetable stock
- 2¼ cups water
- Salt and ground black pepper, to taste
- 3 tablespoons fresh parsley, chopped
- 1 cup Parmesan cheese, grated

Directions:
Set the Instant Pot on Sauté mode, add the oil and butter and heat them up. Add the onion and garlic, stir, and cook for 4 minutes. Add the celery and barley and toss to coat. Add the mushrooms, water, stock, salt, and pepper, stir, cover the Instant Pot and cook on the Multigrain setting for 18 minutes. Release the pressure, uncover the Instant Pot, add the cheese and parsley and more salt and pepper, if needed, stir for 2 minutes, divide into bowls, and serve.

Nutrition:
- Calories: 170
- Fat: 6
- Fiber: 4.5
- Carbs: 30
- Protein: 8

Barley Salad

Preparation time: 10 minutes
Cooking time: 20 minutes
Servings: 4

Ingredients:

- 1 cup hulled barley, rinsed
- 2½ cups water
- ¾ cup jarred spinach pesto
- 1 green apple, chopped
- ¼ cup celery, chopped
- Salt and ground white pepper, to taste

Directions:

Put the barley, water, salt, and pepper into the Instant Pot, stir, cover and cook on the Multigrain setting for 20 minutes. Release the pressure, uncover the Instant Pot, strain the barley, and put in a bowl. Add the celery, apple, spinach pesto, and more salt and pepper, toss to coat, and serve.

Nutrition:

- Calories: 170
- Fat: 7
- Fiber: 7
- Carbs: 0
- Protein: 5

Wheat Berry Salad

Preparation time: 10 minutes
Cooking time: 35 minutes
Servings: 6

Ingredients:

- 1½ cups wheat berries
- 1 tablespoon extra virgin olive oil
- Salt and ground black pepper, to taste
- 4 cups water

For the salad:

- 1 tablespoon balsamic vinegar
- 1 tablespoon extra virgin olive oil
- 1 cup cherry tomatoes, cut into halves
- 2 green onions, chopped
- 2 ounces feta cheese, crumbled
- ½ cup Kalamata olives, pitted and chopped
- ½ cup fresh basil leaves, chopped
- ½ cup fresh parsley, chopped

Directions:

Set the Instant Pot on Sauté mode, add the tablespoon oil and heat it up. Add the wheat berries, stir, and cook for 5 minutes. Add the water, salt, and pepper, cover the Instant Pot, and cook on Multigrain mode for 30 minutes. Release the pressure for 10 minutes, uncover the Instant Pot, drain the wheat berries, and put them in a salad bowl. Add the salt and pepper, 1 tablespoon oil, balsamic vinegar, tomatoes, green onions, olives, cheese, basil, and parsley, toss to coat, and serve.

Nutrition:

- Calories: 240
- Fat: 11
- Fiber: 6.3
- Carbs: 31
- Protein: 5

Cracked Wheat and Vegetables

Preparation time: 10 minutes
Cooking time: 15 minutes
Servings: 4

Ingredients:
- ½ cup cracked whole wheat
- 1½ cups water
- 2 tomatoes, cored and chopped
- 2 small potatoes, cubed
- 5 cauliflower florets, chopped
- Salt and ground black pepper, to taste
- ¼ teaspoon mustard seeds
- ¼ teaspoon cumin seeds
- 1 teaspoon ginger, grated
- 1 tablespoon yellow split peas, rinsed
- 2 garlic cloves, peeled and minced
- 1 yellow onion, peeled and chopped
- 2 curry leaves
- 3 teaspoons vegetable oil
- ¼ teaspoon garam masala
- Cilantro leaves, chopped, for serving

Directions:
Set the Instant Pot on Sauté mode, add the oil and heat it up. Add the cumin and mustard seeds, stir, and cook for 1 minute. Add the onion, garlic, split peas, garam masala, ginger, and curry leaves, stir, and cook for 2 minutes. Add the cauliflower, potatoes, and tomatoes, stir, and cook for 4 minutes. Add the wheat, salt, pepper, and water, stir, cover, and cook on Multigrain mode for 5 minutes. Release the pressure, uncover the Instant Pot, transfer the wheat and vegetables to plates, sprinkle cilantro on top, and serve.

Nutrition:
- Calories: 145
- Fat: 2
- Fiber: 4
- Carbs: 16
- Protein: 7

Cracked Wheat Surprise

Preparation time: 5 minutes
Cooking time: 17 minutes
Servings: 2

Ingredients:
- 2 cups cracked wheat
- 1 teaspoon fennel seeds
- 2½ cups butter
- 2 cups light brown sugar
- 3 cloves
- 1 cup milk
- Salt
- 3 cups water
- Almonds, chopped

Directions:
Set the Instant Pot on Sauté mode, add the butter and heat it up. Add the cracked wheat, stir, and cook for 5 minutes. Add the cloves and fennel seeds, stir, and cook for 2 minutes. Add the sugar, a pinch of salt, milk, and water, stir, cover, and cook on the Multigrain setting for 10 minutes. Release the pressure, uncover the Instant Pot, divide into bowls, and serve with chopped almonds on top.

Nutrition:
- Calories: 120
- Fat: 1
- Fiber: 1
- Carbs: 4
- Protein: 8

Bulgur Salad

Preparation time: 15 minutes
Cooking time: 12 minutes
Servings: 4

Ingredients:
- Zest from 1 orange
- Juice from 2 oranges
- 2 garlic cloves, minced
- 2 teaspoons canola oil
- 2 tablespoons ginger, grated
- 1 cup bulgur, rinsed
- 1 tablespoon soy sauce
- ⅔ cup scallions, chopped
- ⅓ cup almonds, chopped
- Salt, to taste
- 2 teaspoons brown sugar
- ½ cups water

Directions:

Set the Instant Pot on Sauté mode, add the oil and heat it up. Add the ginger and garlic, stir, and cook for 1 minutes. Add the bulgur, sugar, water, and orange juice, stir, cover, and cook on the Multigrain setting for 5 minutes. Release the pressure naturally, uncover the Instant Pot, and set the bulgur aside. Heat up a pan over medium heat, add the almonds, stir, and toast them for 3 minutes. Add the orange zest, salt, soy sauce and scallions, stir, and cook for 1 minute. Add this to bulgur mix, stir with a fork, transfer to a bowl, and serve.

Nutrition:
- Calories: 232
- Fat: 7
- Fiber: 6
- Carbs: 38
- Protein: 7

Bulgur Pilaf

Preparation time: 10 minutes
Cooking time: 21 minutes
Servings: 6

Ingredients:
- 2 cups red onions, peeled and chopped
- 2 tablespoons extra virgin olive oil
- Salt and ground black pepper, to taste
- 2 teaspoons ginger, grated
- ¼ cup dill, chopped
- 1 garlic clove, peeled and minced
- 1½ cups bulgur
- ¼ cup fresh mint, chopped
- ¼ cup fresh parsley, chopped
- 3 tablespoons lemon juice
- ½ teaspoon cumin
- ½ teaspoons turmeric
- 2 cups vegetable stock
- 1½ cups carrot, chopped
- ½ cup walnuts, toasted and chopped

Directions:

Set the Instant Pot on Sauté mode, add the oil and heat it up. Add the onion, stir, and cook on Multigrain temperature for 12 minutes. Add the garlic, stir, and cook for 1 minute. Add the cumin, turmeric, and bulgur, stir, and cook for 1 minute. Add the ginger, stock, carrots, salt, and pepper, stir, cover and cook on the Manual setting for 5 minutes. Release the pressure, uncover the Instant Pot, add the mint, dill, parsley, lemon juice, and more salt and pepper, if needed, and stir gently. Divide among plates, and serve with almonds on top.

Nutrition:
- Calories: 270
- Fat: 12
- Fiber: 8
- Carbs: 38
- Protein: 7

Buckwheat Porridge

Preparation time: 10 minutes
Cooking time: 6 minutes
Servings: 4

Ingredients:

- 3 cups rice milk
- 1 cup buckwheat groats
- 1 banana, sliced
- ¼ cup raisins
- 1 teaspoon ground cinnamon
- ½ teaspoon vanilla extract
- Chopped nuts, for serving

Directions:

Put the buckwheat into the Instant Pot, add the milk, raisins, banana, vanilla, and cinnamon, stir, cover, and cook on Porridge mode for 6 minutes. Release the pressure for 15 minutes, uncover the Instant Pot, stir porridge, divide into bowls, and serve with chopped nuts on top.

Nutrition:

- Calories: 400
- Fat: 3
- Fiber: 13
- Carbs: 30
- Protein: 13

Couscous with Chicken and Vegetables

Preparation time: 10 minutes
Cooking time: 15 minutes
Servings: 4

Ingredients:

- 8 chicken thighs, skinless
- 1½ cups mushrooms, cut into halves
- 1½ cups carrots, chopped
- 1 green bell pepper, seeded and chopped
- 1 yellow onion, peeled and chopped
- 2 garlic cloves, peeled and minced
- 15 ounces canned stewed tomatoes, chopped
- Salt and ground black pepper, to taste
- ¾ cup couscous
- 1 zucchini, chopped
- ½ cup chicken stock
- ½ cup fresh parsley, chopped

Directions:

In the Instant Pot, mix chicken with mushrooms, carrots, bell pepper, onion, garlic, tomatoes and stock, stir, cover and cook on the Manual setting for 8 minutes. Release the pressure fast, uncover the Instant Pot, add couscous, zucchini, salt and pepper, stir, cover again and cook on Low for 6 minutes. Release the pressure again, uncover the Instant Pot, add parsley, stir gently, divide into bowls, and serve.

Nutrition:

- Calories: 300
- Fat: 10
- Fiber: 3
- Carbs: 35
- Protein: 20

Israeli Couscous

Preparation time: 10 minutes
Cooking time: 8 minutes
Servings: 4

Ingredients:
- ½ cup red onion, chopped
- ½ teaspoon sesame oil
- ¼ cup red bell pepper, seeded and chopped
- 1 cup couscous, rinsed
- 1½ cups vegetable stock
- ½ teaspoon ground cinnamon
- ¼ teaspoon coriander
- Salt and ground black pepper, to taste
- 2 tablespoons red wine vinegar

Directions:
Set the Instant Pot on Sauté mode, add the oil, and heat it up. Add the bell pepper and onion, stir, and cook for 5 minutes. Add the couscous, coriander, stock, cinnamon, salt, pepper, and vinegar, stir, cover, and cook on the Multigrain setting for 3 minutes. Release the pressure, uncover the Instant Pot, divide the couscous into bowls, and serve.

Nutrition:
- Calories: 150
- Fat: 1
- Fiber: 5
- Carbs: 33
- Protein: 6

Millet with Vegetables

Preparation time: 10 minutes
Cooking time: 25 minutes
Servings: 4

Ingredients:
- 1 cup onion, chopped
- 2 garlic cloves, peeled and minced
- ½ cup oyster mushrooms, sliced
- ½ cup green lentils, rinsed
- 1 cup millet
- 2¼ cups vegetable stock
- ½ cup bok choy, sliced
- 1 cup snow peas
- 2 tablespoons parsley, chopped
- 2 tablespoons chives, chopped
- 1 cup asparagus, chopped
- 1 tablespoon lemon juice
- Salt and ground black pepper, to taste

Directions:
Set the Instant Pot on Sauté mode, add the onions, garlic, and mushrooms, stir, and cook for 2 minutes. Add the millet and lentils, stir, and cook for 1 minute. Add the stock, stir, cover, and cook on the Multigrain setting for 10 minutes. Release the pressure naturally, uncover the Instant Pot, add the asparagus, bok choy, and peas, stir, cover, and cook on the Manual setting for 3 minutes. Release the pressure again, uncover, add the lemon juice, salt, pepper, parsley, and chives, stir gently, divide into bowls, and serve.

Nutrition:
- Calories: 100
- Fat: 1.2
- Fiber: 7
- Carbs: 20
- Protein: 10

Creamy Millet

Preparation time: 10 minutes
Cooking time: 20 minutes
Servings: 4

Ingredients:

- 1 cup split mung beans
- 1 bay leaf
- 1 cup carrot, chopped
- 1 cup millet, chopped
- 1 cup celery, chopped
- 4 cardamom pods
- 6 cups water
- 1½ cups fresh peas
- 1 tablespoon lime juice
- ¼ cup fresh cilantro, chopped
- 1 tablespoon butter
- 1 teaspoon coriander seeds, ground
- 1 teaspoon fennel seeds, ground
- ½ teaspoon cumin seeds, ground
- ½ teaspoon turmeric
- Salt and ground black pepper, to taste
- ½ teaspoon ginger, grated

Directions:

Set the Instant Pot on Sauté mode, add the mung beans, stir, and cook until they are golden. Add the millet, carrot, bay leaf, celery, cardamom, water, salt, and pepper, stir, cover, and cook on the Multigrain setting for 10 minutes. Release the pressure, uncover the Instant Pot, and set it on simmer mode. Heat up a pan with the butter over medium heat, add the coriander, fennel, cumin, turmeric, and ginger, stir, and cook for 2 minutes. Add this to the Instant Pot, stir, add more salt and pepper, peas, and lime juice, simmer for 5 minutes, divide among plates, sprinkle with cilantro, and serve.

Nutrition:

- Calories: 231
- Fat: 2
- Fiber: 8
- Carbs: 41
- Protein: 11

Oats and Vegetables

Preparation time: 10 minutes
Cooking time: 15 minutes
Servings: 4
Ingredients:

- 1 cup steel-cut oats
- 1½ cups water
- 1 carrot, peeled and chopped
- ½ green bell pepper, seeded and chopped
- 1-inch ginger piece, peeled and grated
- 1 Thai green chili, chopped
- 2 curry leaves
- ¼ teaspoon mustard seeds
- ½ teaspoon black lentils
- Onion powder
- 1½ tablespoons canola oil
- Turmeric
- Salt, to taste

Directions:

Put oats into the Instant Pot, add the water, cover, and cook on the Multigrain setting for 7 minutes. Heat up a pan with the oil over medium heat, add the mustard seeds, lentils, chili pepper, curry leaf, ginger, carrot, bell pepper, and a pinch of onion powder and turmeric, stir, and cook for 5 minutes. Release the pressure from the Instant Pot, uncover, add the oats to the pan with some salt, stir, divide into bowls, and serve.

Nutrition:

- Calories: 211
- Fat: 6.3
- Fiber: 5.6
- Carbs: 32
- Protein: 7.5

Quinoa and Vegetables

Preparation time: 10 minutes
Cooking time: 2 minutes
Servings: 4

Ingredients:
- 1½ cups quinoa
- 1 red bell pepper, seeded and chopped
- 3 celery stalks, chopped
- Salt, to taste
- 4 cups spinach
- 2 tomatoes, cored and chopped
- 1½ cups chicken stock
- ½ cup black olives, pitted and chopped
- ½ cup feta cheese, crumbled
- ⅓ cup jarred pesto sauce
- ¼ cup almonds, sliced

Directions:

In the Instant Pot, mix the quinoa with the bell pepper, celery, spinach, stock, and salt, stir gently, cover, and cook on the Multigrain setting for 2 minutes. Release the pressure for 10 minutes, uncover the Instant Pot, add the tomatoes, pesto, and olives, stir, and transfer to plates. Add the cheese and almonds on top, toss to coat, and serve.

Nutrition:
- Calories: 249
- Fat: 7
- Fiber: 5.4
- Carbs: 20
- Protein: 7.4

Mexican Cranberry Beans

Preparation time: 10 minutes
Cooking time: 20 minutes
Servings: 6

Ingredients:
- 1 pound cranberry beans, soaked for 8 hours and drained
- 3¼ cups water
- 4 garlic cloves, peeled and minced
- 1 yellow onion, peeled and chopped
- 1½ teaspoons cumin
- ⅓ cup fresh cilantro, chopped
- 1 tablespoon chili powder
- 1 teaspoon dried oregano
- Salt and ground black pepper, to taste
- Cooked rice, for serving

Directions:

Put the beans into the Instant Pot, add the water, garlic, and onion, cover, and cook on the Bean/Chili setting for 20 minutes. Release the pressure, uncover the Instant Pot, add the cumin, cilantro, oregano, chili powder, salt, and pepper, stir well, mash a bit using a fork, divide among plates on top of rice, and serve.

Nutrition:
- Calories: 100
- Fat: 1
- Fiber: 4
- Carbs: 10
- Protein: 6

Cranberry Beans and Pasta

Preparation time: 10 minutes
Cooking time: 20 minutes
Servings: 8

Ingredients:

- 2 cups dried cranberry beans, soaked for 8 hours and drained
- 7 garlic cloves, peeled and minced
- 6 cups water
- 2 celery ribs, chopped
- 1 yellow onion, peeled and chopped
- 1 teaspoon rosemary, chopped
- ¼ teaspoon red pepper flakes
- 26 ounces canned diced tomatoes
- 3 teaspoons dried basil
- ½ teaspoon smoked paprika
- 2 teaspoons dried oregano
- Salt and ground black pepper, to taste
- 2 cups small pasta
- 3 tablespoons nutritional yeast
- 10 ounces kale leaves

Directions:

Set the Instant Pot on Sauté mode, add the onion, celery, garlic, red pepper flakes, rosemary, and a pinch of salt, stir, and brown for 2 minutes. Add the tomatoes, basil, oregano and paprika, stir and cook for 1 minute. Add the beans, and water, cover the Instant Pot and cook on the Bean/Chili setting for 10 minutes. Release the pressure, uncover the Instant Pot, add the pasta, yeast, kale, salt, and pepper, stir ,and set the Instant Pot on Sauté mode. Cook for 5 minutes, divide into bowls, and serve.

Nutrition:

- Calories: 330
- Fat: 14
- Fiber: 10
- Carbs: 32
- Protein: 18

Cranberry Beans Mixture

Preparation time: 10 minutes
Cooking time: 15 minutes
Servings: 6

Ingredients:

- 1½ cups cranberry beans, soaked for 8 hours and drained
- 4-inch dried seaweed, sliced
- 4 bacon slices, chopped
- Salt and ground black pepper, to taste
- 8 cups kale, chopped
- 4 ounces shiitake mushrooms, chopped
- ½ teaspoon garlic powder
- 1 teaspoon extra virgin olive oil

Directions:

Put the beans into the Instant Pot, add 2 inches water, salt, pepper, seaweed, cover and cook on the Bean/Chili setting for 8 minutes. Release the pressure, uncover the Instant Pot, transfer the beans and cooking liquid to a bowl and set the dish aside. Set the Instant Pot on Sauté mode, add the oil and heat it up. Add the garlic powder, bacon, mushrooms, salt, pepper, ¾ cup of the cooking liquid from the Instant Pot, stir well, and cook for 1 minute. Cover the Instant Pot, cook on the Manual setting for 3 minutes, and release pressure. Add the beans and kale, stir, and divide into bowls.

Nutrition:

- Calories: 228
- Fat: 2
- Fiber: 14
- Carbs: 41
- Protein: 9

Cranberry Bean Chili

Preparation time: 10 minutes
Cooking time: 40 minutes
Servings: 8

Ingredients:

- 1 pound cranberry beans, soaked in water for 7 hours and drained
- 5 cups water
- 14 ounces canned tomatoes with green chilies, chopped
- ¼ cup millet
- ½ cup bulgur
- 1½ teaspoons cumin
- 2 tablespoons tomato paste
- 1 teaspoon chili powder
- 1 teaspoon garlic, minced
- ½ teaspoon liquid smoke
- 1 teaspoon dried oregano
- ½ teaspoon ancho chili powder
- Salt and ground black pepper, to taste
- Hot sauce, for serving
- Pickled jalapeños, for serving

Directions:

Put the beans and 3 cups water into the Instant Pot, cover, and cook on the Bean/Chili setting for 25 minutes. Release the pressure, add the rest of the water, tomatoes with chilies, millet, bulgur, cumin, tomato paste, chili powders, garlic, liquid smoke, oregano, salt, and pepper, stir, cover, and cook on Manual for 10 minutes. Release the pressure, uncover, divide into bowls, and serve with hot sauce on top and pickled jalapeños on the side.

Nutrition:

- Calories: 200
- Fat: 13
- Fiber: 4
- Carbs: 14
- Protein: 15

Lentil Tacos

Preparation time: 10 minutes
Cooking time: 15 minutes
Servings: 4

Ingredients:

- 4 ounces tomato sauce
- ½ teaspoon cumin
- 1 teaspoon salt
- 1 teaspoon garlic powder
- 1 teaspoon chili powder
- 1 teaspoon onion powder
- 4 cups water
- 2 cups brown lentils
- Taco shells, for serving

Directions:

In the Instant Pot, mix the lentils with the water, tomato sauce, cumin, garlic powder, chili powder, and onion powder, stir, cover, and cook on the Bean/Chili setting for 15 minutes. Release the pressure, uncover the Instant Pot, divide the lentils into taco shells, and serve.

Nutrition:

- Calories: 157
- Fat: 4
- Fiber: 8
- Carbs: 24
- Protein: 6.4

Italian Lentils

Preparation time: 10 minutes
Cooking time: 15 minutes
Servings: 4

Ingredients:
- ½ cup brown rice, soaked overnight and drained
- ¾ cup green lentils, soaked overnight and drained
- 2½ cups chicken stock
- 1 cup tomato sauce
- ¾ cup onion, chopped
- 1 cup green and red bell pepper, chopped
- 2 cups chicken, already cooked and shredded
- 3 carrots, peeled and chopped
- ½ cup greens
- Salt and ground black pepper, to taste
- 3 teaspoons Italian seasoning
- 2 garlic cloves, peeled and crushed
- 1 cup mozzarella cheese, shredded

Directions:

In the Instant Pot, mix the lentils with the rice, salt, pepper, stock, tomato sauce, onion, red and green pepper, chicken, carrots, greens, Italian seasoning and garlic, stir, cover and cook on Rice mode for 15 minutes. Release the pressure, uncover the Instant Pot, add the cheese, stir, divide among bowls, and serve.

Nutrition:
- Calories: 186
- Fat: 2
- Fiber: 3.3
- Carbs: 28
- Protein: 14.4

Lentils and Tomato Sauce

Preparation time: 10 minutes
Cooking time: 20 minutes
Servings: 4

Ingredients:
- 1 tablespoon olive oil
- 1 green bell pepper, seeded and chopped
- 1 yellow onion, peeled and chopped
- 1 celery stalk, chopped
- 1½ cups tomatoes, chopped
- Salt and ground black pepper, to taste
- 1 teaspoon curry powder
- 2 cups water
- 1½ cups lentils

Directions:

Set the Instant Pot on Sauté mode, add the oil and heat it up. Add the celery, bell pepper, onion, and tomatoes, stir, and cook for 4 minutes. Add the curry, salt, pepper, lentils, and water, stir, cover and cook on the Bean/Chili setting for 15 minutes. Release the pressure, uncover the Instant Pot, divide the lentils among bowls, and serve.

Nutrition:
- Calories: 105
- Fat: 3
- Fiber: 4.6
- Carbs: 1.7
- Protein: 6

Indian Lentils

Preparation time: 10 minutes
Cooking time: 20 minutes
Servings: 4

Ingredients:
- 3 teaspoons butter
- 1 teaspoon extra virgin olive oil
- 1 cup red lentils
- 1 yellow onion, peeled and chopped
- 2 teaspoons cumin
- ¼ teaspoon coriander
- ¼ teaspoon garlic powder
- ¼ teaspoon turmeric
- ¼ teaspoon paprika
- ¼ teaspoon red pepper flakes
- Salt and ground black pepper, to taste
- 3 cups chicken stock

Directions:
Set the Instant Pot on Sauté mode, add the butter and oil and heat up. Add the onions, stir, and cook for 4 minutes. Add the cumin, coriander, garlic powder, turmeric, paprika, and pepper flakes, stir, and cook for 2 minutes. Add the lentils and stock, stir, cover, and cook on the Bean/Chili setting for 15 minutes. Release the pressure, uncover the Instant Pot, divide into bowls, and serve.

Nutrition:
- Calories: 198
- Fat: 6
- Fiber: 8.7
- Carbs: 26
- Protein: 10.4

Lentils Salad

Preparation time: 10 minutes
Cooking time: 8 minutes
Servings: 4

Ingredients:
- 2 cups chicken stock
- 1 cup lentils
- 1 bay leaf
- ½ teaspoon dried thyme
- ¼ cup red onion, chopped
- ½ cup celery, chopped
- ¼ cup red bell pepper, chopped
- 2 tablespoons extra virgin olive oil
- 1 tablespoon garlic, minced
- ½ teaspoon dried oregano
- Juice of 1 lemon
- 2 tablespoons fresh parsley
- Salt and ground black pepper, to taste

Directions:
Put the lentils into the Instant Pot. Add the bay leaf, stock and thyme, stir, cover, and cook on the Bean/Chili setting for 8 minutes. Release the pressure, uncover the Instant Pot, drain the lentils and put them in a bowl. Add the celery, onion, bell pepper, garlic, parsley, oregano, lemon juice, olive oil, salt and pepper, toss to coat, and serve.

Nutrition:
- Calories: 165
- Fat: 5
- Fiber: 10
- Carbs: 20
- Protein: 9

Chickpeas Curry

Preparation time: 10 minutes
Cooking time: 21 minutes
Servings: 6

Ingredients:
- 4 teaspoons cumin seeds
- 8 teaspoons olive oil
- 4 teaspoons garlic, minced
- 1 yellow onion, diced
- 2 teaspoons garam masala
- 2 teaspoons coriander
- 2 teaspoons turmeric
- 3 cups chickpeas, already cooked, drained and rinsed
- 28 ounces canned diced tomatoes
- 3 potatoes, cubed
- ½ cup water
- Salt and ground black pepper, to taste
- Basmati rice, already cooked, for serving
- Cilantro, chopped, for serving

Directions:
Set the Instant Pot on Sauté mode, add the oil and heat it up. Add the cumin seeds, stir, and cook for 30 seconds. Add the onion, stir, and cook for 5 minutes. Add the garlic, garam masala, coriander, turmeric, tomatoes, potatoes, chickpeas, water, salt, and pepper, stir, cover and cook on the Bean/Stew setting for 15 minutes. Release the pressure, uncover the Instant Pot, divide the chickpeas onto plates, and serve with rice on the side and cilantro on top.

Nutrition:
- Calories: 384
- Fat: 8.3
- Fiber: 12
- Carbs: 69
- Protein: 11.5

Chickpeas and Dumplings

Preparation time: 10 minutes
Cooking time: 17 minutes
Servings: 4

Ingredients:
- 4 carrots, peeled and chopped
- 1 yellow onion, peeled and chopped
- 4 red baby potatoes, chopped
- 2 garlic cloves, peeled and minced
- 28 ounces vegetable stock
- 1 vegetable bouillon cube
- 2 cans chickpeas, drained
- Salt and ground black pepper, to taste
- Cayenne pepper
- 2 green onions, chopped
- 2 celery stalks, chopped
- 1 ¾ teaspoons baking powder
- ¾ cup white flour
- ½ teaspoon dried dill
- ½ cup milk

Directions:
Set the Instant Pot on Sauté mode, add the onion, garlic, and a splash of stock, stir, and cook for 3 minutes. Add the potatoes, carrots, chickpeas, stock, bouillon cube, salt, pepper, and cayenne pepper, stir, cover, and cook on the Bean/Chili setting for 7 minutes. Release the pressure, uncover the Instant Pot, add the celery and green onions, stir and set aside. In a bowl, mix the flour with baking powder, a pinch of salt, dill, and milk and stir well. Shape 10 dumplings, heat up the soup on Manual mode, drop the dumplings into the Instant Pot, cover it, and cook on Steam mode for 10 minutes. Uncover the Instant Pot, add more salt and pepper, if needed, stir, divide into bowls, and serve.

Nutrition:
- Calories: 300
- Fat: 5
- Fiber: 10
- Carbs: 56
- Protein: 12

Chickpeas and Garlic

Preparation time: 10 minutes
Cooking time: 35 minutes
Servings: 4

Ingredients:

- 2 bay leaves
- 4 garlic cloves, peeled
- 2 cups chickpeas, rinsed
- Water
- 2 tomatoes, cored and chopped
- 2 small cucumbers, chopped
- 1 teaspoon olive oil
- Salt and ground black pepper, to taste

Directions:

Put the chickpeas into the Instant Pot. Add the water, garlic, and bay leaves, stir, cover, and cook on the Bean/Stew setting for 35 minutes. Release the pressure naturally for 10 minutes, uncover the Instant Pot, drain the water and put the chickpeas and garlic in a bowl. Add the cucumber, tomatoes, salt, pepper, and oil, toss to coat, and serve.

Nutrition:

- Calories: 110
- Fat: 7
- Fiber: 0.6
- Carbs: 17
- Protein: 8

Chickpeas and Pesto

Preparation time: 10 minutes
Cooking time: 20 minutes
Servings: 4

Ingredients:

For the pesto:
- ¼ cup extra virgin olive oil
- 1½ cups fresh basil
- 1 garlic clove, peeled and minced
- ¼ cup Parmesan cheese, grated
- 1 tablespoon pine nuts, roasted

For the chickpeas:
- 12 ounces chickpeas, soaked for 8 hours

- 1 yellow onion, peeled and chopped
- 2 tablespoons extra virgin olive oil
- 2 carrots, peeled and chopped
- 14 ounces canned tomatoes
- 4 cups chicken stock
- ¼ cup Parmesan cheese, grated

Directions:

In a blender, mix the basil with the cheese, garlic, pine nuts, ¼ cup oil, and some salt and blend well. Transfer to a bowl and set the dish aside. Set the Instant Pot on Sauté mode, add 2 tablespoons oil and heat it up. Add the onion and some salt, stir, and cook for 3 minutes. Add the carrots, chickpeas, tomatoes, stock, salt, and pepper, stir, cover, and cook on the Bean/Stew setting for 10 minutes. Release the pressure, uncover the Instant Pot and transfer the chickpeas mix into bowls. Add the pesto on top, sprinkle with cheese, and serve.

Nutrition:

- Calories: 100
- Fat: 3.5
- Fiber: 3
- Carbs: 13
- Protein: 3.2

Kidney Beans Étouffée

Preparation time: 10 minutes
Cooking time: 30 minutes
Servings: 4

Ingredients:

- 1 tablespoon vegetable oil
- 2 cups bell pepper, chopped
- 1 cup yellow onion, chopped
- 2 teaspoons garlic, chopped
- 1 cup water
- 3 bay leaves
- 1 cup red kidney beans, soaked for 12 hours and drained
- 2 teaspoons smoked paprika
- 1½ teaspoons dried thyme
- Cayenne pepper
- 2 teaspoons marjoram
- 1 teaspoon dried oregano
- 14 ounces canned crushed tomatoes
- ½ teaspoon liquid smoke
- Salt and ground black pepper, to taste
- Rice, already cooked, for serving

Directions:

Set the Instant Pot on Sauté mode, add the oil, and heat it up. Add the onion, stir, and cook for 5 minutes. Add the bell pepper and garlic, stir, and cook 5 minutes. Add the beans, bay leaves, water, thyme, paprika, cayenne, and marjoram, stir, cover, and cook on the Bean/Chili setting for 15 minutes. Release the pressure, uncover the Instant Pot, discard the bay leaves, add the oregano, tomatoes, liquid smoke, salt, and pepper, stir, cover the Instant Pot again and cook for 3 minutes. Release the pressure, uncover the Instant Pot, and divide beans mix among plates on top of already cooked rice.

Nutrition:

- Calories: 189
- Fat: 3
- Fiber: 10
- Carbs: 32
- Protein: 11.3

Kidney Bean Curry

Preparation time: 10 minutes
Cooking time: 1 hour and 10 minutes
Servings: 8

Ingredients:

- 2 cups red kidney beans, soaked for 8 hours and drained
- 1-inch piece ginger, chopped
- 1 yellow onion, peeled and chopped
- 4 garlic cloves, peeled and chopped
- 2 tablespoons vegetable oil
- 2 teaspoons butter
- 2 red chili peppers, dried and crushed
- Salt and ground black pepper, to taste
- 6 cloves
- 1 teaspoon cumin seeds
- 1 teaspoons turmeric
- 1 teaspoon cumin
- 1 teaspoon coriander
- 2 tomatoes, cored and chopped
- 2 cups water
- 1 teaspoon sugar
- 1 teaspoon cayenne pepper
- 2 teaspoons garam masala
- ¼ cup fresh cilantro, chopped

Directions:

Grind the ginger, garlic, and onion using a mortar and pestle and transfer the paste to a bowl. Set the Instant Pot on Sauté mode, add the butter and oil and heat it up. Add the red chili peppers, cloves, and cumin seeds, stir, and fry for 3 minutes. Add the onion paste, stir, and cook for 3 minutes. Add the coriander, cumin, and turmeric, stir, and cook for 30 seconds. Add the tomatoes, stir, and cook 5 minutes. Add the beans, water, salt, pepper, and sugar, stir, cover, and cook on the Bean/Chili setting for 40 minutes. Switch Instant Pot to Manual and cook for 10 minutes. Release the pressure, uncover the Instant Pot, add the red pepper, garam masala, and cilantro, stir, divide among plates, and serve.

Nutrition:

- Calories: 224
- Fat: 4
- Fiber: 7
- Carbs: 30
- Protein: 12

Kidney Beans and Ham

Preparation time: 10 minutes
Cooking time: 25 minutes
Servings: 8

Ingredients:

- 1 pound red kidney beans, soaked for 8 hours and drained
- 2 yellow onions, peeled and chopped
- 8 ounces smoked Tasso ham, chopped
- 1 celery rib, chopped
- 2 tablespoons garlic, minced
- 1 green bell pepper, seeded and chopped
- 2 teaspoons dried thyme
- 3 tablespoons extra virgin olive oil
- 2 bay leaves
- Cajun seasoning, to taste
- 4 green onions, chopped
- Hot sauce, to taste

Directions:

Set the Instant Pot on Sauté mode, add the oil, and heat it up. Add the ham, stir, cook for 5 minutes, and transfer to a bowl. Add the onions and Cajun seasoning to the Instant Pot, stir, and cook for 10 minutes. Add the garlic, stir, and cook 5 minutes. Add the bell pepper and celery, stir, and cook 5 minutes. Add the beans, enough water to cover everything, bay leaves, thyme, cover the Instant Pot and cook on the Bean/Chili setting for 15 minutes. Release the pressure fast, uncover the Instant Pot, add the ham and set aside for 5 minutes. Divide the beans and ham mix on plates, garnish with green onions, and serve with hot sauce to the taste.

Nutrition:

- Calories: 240
- Fat: 3
- Fiber: 4
- Carbs: 16
- Protein: 5

Black Beans and Chorizo

Preparation time: 10 minutes
Cooking time: 45 minutes
Servings: 6
Ingredients:

- 1 tablespoon vegetable oil
- 6 ounces chorizo, chopped
- 1 yellow onion, peeled and cut into half
- 1 pound black beans, soaked for 8 hours and drained
- 6 garlic cloves, peeled and minced
- 2 bay leaves
- 1 orange, cut into half
- 2 quarts chicken stock
- Salt, to taste
- Fresh cilantro, chopped for serving

Directions:

Set the Instant Pot on Sauté mode, add the oil and heat it up. Add the chorizo, stir, and cook for 2 minutes. Add the onion, beans, garlic, bay leaves, orange, salt, and stock, stir, cover, and cook on the Bean/Chili setting for 40 minutes. Release the pressure naturally, uncover the Instant Pot, discard the bay leaves, onion, and orange, add more salt and cilantro, stir, divide into bowls, and serve.

Nutrition:

- Calories: 230
- Fat: 7.7
- Fiber: 8
- Carbs: 30
- Protein: 12.5

Black Beans

Preparation time: 10 minutes
Cooking time: 30 minutes
Servings: 4

Ingredients:
- 1 pound ham hock
- 4 tablespoons extra virgin olive oil
- 1 yellow onion, peeled and chopped
- 1 bay leaf
- 2 garlic cloves, peeled and minced
- 2 cups black beans, soaked for 8 hours and drained
- Salt and ground black pepper, to taste
- 6 cups water

Directions:

Set the Instant Pot on Sauté mode, add 3 tablespoons oil and heat up. Add the ham hock and onions, stir, and cook for 5 minutes. Add the bay leaf and garlic, stir, and cook for 1 minute. Add the beans and stir well. Add the water, the rest of the oil, salt, and pepper, stir, cover, and cook on the Bean/Chili setting for 25 minutes. Release the pressure, set aside for 5 minutes, uncover the Instant Pot, discard the bay leaf and ham hock bone, add more salt and pepper, if needed, stir, divide into bowls, and serve.

Nutrition:
- Calories: 500
- Fat: 4
- Fiber: 21
- Carbs: 35
- Protein: 32

Black Beans in Sauce

Preparation time: 10 minutes
Cooking time: 35 minutes
Servings: 8

Ingredients:
- 16 ounces black beans, soaked overnight and drained
- 2 tablespoons chili powder
- 1 yellow onion, peeled and chopped
- 4 garlic cloves, peeled and minced
- 2 teaspoons cumin
- 1 teaspoon chipotle powder
- 2 teaspoons dried oregano
- 8 ounces tomato paste
- 2 quarts water
- 4 tablespoons sunflower oil
- Salt, to taste

Directions:

In the Instant Pot, mix the beans with garlic, onion, chili powder, chipotle powder, cumin, oregano, tomato paste, water, oil, and salt, stir, cover, and cook on the Bean/Chili setting for 30 minutes. Release the pressure, uncover the Instant Pot, and set it on Manual mode. Add more salt, if needed, stir, cook for 3 minutes, divide into bowls, and serve.

Nutrition:
- Calories: 180
- Fat: 3
- Fiber: 7
- Carbs: 7
- Protein: 10

Chili Lime Black Beans

Preparation time: 10 minutes
Cooking time: 42 minutes
Servings: 4

Ingredients:

- 2 cups black beans, soaked for 8 hours and drained
- 2 teaspoons red palm oil
- 1 yellow onion, peeled and chopped
- Salt, to taste
- 4 garlic cloves, peeled and minced
- 1 tablespoon chili powder
- 1 teaspoon smoked paprika
- 3 cups water
- Juice from 1 lime

Directions:

Set the Instant Pot on Sauté mode, add the oil and heat it up. Add the garlic and onion, stir, and cook for 2 minutes. Add the beans, chili powder, paprika, salt, and water, stir, cover, and cook on Bean/Chili for 40 minutes. Release the pressure naturally, uncover the Instant Pot, add the lime juice and more salt, stir, divide into bowls, and serve.

Nutrition:

- Calories: 200
- Fat: 3
- Fiber: 5
- Carbs: 22
- Protein: 7

Marrow Beans with Lemon

Preparation time: 10 minutes
Cooking time: 45 minutes
Servings: 4

Ingredients:

- 2 cups marrow beans, soaked for 8 hours and drained
- 1 cup yellow onion, peeled and chopped
- 1 tablespoon extra virgin olive oil
- 1 tablespoon fresh rosemary, chopped
- 4 garlic cloves, peeled and minced
- 1 carrot, peeled and chopped
- Salt and ground black pepper, to taste
- 4 cups water
- 1 bay leaf
- 2 tablespoons lemon juice
- Quinoa, already cooked, for serving

Directions:

Set the Instant Pot on Sauté mode, add the oil and heat it up. Add the onion, carrot, garlic, and rosemary, stir, and cook for 3 minutes. Add the water, bay leaf, beans, and some salt, stir, cover, and cook on the Bean/Chili setting for 45 minutes. Release the pressure naturally, uncover the Instant Pot, discard the bay leaf, add salt and pepper to taste and lemon juice, stir well and divide into bowls over already cooked quinoa.

Nutrition:

- Calories: 165
- Fat: 2
- Fiber: 6
- Carbs: 28
- Protein: 9

White Beans and Shrimp

Preparation time: 10 minutes
Cooking time: 35 minutes
Servings: 8

Ingredients:
- 1 pound white beans, soaked for 8 hours and drained
- 1 garlic clove, peeled and minced
- 2 yellow onions, peeled and chopped
- 1 green bell pepper, seeded and chopped
- 1 celery rib, chopped
- Fresh parsley, chopped
- 2 cups seafood stock
- 2 bay leaves
- 3 tablespoons canola oil
- Creole seasoning, to taste
- 1 pound shrimp, peeled and deveined
- Cooked rice, for serving
- Hot sauce, for serving

Directions:
Set the Instant Pot on Sauté mode, add the oil and heat it up. Add the onions and some Creole seasoning, stir, and cook for 5 minutes. Add the garlic, stir, and cook 5 minutes. Add the bell pepper and celery, stir, and cook for 5 minutes. Add the beans, stock, and some water to cover everything in the Instant Pot. Add the bay leaves and parsley, stir, cover, and cook on the Bean/Chili setting for 15 minutes. Release the pressure, uncover the Instant Pot, add the shrimp, cover the Instant Pot and set it aside for 10 minutes. Divide the beans and shrimp among plates on top of cooked rice, and serve with hot sauce.

Nutrition:
- Calories: 340
- Fat: 13
- Fiber: 11
- Carbs: 38
- Protein: 21

Baked Beans

Preparation time: 10 minutes
Cooking time: 55 minutes
Servings: 4

Ingredients:
- 1 pound white beans, soaked for 8 hours and drained
- ½ cup molasses
- 2 garlic cloves, peeled and minced
- 1 yellow onion, peeled and chopped
- ½ cup maple syrup
- 1 tablespoon dry mustard
- Salt and ground black pepper, to taste
- 7 cups water
- ⅛ cup balsamic vinegar

Directions:
Put the beans and 3 cups water into the Instant Pot, cover, and cook on the Bean/Chili setting for 10 minutes. Release the pressure, uncover the Instant Pot, drain the beans and return them to the Instant Pot. Add 4 cups of water, molasses, garlic, onion, maple syrup, vinegar, salt, and pepper, stir, cover, and cook on Manual for 45 minutes. Release the pressure again, uncover the Instant Pot, divide into bowls, and serve.

Nutrition:
- Calories: 152
- Fat: 5.5
- Fiber: 5.4
- Carbs: 21
- Protein: 5.5

Creamy White Beans

Preparation time: 10 minutes
Cooking time: 35 minutes
Servings: 8

Ingredients:

- 1 yellow onion, peeled and chopped
- 1 pound white beans
- 5 cups water
- 2 celery ribs, chopped
- 2 bay leaves
- 4 garlic cloves, peeled and minced
- 1 green bell pepper, seeded and chopped
- 1 teaspoon dried oregano
- 1 teaspoon dried thyme
- Salt and ground white pepper, to taste
- 1 tablespoon soy sauce
- 1 tablespoon Tabasco sauce

Directions:

Put the beans and water into the Instant Pot. Add the onion, celery, garlic, bell pepper, oregano, thyme, salt, white pepper, and soy sauce, stir, cover, and cook on the Bean/Chili setting for 15 minutes. Release the pressure naturally for 15 minutes, uncover the Instant Pot, and set it on Manual mode. Add more salt and pepper to taste and Tabasco sauce, stir, and cook for 20 minutes. Divide into bowls, and serve.

Nutrition:

- Calories: 170
- Fat: 0.6
- Fiber: 10
- Carbs: 31
- Protein: 10.5

Mung Beans

Preparation time: 10 minutes
Cooking time: 17 minutes
Servings: 4

Ingredients:

- ¾ cup mung beans, soaked for 15 minutes and drained
- 1 small red onion, peeled and chopped
- ½ teaspoon cumin seeds
- ½ teaspoon coconut oil
- ½ cup brown rice, soaked for 15 minutes and drained
- 28 ounces canned crushed tomatoes
- 5 garlic cloves, peeled and minced
- 1-inch ginger piece, peeled and chopped
- 1 teaspoon coriander
- 1 teaspoon turmeric
- ½ teaspoon garam masala
- Cayenne pepper
- Salt and ground black pepper, to taste
- 1 teaspoon lemon juice
- 4 cups water

Directions:

In a food processor, mix the tomatoes with the onions, ginger, garlic, coriander, turmeric, cayenne, salt, pepper, and garam masala, and blend well. Set the Instant Pot on Sauté mode, add the oil and heat up. Add the cumin seeds, stir, and fry for 2 minutes. Add the tomatoes, stir, and cook for 15 minutes. Add the beans, rice, water, salt, pepper, and lemon juice, stir, cover, and cook on the Bean/Chili setting for 15 minutes. Release the pressure for 10 minutes, uncover the Instant Pot, stir again, divide into bowls, and serve.

Nutrition:

- Calories: 180
- Fat: 1
- Fiber: 15
- Carbs: 39
- Protein: 7

Indian-style Mung Beans

Preparation time: 10 minutes
Cooking time: 1 hour
Servings: 4

Ingredients:

- 1 cup mung beans, soaked for 6 hours and drained
- 1 teaspoon cumin seeds
- 2 teaspoons butter
- Cayenne pepper
- 2 teaspoons turmeric
- ½ tablespoon coriander
- 1 teaspoon cumin
- 1 tablespoon ginger, grated
- 1 yellow onion, peeled and chopped
- 1 tomato, cored and chopped
- 1½ cups water
- 4 jalapeño peppers, chopped
- ¼ cup fresh cilantro, chopped
- Salt and ground black pepper, to taste

Directions:

Set the Instant Pot on Sauté mode, add the butter, and heat it up. Add the cumin seeds, stir, and cook for 1 minute. Add the cayenne, turmeric, coriander, cumin, and ginger, stir, and cook for 2 minutes. Add jalapeños and onion, stir, and cook for 4 minutes. Add the beans and water, salt and pepper, stir, cover, and cook on the Bean/Chili setting for 20 minutes. Release the pressure, uncover the Instant Pot, add the tomatoes, more salt and pepper, if needed, and set the Instant Pot on Manual mode. Stir and simmer for 20 minutes, add the cilantro, divide into bowls, and serve.

Nutrition:

- Calories: 210
- Fat: 4.3
- Fiber: 8.7
- Carbs: 33
- Protein: 13

Navy Beans and Cabbage

Preparation time: 10 minutes
Cooking time: 40 minutes
Servings: 8

Ingredients:

- 6 bacon slices, chopped
- 1 yellow onion, peeled and chopped
- 1½ cups navy beans, soaked for 8 hours and drained
- ¼ teaspoon cloves
- 3 cups chicken stock
- 1 bay leaf
- 1 cabbage head, chopped
- 3 tablespoons honey
- 3 tablespoons white wine vinegar
- Salt and ground black pepper, to taste

Directions:

Set the Instant Pot on Sauté mode, add the bacon, stir, and brown it for 4 minutes. Add the onions, stir, and cook for 4 minutes. Add the stock, beans, clove, and bay leaf, stir, cover, and cook on the Bean/Chili setting for 35 minutes. Release the pressure, uncover, add the vinegar, honey, and cabbage, stir, cover, and cook on the Manual setting for 12 minutes. Release the pressure, uncover, add salt and pepper, stir, divide into bowls, and serve.

Nutrition:

- Calories: 150
- Fat: 1
- Fiber: 9.5
- Carbs: 27
- Protein: 7

Black-eyed Pea Curry

Preparation time: 10 minutes
Cooking time: 45 minutes
Servings: 4

Ingredients:

- 1 cup black-eyed peas, soaked for 3 hours and drained
- ½ teaspoon cumin seeds
- 2 tablespoons avocado oil
- 1 bay leaf
- 1 yellow onion, peeled and chopped
- 6 garlic cloves, peeled and minced
- 1-inch ginger piece, peeled and grated
- 1 teaspoon turmeric
- Cayenne pepper
- 2 tomatoes, cored and chopped
- Salt and ground black pepper, to taste
- 1 teaspoon garam masala
- 3 cups water
- Cilantro leaves, chopped, for serving

Directions:

Set the Instant Pot on Sauté mode, add the oil and heat it up. Add the cumin seeds, stir, and fry for 2 minutes. Add the onion and bay leaf, stir, and cook for 8 minutes. Add the ginger, garlic, turmeric, cayenne, salt, pepper, and garam masala, stir, and cook for 2 minutes. Add the peas, tomatoes and water, stir, cover and cook on the Bean/Chili setting for 30 minutes. Release the pressure, uncover the Instant Pot, add the cilantro, more salt and pepper, if needed, stir, divide into bowls, and serve.

Nutrition:

- Calories: 200
- Fat: 6
- Fiber: 12
- Carbs: 33
- Protein: 12

Fava Bean Dip

Preparation time: 10 minutes
Cooking time: 30 minutes
Servings: 6

Ingredients:

- 2 cups fava beans, soaked
- 2 garlic cloves, peeled and crushed
- 3 cups water
- 2 teaspoons tahini
- 2 tablespoons vegetable oil
- 2 teaspoons cumin
- 1 teaspoon harissa
- Zest from 1 lemon
- Juice of 1 lemon
- Salt and ground black pepper, to taste
- 1 tablespoon olive oil
- 1 teaspoon paprika

Directions:

Set the Instant Pot on Sauté mode, add the vegetable oil and heat it up. Add the garlic, stir, and cook for 3 minutes. Add the fava beans and water, stir, cover, and cook on the Bean/Chili setting for 12 minutes. Release the pressure naturally for 10 minutes, uncover the Instant Pot, drain most of the liquid, and set the Instant Pot on Sauté mode. Add the cumin, harissa, tahini, salt, pepper, and lemon zest, stir, and blend everything using an immersion blender. Add the paprika, lemon juice, and olive oil and stir gently. Divide into bowls, and serve.

Nutrition:

- Calories: 60
- Fat: 1
- Fiber: 0
- Carbs: 9
- Protein: 3

Fava Bean Puree

Preparation time: 10 minutes
Cooking time: 25 minutes
Servings: 6

Ingredients:
- 1 pound fava bean, rinsed
- 1 cup yellow onion, peeled and chopped
- 4½ cups water
- 1 bay leaf
- ¼ cup extra virgin olive oil
- 1 garlic clove, peeled and minced
- 2 tablespoons lemon juice
- Salt, to taste

Directions:

Put fava beans into the Instant Pot, add 4 cups water, some salt, and bay leaf, cover, and cook on the Bean/Chili setting for 18 minutes. Release the pressure naturally, uncover the Instant Pot, drain the beans, and discard bay leaf. Return the beans to the Instant Pot, add the remaining water, garlic, onion, and salt, stir, cover, and cook 5 minutes. Release the pressure, uncover the Instant Pot, transfer beans mixture to your food processor, add the olive oil and lemon juice and blend well. Divide into bowls, and serve cold.

Nutrition:
- Calories: 330
- Fat: 4
- Fiber: 1
- Carbs: 30
- Protein: 10

Full Mudammas

Preparation time: 10 minutes
Cooking time: 25 minutes
Servings: 2

Ingredients:
- 2 cups fava beans, already cooked
- 4 roasted garlic cloves, peeled and chopped
- 1 red onion, peeled and chopped
- 1 tablespoon olive oil
- 1 teaspoon cumin
- ½ cup water
- Salt and ground black pepper, to taste
- Juice from 2 lemons
- 1 egg, hard boiled, peeled and sliced
- 1 tomato, diced
- 1 yellow onion, peeled and cut into thin rings
- Red chili flakes
- Paprika

Directions:

Set the Instant Pot on Sauté mode, add the oil and heat it up. Add the red onion, stir, and cook for 3 minutes. Add the cumin and garlic, stir, and cook for 1 minute. Add the beans, salt, pepper and water, stir, cover, and cook on the Bean/Chili setting for 15 minutes. Release the pressure, uncover the Instant Pot, set it on Manual mode and cook for 10 more minutes. Transfer to a bowl, add more salt, pepper, and lemon juice and mash using a potato masher. Garnish with egg slices, tomato pieces, yellow onion rings, red chili flakes, and paprika sprinkled on top.

Nutrition:
- Calories: 154
- Fat: 1.4
- Fiber: 3
- Carbs: 30
- Protein: 8.6

Butter Beans with Bacon

Preparation time: 10 minutes
Cooking time: 1 hour
Servings: 8

Ingredients:

- 1 pound butter beans, soaked for 8 hours and drained
- 1 pound bacon, chopped
- 4 cups water
- 1 garlic clove, minced
- 1 jalapeño pepper, chopped
- ½ teaspoon cumin, ground
- 12 ounces beer
- Salt and ground black pepper, to taste

Directions:

Set the Instant Pot on Sauté mode, add bacon and brown it for 10 minutes. Transfer bacon to paper towels, drain the grease, put in a bowl and set aside. Add the water, cumin, and beer to the Instant Pot and stir. Add the beans, stir, cover and cook on the Bean/Chili setting for 30 minutes. Release the pressure, uncover the Instant Pot, add the garlic, bacon, jalapeño, salt, and pepper, stir, cover again and cook on the Manual setting for 3 minutes. Release the pressure, uncover, transfer to bowls, and serve.

Nutrition:

- Calories: 156
- Fat: 4
- Fiber: 3
- Carbs: 6
- Protein: 1

Split Pea Curry

Preparation time: 10 minutes
Cooking time: 35 minutes
Servings: 4

Ingredients:

- 1 cup split peas, soaked in water for a few hours and drained
- 1 tablespoon olive oil
- 2 yellow onions, peeled and chopped
- 2 bell peppers, seeded and chopped
- 4 tablespoons curry paste
- 2 teaspoons cumin seeds
- 15 ounces canned diced tomatoes
- 15 ounces canned coconut milk
- Cilantro leaves, chopped
- Zest and juice of 1 lime
- Salt and ground black pepper, to taste
- 5 ounces coconut-flavored yogurt
- Naan bread, for serving

Directions:

Set the Instant Pot on Sauté mode, add the oil and heat it up. Add the onions and bell peppers, stir, and cook for 10 minutes. Add the curry paste and cumin seeds, stir, and cook for 1 minute. Add the split peas, coconut milk, tomatoes, and cilantro. Also, add some salt and pepper, stir, cover, and cook on the Bean/Chili setting for 25 minutes. Release the pressure, uncover the Instant Pot, add more salt and pepper, if needed, lime zest, and juice and yogurt and stir. Divide into bowls, and serve with naan bread on the side.

Nutrition:

- Calories: 435
- Fat: 18
- Fiber: 8
- Carbs: 47
- Protein: 16

Split Pea and Squash Curry

Preparation time: 10 minutes
Cooking time: 25 minutes
Servings: 4

Ingredients:
- 1 cup split peas, soaked in water for a few hours and drained
- ¼ teaspoon black lentils
- 1 tablespoon peanut oil
- ¾ teaspoon mustard seeds
- 1 tablespoon ginger, minced
- 2 garlic cloves, peeled and minced
- ½ cup onion, chopped
- 2 cups squash, peeled and chopped
- ⅓ cup tomato, cored and cut into chunks
- 2 cups water
- Salt and ground black pepper, to taste
- ½ teaspoon turmeric
- 1 teaspoon cumin
- 1 teaspoon coriander
- 2 teaspoons garam masala
- ½ cup fresh cilantro, chopped

Directions:
Set the Instant Pot on Sauté mode, add the oil and heat it up. Add black lentils and mustard seeds, stir and fry for 1 minute. Add onions, ginger, garlic, stir and cook for 3 minutes. Add the split peas, water, tomato, turmeric, salt, pepper, coriander, cumin, squash and half of the cilantro, stir, cover, and cook on the Bean/Chili setting for 10 minutes. Release the pressure naturally, uncover the Instant Pot, add the rest of the cilantro and garam masala, stir, divide into bowls, and serve.

Nutrition:
- Calories: 275
- Fat: 2.7
- Fiber: 12.5
- Carbs: 53
- Protein: 12

Pea and Pineapple Curry

Preparation time: 10 minutes
Cooking time: 35 minutes
Servings: 4

Ingredients:

- 1 cup peas, soaked in water for a few hours and drained
- 4 cups water
- 3 tablespoons extra virgin olive oil
- 1 yellow onion, peeled and chopped
- 1 cup brown lentils
- 1 teaspoon curry powder
- ½ teaspoon turmeric
- ¼ teaspoon ground cinnamon
- ½ teaspoon cumin
- ⅔ cup canned pineapple, cut into chunks
- ¼ cup cashew butter

Directions:

In a bowl, mix the cashew butter with some water, stir well set aside and set the dish aside. Put the lentils and peas in you Instant Pot, add 3½ cups water, stir, cover, and cook on the Bean/Chili setting for 25 minutes. Release the pressure, drain the peas and lentils and put them in a bowl. Set the Instant Pot on Sauté mode, add the oil and heat it up. Add the turmeric, cumin, curry powder, and cinnamon, stir and cook for 3 minutes. Add the onions, stir and cook for 4 minutes. Set the Instant Pot on Manual mode, add the peas and lentils, cashew butter, pineapple½ cup water, stir, simmer for 5 minutes, divide into bowls, and serve.

Nutrition:

- Calories: 333
- Fat: 11
- Fiber: 17
- Carbs: 43
- Protein: 16

Instant Pot Sauce Recipes

Simple Spaghetti Sauce

Preparation time: 10 minutes
Cooking time: 40 minutes
Servings: 6

Ingredients:

- 1 and ⅔ pounds beef, ground
- 2 carrots, peeled and chopped
- 4 garlic cloves, peeled and minced
- 2 celery ribs, chopped
- 28 ounces canned crushed tomatoes
- 1 yellow onion, peeled and chopped
- 2 bay leaves
- 1 tablespoon olive oil
- Dried basil
- Dried oregano
- Red wine
- Salt and ground black pepper, to taste

For the chicken stock mix:

- 1 cup chicken stock
- 2 tablespoons soy sauce
- 3 tablespoons tomato paste
- 2 tablespoons fish sauce
- 1 tablespoon Worcestershire sauce

Directions:

Set the Instant Pot on Sauté mode, add the beef, salt, pepper, and oil, stir and brown for 7 minutes. Transfer the beef to a bowl when it's brown and set it aside for now. In a bowl, mix the stock with the fish sauce, soy sauce, tomato paste, and Worcestershire sauce and stir well. Heat up you Instant Pot again, add the onions, garlic, bay leaves, basil, and oregano, stir and cook for 5 minutes. Add the celery, carrots, salt, and pepper, stir and cook for 3 minutes. Add the wine, chicken stock, beef, and crushed tomatoes on top. Cover the Instant Pot and cook on the Manual setting for 10 minutes. Release the pressure, uncover the Instant Pot, add more salt and pepper, if needed, set the Instant Pot on Manual mode and cook the sauce for 4 minutes. Serve with your favorite pasta.

Nutrition:

- Calories: 281
- Fat: 16
- Fiber: 5
- Carbs: 20
- Protein: 17

Marinara Sauce

Preparation time: 10 minutes
Cooking time: 20 minutes
Servings: 8

Ingredients:

- 56 ounces canned crushed tomatoes
- 3 garlic cloves, peeled and minced
- ½ cup red lentils
- 1 cup sweet potato, diced
- Salt and ground black pepper, to taste
- 1½ cups water

Directions:

Set the Instant Pot on Sauté mode, add the lentils, sweet potatoes, salt, pepper, and garlic, stir and cook them for 2 minutes. Add the water and tomatoes, stir, cover the Instant Pot and cook on the Manual setting for 13 minutes. Release the pressure, uncover the Instant Pot, puree everything using an immersion blender, add more salt and pepper, if needed, set the Instant Pot on Manual mode, and cook the sauce for 4 minutes.

Nutrition:

- Calories: 60
- Fat: 2
- Fiber: 2
- Carbs: 9
- Protein: 2

Applesauce

Preparation time: 10 minutes
Cooking time: 8 minutes
Servings: 4

Ingredients:
- 8 apples, cored and chopped
- 2 drops cinnamon oil
- 1 cup water
- 1 teaspoon ground cinnamon

Directions:

Put apples into the Instant Pot, add the water, cover the Instant Pot and cook on the Manual setting for 8 minutes. Release the pressure, uncover the Instant Pot, add the oil and cinnamon and puree using an immersion blender. Serve chilled.

Nutrition:
- Calories: 70
- Fat: 1
- Fiber: 1.2
- Carbs: 17
- Protein: 0.3

Cranberry Sauce

Preparation time: 10 minutes
Cooking time: 15 minutes
Servings: 4

Ingredients:
- 2½ teaspoons orange zest
- 12 ounces cranberries
- ¼ cup orange juice
- 2 tablespoons maple syrup
- Salt
- 1 cup sugar

Directions:

In the Instant Pot, mix the orange juice with maple syrup and stir well. Add the orange zest and almost all of the cranberries, stir, cover and cook on the Manual setting for 2 minutes. Release the pressure, uncover the Instant Pot, and set it on Sauté mode. Add the rest of the cranberries, a pinch of salt, and the sugar, stir and cook until sugar dissolves. Serve chilled.

Nutrition:
- Calories: 151
- Fat: 0.4
- Fiber: 1
- Carbs: 39
- Protein: 0.4

Ancho Chili Sauce

Preparation time: 10 minutes
Cooking time: 10 minutes
Servings: 8

Ingredients:

- 5 ancho chilies, dried, seedless and chopped
- 2 garlic cloves, peeled and crushed
- Salt and ground black pepper, to taste
- 1½ cups water
- 1½ teaspoons sugar
- ½ teaspoon dried oregano
- ½ teaspoon cumin
- 2 tablespoons apple cider vinegar

Directions:

In the Instant Pot mix the water chilies, garlic, salt, pepper, sugar, cumin, and oregano, stir, cover and cook on the Manual setting for 8 minutes. Release the pressure for 5 minutes, uncover the Instant Pot, and pour sauce into a blender. Add the vinegar, blend well and transfer everything to a bowl.

Nutrition:

- Calories: 50
- Fat: 2
- Fiber: 0
- Carbs: 2

Orange and Ginger Sauce

Preparation time: 5 minutes
Cooking time: 7 minutes.
Servings: 4

Ingredients:

- 1 cup fish stock
- Salt and ground black pepper, to taste
- 1 tablespoon olive oil
- 4 green onions, chopped
- 1-inch ginger piece, chopped
- Zest and juice from 1 orange

Directions:

In the Instant Pot, mix the fish stock with the salt, pepper, olive oil, onions, ginger, orange juice, and zest and stir well. Cover the Instant Pot and cook on the Manual setting for 7 minutes. Release the pressure, uncover the Instant Pot, and serve your sauce.

Nutrition:

- Calories: 100
- Fat: 1
- Fiber: 1
- Carbs: 2
- Protein: 4

Barbecue Sauce

Preparation time: 10 minutes
Cooking time: 10 minutes
Servings: 8

Ingredients:

- 1 tablespoon sesame seed oil
- ½ cup tomato puree
- 1 yellow onion, peeled and chopped
- ½ cup water
- 4 tablespoons white wine vinegar
- 4 tablespoons honey
- 1 teaspoon salt
- ½ teaspoon garlic powder
- 1 teaspoon liquid smoke
- 1 teaspoon Tabasco sauce
- 1/8 teaspoon cumin
- 1/8 teaspoon ground cloves
- 5 ounces dried seedless plums

Directions:

Set the Instant Pot on Sauté mode, add the oil and heat it up. Add the onion, stir and cook for 5 minutes. Add the tomato puree, honey, water, vinegar, salt, garlic, Tabasco sauce, liquid smoke, cumin, and cloves and stir everything very well. Add the plums and stir well. Cover the Instant Pot and cook on the Manual setting for 10 minutes. Release the pressure, uncover the Instant Pot, blend everything with an immersion blender, transfer sauce to a bowl, and serve.

Nutrition:

- Calories: 20
- Fat: 0.4
- Fiber: 0.4
- Carbs: 3.5
- Protein: 0.1

Gravy

Preparation time: 10 minutes
Cooking time: 1 hour and 30 minutes
Servings: 2

Ingredients:

- Turkey neck, gizzard, livers, and heart
- 1 tablespoon vegetable oil
- ½ cup dry vermouth
- 1 yellow onion, peeled and chopped
- 1 quart turkey stock
- 1 bay leaf
- 4 tablespoons butter
- 2 thyme sprigs
- 4 tablespoons white flour
- Salt and ground black pepper, to taste

Directions:

Set the Instant Pot on Sauté mode, add the oil and heat it up. Add the turkey pieces and onion, stir and cook for 3 minutes. Stir again and cook for 3 minutes. Add the vermouth, stock, bay leaf, and thyme and stir. Cover the Instant Pot and cook on the Manual setting for 36 minutes. Release the pressure for 20 minutes, strain the stock, reserve the turkey giblets and let them cool down, remove gristle and dice them into small pieces. Heat up a pan with the butter over medium heat, add the flour, stir, and cook for 3 minutes. Add the strained stock, stir well, increase heat to medium high and simmer for 20 minutes, stirring frequently. Add salt, pepper, and the giblets, stir well, and serve.

Nutrition:

- Calories: 181
- Fat: 10
- Fiber: 1
- Carbs: 11.4
- Protein: 10.5

Zucchini Pesto

Preparation time: 10 minutes
Cooking time: 10 minutes
Servings: 4

Ingredients:
- 1 yellow onion, peeled and chopped
- 1 tablespoon extra virgin olive oil
- 1½ pounds zucchini, chopped
- Salt, to taste
- ½ cup water
- 1 bunch fresh basil, chopped
- 2 garlic cloves, peeled and minced

Directions:
Set the Instant Pot on Sauté mode, add the oil and heat it up. Add the onion, stir and cook 4 minutes. Add the zucchini, salt and water, stir, cover, and cook on the Manual setting for 3 minutes. Release the pressure, uncover the Instant Pot, add the garlic and basil and blend everything using an immersion blender. Transfer to a bowl, and serve.

Nutrition:
- Calories: 71
- Fat: 5
- Fiber: 2.3
- Carbs: 2
- Protein: 1.

Vegetarian Sauce

Preparation time: 10 minutes
Cooking time: 20 minutes
Servings: 8

Ingredients:
- 1 yellow onion, peeled and chopped
- 2 tablespoons olive oil
- 5 celery ribs
- 8 carrots, peeled and chopped
- 4 beets, peeled and chopped
- 1 butternut squash, peeled and chopped
- 8 garlic cloves, peeled and minced
- 1 cup vegetable stock
- ¼ cup lemon juice
- 1 bunch fresh basil, chopped
- 2 bay leaves
- Salt and ground black pepper, to taste

Directions:
Set the Instant Pot on Sauté mode, add the oil and heat it up. Add the celery, onion, and carrots, stir and cook for 4 minutes. Add the beets, squash, garlic, stock, lemon juice, basil, bay leaves, salt, and pepper, stir, cover and cook for 12 minutes at Manual. Release the pressure, uncover the Instant Pot, discard the bay leaves, puree sauce using an immersion blender, transfer to a bowl, and serve.

Nutrition:
- Calories: 79
- Fat: 1
- Fiber: 0.4
- Carbs: 5
- Protein: 3

Cheese Sauce

Preparation time: 10 minutes
Cooking time: 5 minutes
Servings: 4

Ingredients:
- 2 cups processed cheese, cut into chunks
- 1 cup Italian sausage, cooked and chopped
- 5 ounces canned tomatoes and green chilies, diced
- 4 tablespoons water

Directions:

In the Instant Pot, mix sausage with cheese, tomatoes, and chilies and water. Stir, cover and cook on the Manual setting for 5 minutes. Release the pressure, uncover the Instant Pot, transfer sauce to a bowl, and serve with your favorite pasta or vegetables.

Nutrition:
- Calories: 110
- Fat: 8.5
- Fiber: 0.4
- Carbs: 4.3
- Protein: 4.32

Mushroom Sauce

Preparation time: 10 minutes
Cooking time: 35 minutes
Servings: 6

Ingredients:
- 1 yellow onion, peeled and chopped
- ¼ cup olive oil
- 1 tablespoon flour
- Salt and ground black pepper, to taste
- 1 tablespoon thyme, chopped
- 3 garlic cloves, peeled and minced
- 1¼ cup chicken stock
- ¼ cup dry sherry
- 10 ounces shiitake mushrooms, chopped
- 10 ounces cremini mushrooms, chopped
- 10 ounces button mushrooms, chopped
- 1-ounce Parmesan cheese, grated
- ½ cup heavy cream
- 1 tablespoons parsley, diced

Directions:

Set the Instant Pot on Sauté mode, add the oil and heat it up. Add the onion, salt, and pepper, stir and cook for 5 minutes. Add the garlic, flour, and thyme, stir and cook for 1 minute. Add sherry, stock, and the mushrooms, stir, cover, and cook on the Manual setting for 25 minutes. Release pressure, uncover the Instant Pot, add the cream, cheese, and parsley, stir, and set the Instant Pot on Manual mode. Cook for 5 minutes, transfer to a bowl, and serve.

Nutrition:
- Calories: 140
- Fat: 5.7
- Fiber: 3.1
- Carbs: 13
- Protein: 7.4

Cauliflower Sauce

Preparation time: 10 minutes
Cooking time: 10 minutes
Servings: 6

Ingredients:
- 2 tablespoons butter
- 8 garlic peeled and cloves, minced
- 7 cups vegetable stock
- 6 cups cauliflower florets
- Salt and ground black pepper, to taste
- ½ cup milk

Directions:
Set the Instant Pot on Sauté mode, add the butter and melt it. Add garlic, salt, and pepper, stir, cook for 5 minutes and transfer to a bowl. Add the stock and cauliflower to the Instant Pot, heat up, cover, and cook on the Manual setting for 7 minutes. Release the pressure, transfer the cauliflower and 1 cup stock to your blender, add the salt, pepper, milk, and garlic and puree for a few minutes. Serve with pasta.

Nutrition:
- Calories: 119
- Fat: 5
- Fiber: 1
- Carbs: 10
- Protein: 8

Mango Sauce

Preparation time: 10 minutes
Cooking time: 30 minutes
Servings: 4

Ingredients:
- 1 shallot, peeled and chopped
- 1 tablespoon vegetable oil
- ¼ teaspoon cardamom
- 2 tablespoons ginger, minced
- ½ teaspoon ground cinnamon
- 2 mangos, chopped
- 2 red hot chilies, chopped
- 1 apple, cored and chopped
- 2 teaspoons salt
- ¼ cup raisins
- 1¼ cup raw sugar
- 1¼ apple cider vinegar

Directions:
Set the Instant Pot on Sauté mode, add the oil and heat it up. Add the ginger and shallot, stir and cook for 5 minutes. Add the cinnamon, hot peppers, and cardamom, stir and cook for 2 minutes. Add the mangos, apple, raisins, sugar, and cider, stir and cook until the sugar melts. Cover the Instant Pot and cook on the Manual setting for 7 minutes. Release the pressure, uncover the Instant Pot, transfer to a pan, and simmer on medium heat for 15 minutes, stirring occasionally. Transfer to jars, and serve when needed.

Nutrition:
- Calories: 80
- Fat: 0.3
- Fiber: 1
- Carbs: 9
- Protein: 0.9

Hot Sauce

Preparation time: 10 minutes
Cooking time: 2 minutes
Servings: 6

Ingredients:
- 12 ounces hot peppers, chopped
- 2 teaspoons salt
- 1¼ cups apple cider vinegar

Directions:
Put peppers into the Instant Pot. Add the vinegar and salt, stir, cover, and cook on the Manual setting for 2 minutes. Release the pressure for 15 minutes, uncover the Instant Pot, and puree everything using your immersion blender. Transfer to jars, and serve when needed.

Nutrition:
- Calories: 12
- Fat: 0.04
- Fiber: 0
- Carbs: 0.04
- Protein: 0.06

Strawberry Sauce

Preparation time: 10 minutes
Cooking time: 2 minutes
Servings: 8

Ingredients:
- 1 ounce orange juice
- ⅛ cup sugar
- 1 pound strawberries, cored and cut into halves
- Ground ginger
- ½ teaspoon vanilla extract

Directions:
In the Instant Pot, mix the strawberries with sugar, stir, and leave them aside for 10 minutes. Add the orange juice, stir, cover, and cook on the Manual setting for 2 minutes. Release the pressure for 15 minutes, uncover the Instant Pot, add the vanilla extract, and ginger, puree using an immersion blender and refrigerate until ready for use.

Nutrition:
- Calories: 60
- Fat: 0
- Carbs: 13
- Protein: 1

Tomato Chutney

Preparation time: 10 minutes
Cooking time: 10 minutes
Servings: 6

Ingredients:
- 3 pounds tomatoes, cored, peeled, and chopped
- 1 cup red wine vinegar
- 1¾ cups sugar
- 1-inch ginger piece, peeled and grated
- 3 garlic cloves, peeled and minced
- 2 onions, peeled and chopped
- ¼ cup raisins
- ¾ teaspoon ground cinnamon
- ¼ teaspoon ground cloves
- ½ teaspoon coriander
- ¼ teaspoon nutmeg
- ¼ teaspoon ground ginger
- Paprika
- 1 teaspoon chili powder

Directions:

Mix the tomatoes and the grated ginger into the blender, pulse well, and transfer to the Instant Pot. Add the vinegar, sugar, garlic, onions, raisins, cinnamon, cloves, coriander, nutmeg, ground ginger, paprika, and chili powder, stir, cover, and cook on the Manual setting for 10 minutes. Release the pressure, uncover the Instant Pot, transfer to jars, and serve when needed.

Nutrition:
- Calories: 140
- Fat: 10
- Fiber: 0
- Carbs: 10
- Protein: 4

Tomato Sauce

Preparation time: 10 minutes
Cooking time: 15 minutes
Servings: 20

Ingredients:
- 2 pounds tomatoes, cored, peeled, and chopped
- 1 apple, cored and chopped
- 1 yellow onion, peeled and chopped
- 6 ounces raisins, chopped
- 3 ounces dates, chopped
- Salt, to taste
- 3 teaspoons allspice
- ½ pint vinegar
- ½ pound brown sugar

Directions:

Put the tomatoes into the Instant Pot. Add the apple, onion, raisins, dates, salt, allspice, and half of the vinegar, stir, cover, and cook on the Manual setting for 10 minutes. Release the pressure, uncover the Instant Pot, set it on Manual mode, add the rest of the vinegar and sugar, stir, and simmer until the sugar dissolves. Transfer to jars, and serve when needed.

Nutrition:
- Calories: 70
- Fat: 4
- Fiber: 1
- Carbs: 8
- Protein: 1.7

Green Tomato Sauce

Preparation time: 5 minutes
Cooking time: 10 minutes
Servings: 12

Ingredients:

- 2 pounds green tomatoes, cored and chopped
- 1 white onion, peeled and chopped
- ¼ cup currants
- 1 Anaheim chili pepper, chopped
- 4 red chili peppers, chopped
- 2 tablespoons ginger, grated
- ¾ cup brown sugar
- ¾ cup white vinegar

Directions:

In the Instant Pot, mix green tomatoes with onion, currants, Anaheim pepper, chili pepper, ginger, sugar, and vinegar, stir, cover and cook on the Manual setting for 10 minutes. Release the pressure for 5 minutes, uncover the Instant Pot, transfer sauce to jars, and serve.

Nutrition:

- Calories: 50
- Fat: 2
- Fiber: 2.4
- Carbs: 10
- Protein: 1.5

Plum Sauce

Preparation time: 10 minutes
Cooking time: 15 minutes
Servings: 20

Ingredients:

- 3 pounds plums, pitted and chopped
- 2 onions, peeled and chopped
- 2 apples, cored and chopped
- 4 tablespoons ground ginger
- 4 tablespoons ground cinnamon
- 4 tablespoons allspice
- 1½ tablespoons salt
- 1 pint vinegar
- ¾ pound sugar

Directions:

Put the plums, apples, and onions into the Instant Pot. Add the ginger, cinnamon, allspice, salt, and almost all the vinegar, stir, cover, and cook on the Manual setting for 10 minutes. Release the pressure, uncover the Instant Pot, set it on Manual mode, add the rest of the vinegar and the sugar, stir, and cook until sugar dissolves. Keep sauce refrigerated until ready to use.

Nutrition:

- Calories: 100
- Fat: 10
- Fiber: 3
- Carbs: 23
- Protein: 26

Pineapple Sauce

Preparation time: 10 minutes
Cooking time: 3 minutes
Servings: 4

Ingredients:
- 3 cups pineapple chunks
- 3 tablespoons rum
- 3 tablespoons butter
- 4 tablespoons brown sugar
- 1 teaspoon ground cinnamon
- 1 teaspoon allspice
- 1 teaspoon nutmeg
- 1 teaspoon ground ginger

Directions:
Set the Instant Pot on sauté mode, add the butter and melt it. Add the sugar, pineapple, rum, allspice, nutmeg, cinnamon, and ginger, stir, cover, and cook on the Manual setting for 3 minutes. Release the pressure, uncover the Instant Pot, stir sauce one more time, and serve.

Nutrition:
- Calories: 160
- Fat: 0
- Fiber: 0
- Carbs: 23
- Protein: 0

Onion Sauce

Preparation time: 10 minutes
Cooking time: 30 minutes
Servings: 8

Ingredients:
- 6 tablespoons butter
- 3 pounds yellow onion, peeled and chopped
- Salt and ground black pepper, to taste
- ½ teaspoon baking soda

Directions:
Set the Instant Pot on Sauté mode, add the butter and heat it up. Add the onions and baking soda, stir, and cook for 3 minutes. Cover the Instant Pot and cook on the Manual setting for 20 minutes. Release the pressure, uncover the Instant Pot, set it on Sauté mode again, and cook for 5 minutes, stirring often. Serve when needed.

Nutrition:
- Calories: 100
- Fat: 0.4
- Fiber: 0
- Carbs: 9
- Protein: 0

Clementine Sauce

Preparation time: 10 minutes
Cooking time: 6 minutes
Servings: 4

Ingredients:

- 12 ounces cranberries
- 1 cup water
- Juice and peel from 1 clementine
- 1 cup sugar

Directions:

In the Instant Pot, mix the cranberries with clementine juice and peel, water, and sugar, stir, cover and cook on the Manual setting for 6 minutes. Release the pressure, uncover the Instant Pot, and serve.

Nutrition:

- Calories: 50
- Fat: 0
- Fiber: 0
- Carbs: 0.3
- Protein: 0

Orange Sauce

Preparation time: 10 minutes
Cooking time: 7 minutes
Servings: 6

Ingredients:

- ¼ cup white wine vinegar
- 1 teaspoon ginger paste
- 2 tablespoons tomato paste
- 3 tablespoons sugar
- 1 cup orange juice
- 1 teaspoon garlic, diced
- 2 tablespoons agave nectar
- 1 teaspoon sesame oil
- 1 teaspoon chili sauce
- 2 tablespoons soy sauce
- ¼ cup vegetable stock
- 2 tablespoons cornstarch

Directions:

Set the Instant Pot on Sauté mode, add the oil and heat it up. Add the garlic and ginger paste, stir, and cook for 2 minutes. Add the tomato paste, sugar, orange juice, vinegar, agave nectar, soy sauce, and chili sauce, stir, cover, and cook on the Manual setting for 3 minutes. Release the pressure, uncover the Instant Pot, add the stock and cornstarch, stir, cover again, and cook on the Manual setting for 4 minutes. Release the pressure again, and serve your sauce.

Nutrition:

- Calories: 80
- Fat: 7
- Fiber: 1.4
- Carbs: 5
- Protein: 13

Bread Sauce

Preparation time: 10 minutes
Cooking time: 10 minutes
Servings: 12

Ingredients:
- 1 yellow onion, peeled and chopped
- 2 garlic cloves, peeled and crushed
- 6 cloves
- 26 ounces milk
- 6 bread slices, torn
- 2 bay leaves
- Salt, to taste
- 2 tablespoons butter
- Heavy cream

Directions:
Set the Instant Pot on Manual mode, add the milk and heat it up. Add the garlic, cloves, onion, bay leaves, and salt, stir well, and cook for 3 minutes. Add the bread, stir, cover, and cook on the Manual setting for 4 minutes. Release the pressure, uncover the Instant Pot, transfer the sauce to a blender, add the butter and cream, discard the bay leaves, and blend well. Return the sauce to the Instant Pot set it on Manual mode and simmer sauce for 3 minutes.

Nutrition:
- Calories: 113
- Fat: 5
- Fiber: 2.4
- Carbs: 11
- Protein: 3

Chili Jam

Preparation time: 10 minutes
Cooking time: 40 minutes
Servings: 12

Ingredients:
- 4 garlic cloves, peeled and minced
- 2 red onions, peeled and diced
- 4 red chili peppers, seeded and chopped
- 17 ounces cranberries
- 4 ounces sugar
- Olive oil
- Salt and ground black pepper, to taste
- 2 tablespoons red wine vinegar
- 3 tablespoons water

Directions:
Set the Instant Pot on Sauté mode, add the oil and heat it up. Add the onions, garlic, and chilies, stir, and cook for 8 minutes. Add the cranberries, vinegar, water, and sugar, stir, cover the Instant Pot, and cook on the Manual setting for 14 minutes. Release the pressure, uncover the Instant Pot, puree sauce using an immersion blender, set the Instant Pot on Manual mode, and cook the sauce for 15 minutes. Add the salt and pepper, transfer to jars, and serve when needed.

Nutrition:
- Calories: 20
- Fat: 0.2
- Fiber: 0.4
- Carbs: 4
- Protein: 0.2

Sriracha Sauce

Preparation time: 10 minutes
Cooking time: 17 minutes
Servings: 6

Ingredients:

- 4 ounces red chilies, seeded and chopped
- 3 tablespoons brown sugar
- 3 ounces arbol chilies, dried
- 12 garlic cloves, peeled and minced
- 5 ounces distilled vinegar
- 5 ounces water

Directions:

In the Instant Pot, mix the water with the brown sugar and stir. Add all the chilies and garlic, stir, cover and cook on the Manual setting for 7 minutes. Release the pressure, uncover the Instant Pot, blend sauce using an immersion blender, add the vinegar, stir, set the Instant Pot on Manual mode, and cook the sauce for 10 minutes. Serve when needed.

Nutrition:

- Calories: 90
- Fat: 0.4
- Fiber: 0.3
- Carbs: 19
- Protein: 2.4

Grape Sauce

Preparation time: 10 minutes
Cooking time: 10 minutes
Servings: 6

Ingredients:

- 6 ounces black grapes
- ½ cup water
- 2½ tablespoons sugar
- 1 cup corn flour
- Lemon juice

Directions:

Put grapes into the Instant Pot, add enough water to cover, cook on the Manual setting for 7 minutes, release the pressure, set the mixture aside to cool down, blend using an immersion blender, strain the sauce, and set the dish aside. Heat up a pan over medium heat, add the grapes, sugar, water, and corn flour, stir, and boil until it thickens. Add the lemon juice, stir, take off heat, and serve.

Nutrition:

- Calories: 60
- Fiber: 0.3
- Carbs: 0
- Protein: 3

Pomegranate Sauce

Preparation time: 10 minutes
Cooking time: 25 minutes
Servings: 4

Ingredients:
- 5 cups pomegranate juice
- ½ cup lemon juice
- 1 cup white sugar

Directions:

In the Instant Pot, mix the pomegranate juice with sugar, and lemon juice, stir, cover, and cook on the Manual setting for 25 minutes. Release the pressure, uncover the Instant Pot, divide sauce into jars, and serve when needed.

Nutrition:
- Calories: 136
- Fat: 0.4
- Fiber: 0.8
- Carbs: 35
- Protein: 1.2

Apricot Sauce

Preparation time: 10 minutes
Cooking time: 20 minutes
Servings: 6

Ingredients:
- 3 ounces apricots, dried and cut into halves
- 2 cups water
- ⅔ cup sugar
- 1 teaspoon vanilla extract

Directions:

In the Instant Pot, mix the apricots with water, sugar, and vanilla, stir, cover, and cook on Manual for 20 minutes. Release the pressure, uncover the Instant Pot, transfer the sauce to a blender, and pulse well. Divide into jars, and serve with a poultry dish.

Nutrition:
- Calories: 100
- Fat: 0.6
- Fiber: 0
- Carbs: 10
- Protein: 1

Mustard Sauce

Preparation time: 10 minutes
Cooking time: 7 minutes
Servings: 4

Ingredients:

- 6 ounces mushrooms, chopped
- 3 tablespoon olive oil
- 3.5 ounces dry sherry
- 1 thyme sprig
- 1 garlic clove, peeled and minced
- 3.5 ounces beef stock
- 1 tablespoon balsamic vinegar
- 1 tablespoon mustard
- 2 tablespoon crème fraiche
- 2 tablespoons fresh parsley, diced

Directions:

Set the Instant Pot on Sauté mode, add the oil and heat it up. Add the garlic, thyme, and mushrooms, stir, and cook for 5 minutes. Add the sherry, vinegar, and stock, stir, cover, and cook on the Manual setting for 3 minutes. Release the pressure, uncover the Instant Pot, discard the thyme, add the crème fraiche, mustard, and parsley, stir, set the Instant Pot on Manual mode, and cook the sauce for 3 minutes, and serve.

Nutrition:

- Calories: 67
- Fat: 0.4
- Fiber: 0.2
- Carbs: 4
- Protein: 1

Eggplant Sauce

Preparation time: 10 minutes
Cooking time: 20 minutes
Servings: 6

Ingredients:

- 1 pound ground beef
- 28 ounces canned diced tomatoes
- 5 garlic cloves, peeled and minced
- 5 ounces canned tomato paste
- 1 onion, peeled and chopped
- 1 eggplant, chopped
- ½ cup olive oil
- ½ teaspoon turmeric
- 1 cup vegetable stock
- 1 tablespoon apple cider vinegar
- ½ teaspoon dried dill
- Salt and ground black pepper, to taste
- ¼ cup fresh parsley, chopped

Directions:

Set the Instant Pot on Sauté mode, add the beef, brown for a few minutes, and transfer to a bowl. Heat up the oil into the Instant Pot, add the onion and some salt, and cook for 2 minutes. Add the eggplant and garlic, stir, and cook for 1 minute. Add the vinegar, stir, and cook for 2 minutes. Add the tomato paste, tomatoes, meat, salt, pepper, parsley, dill, turmeric, and stock, stir, cover, and cook on the Manual setting for 15 minutes. Release the pressure, uncover the Instant Pot, add more salt and pepper, and a splash of lemon juice, stir well, and serve.

Nutrition:

- Calories: 142
- Fat: 11
- Fiber: 4.4
- Carbs: 10
- Protein: 2.1

Broccoli Sauce

Preparation time: 10 minutes
Cooking time: 6 minutes
Servings: 4

Ingredients:
- 6 cups water
- 3 cups broccoli florets
- 2 garlic cloves, minced
- Salt and ground black pepper, to taste
- ⅓ cup coconut milk
- 1 tablespoon white wine vinegar
- 1 tablespoons nutritional yeast
- 1 tablespoon olive oil

Directions:

Put the water into the Instant Pot. Add the broccoli, salt, pepper, and garlic, stir, cover, and cook on the Manual setting for 6 minutes. Release the pressure, uncover the Instant Pot, strain the broccoli and garlic, and transfer to a food processor. Add the coconut milk, vinegar, yeast, olive oil, salt, and pepper and blend well. Serve over pasta.

Nutrition:
- Calories: 128
- Fat: 10
- Fiber: 1.4
- Carbs: 6
- Protein: 5.4

Carrot Sauce

Preparation time: 10 minutes
Cooking time: 15 minutes
Servings: 6

Ingredients:
- 4 tablespoons butter
- 2 cups carrot juice
- Ground cinnamon
- Salt and ground black pepper, to taste
- Cayenne pepper
- 1 teaspoon dried chervil
- 1 teaspoon dried chives
- 1 teaspoon dried tarragon

Directions:

Put the carrot juice into the Instant Pot, set the Instant Pot on Manual mode, and bring to a boil. Add the butter, salt, pepper, cayenne and cinnamon, stir, cover and cook on the Manual setting for 5 minutes. Release the pressure, uncover the Instant Pot, add the chervil, chives, and tarragon, stir, and serve.

Nutrition:
- Calories: 149
- Fat: 7
- Fiber: 4
- Carbs: 19
- Protein: 2
- Sugars 8

Cherry Sauce

Preparation time: 10 minutes
Cooking time: 5 minutes
Servings: 4

Ingredients:
- 1 tablespoon lemon juice
- ¼ cup water
- 1 teaspoon kirsch
- Salt
- 1 tablespoon sugar
- 2 tablespoons cornstarch
- 2 cups cherries

Directions:

In the Instant Pot, mix the water with lemon juice, salt, sugar, kirsch, and cornstarch. Add the cherries, stir, cover, and cook on the Manual setting for 5 minutes. Release the pressure, uncover the Instant Pot, transfer the sauce to a bowl, and serve after chilling.

Nutrition:
- Calories: 60
- Fat: 0
- Fiber: 0
- Carbs: 13
- Protein: 0

Date Sauce

Preparation time: 10 minutes
Cooking time: 9 minutes
Servings: 6

Ingredients:
- 2 cups apple juice
- 2 cups dates, dried
- 1 tablespoon lemon juice

Directions:

In the Instant Pot, mix the apple juice with the lemon juice and dates, stir, cover and cook on the Manual setting for 9 minutes. Release the pressure, uncover the Instant Pot, blend using an immersion blender, and transfer to a container. Serve when needed.

Nutrition:
- Calories: 30
- Fat: 0
- Fiber: 1
- Carbs: 5
- Protein: 0
- Sugar: 5

Elderberry Sauce

Preparation time: 10 minutes
Cooking time: 10 minutes
Servings: 20

Ingredients:
- 4 cups water
- 1 cup elderberries
- 1-inch ginger piece, grated
- 1 cinnamon stick
- 1 vanilla bean, split
- 5 cloves
- 1 cup honey

Directions:

In the Instant Pot, mix the elderberries with the water, ginger, cinnamon, vanilla and cloves, stir, cover and cook on the Manual setting for 10 minutes. Release the pressure, strain the sauce and keep in a jar until needed.

Nutrition:
- Calories: 55
- Fat: 0
- Fiber: 0
- Carbs: 13
- Protein: 0

Fennel Sauce

Preparation time: 10 minutes
Cooking time: 10 minutes
Servings: 6

Ingredients:
- 1 fennel bulb, cut into pieces
- 2 pints grape tomatoes, cut into halves
- ¼ cup dry white wine
- 5 thyme sprigs
- 3 tablespoons olive oil
- Sugar
- Salt and ground black pepper, to taste

Directions:

Set the Instant Pot in Sauté mode, add the oil and heat it up. Add the fennel, tomatoes, thyme, sugar, salt, and pepper, stir, and sauté for 5 minutes. Add the white wine, cover the Instant Pot, and cook for 4 minutes. Release the pressure, uncover, discard the thyme, stir the sauce, and serve.

Nutrition:
- Calories: 76
- Fat: 0.6
- Fiber: 0.6
- Carbs: 4
- Protein: 5

Pear Sauce

Preparation time: 10 minutes
Cooking time: 15 minutes
Servings: 5 pints

Ingredients:
- 10 cups pears, sliced
- 2 teaspoons ground cinnamon
- 1 cup pear juice
- ½ teaspoon nutmeg

Directions:
Put pear pieces into the Instant Pot, add the cinnamon, nutmeg, and pear juice. Stir, cover the Instant Pot, and cook on the Manual setting for 10 minutes. Release the pressure, uncover the Instant Pot, blend using an immersion blender, and serve when needed.

Nutrition:
- Calories: 80
- Fat: 0.1
- Fiber: 0
- Carbs: 20
- Protein: 0.1

Guava Sauce

Preparation time: 10 minutes
Cooking time: 20 minutes
Servings: 6

Ingredients:
- 1 can guava shells and syrup
- 2 onions, peeled and chopped
- ¼ cup vegetable oil
- Juice from 2 lemons
- 2 garlic cloves, peeled and chopped
- 1-inch ginger piece, peeled and minced
- ½ teaspoon nutmeg
- 2 Serrano chilies, chopped

Directions:
Put guava shells and syrup into the blender, pulse well and set aside. Set the Instant Pot on Sauté mode, add the oil and heat it up. Add the onion and garlic, stir and cook for 4 minutes. Add the guava mix, ginger, lemon juice, chilies, and nutmeg, stir, cover, and cook on High for 15 minutes. Release the pressure, uncover the Instant Pot, and serve sauce with fish.

Nutrition:
- Calories: 85
- Fat: 2.3
- Fiber: 8
- Carbs: 22
- Protein: 3

Melon Sauce

Preparation time: 5 minutes
Cooking time: 10 minutes
Servings: 6

Ingredients:
- Flesh from 1 small melon
- 1 ounce sugar
- 1 cup sweet wine
- 1 tablespoon butter
- 1 teaspoon starch
- Juice of 1 lemon

Directions:

Put the melon and sweet wine into the Instant Pot, cover, and cook on the Manual setting for 7 minutes. Release the pressure, transfer the sauce to a blender, add the lemon juice, sugar, butter, and starch and blend very well. Return the sauce to the Instant Pot, set it on Manual mode, cook the sauce until it thickens for 3 minutes, and serve.

Nutrition:
- Calories: 68
- Fat: 0.3
- Carbs: 1
- Protein: 1

Peach Sauce

Preparation time: 5 minutes
Cooking time: 3 minutes
Servings: 6

Ingredients:
- 10 ounces peaches, pitted and chopped
- 1/8 teaspoon nutmeg
- 2 tablespoons cornstarch
- 3 tablespoons sugar
- ½ cup water
- Salt
- 1/8 teaspoon ground cinnamon
- 1/8 teaspoon almond extract

Directions:

In the Instant Pot, mix the peaches with the nutmeg, cornstarch, sugar, cinnamon, and salt, stir, cover, and cook on the Manual setting for 3 minutes. Release the pressure, uncover the Instant Pot, add the almond extract, stir, and serve sauce.

Nutrition:
- Calories: 100
- Fat: 1
- Fiber: 0.6
- Carbs: 4
- Protein: 6

Peach and Whiskey Sauce

Preparation time: 10 minutes
Cooking time: 10 minutes
Servings: 6

Ingredients:
- 1 cup brown sugar
- 3 cups peaches, pureed
- 6 tablespoons whiskey
- 1 cup white sugar
- 2 teaspoons lemon zest, grated

Directions:
In the Instant Pot mix the peaches with brown sugar, white sugar, whiskey, and lemon zest, stir, cover, and cook on the Manual setting for 10 minutes. Release the pressure, uncover the Instant Pot, stir the sauce, and transfer it to jars. Serve when needed.

Nutrition:
- Calories: 100
- Fat: 0.7
- Fiber: 0.6
- Carbs: 7
- Protein: 7

Leek Sauce

Preparation time: 5 minutes
Cooking time: 7 minutes
Servings: 8

Ingredients:
- 2 leeks, sliced thin
- 2 tablespoons butter
- 1 cup whipping cream
- 3 tablespoons lemon juice
- Salt and ground black pepper, to taste

Directions:
Set the Instant Pot on Sauté mode, add the butter and melt it. Add the leeks, stir and cook for 2 minutes. Add the lemon juice, stir, cover, and cook on the Manual setting for 3 minutes. Release the pressure, uncover the Instant Pot, transfer the sauce to your blender, add whipping cream and blend everything together. Return the sauce to the Instant Pot, set on Manual mode, add the salt and pepper, stir, and cook for 2 minutes. Serve with fish.

Nutrition:
- Calories: 140
- Fat: 13
- Fiber: 0.4
- Carbs: 5
- Protein: 1

Parsley Sauce

Preparation time: 10 minutes
Cooking time: 7 minutes
Servings: 6

Ingredients:

- 2 cups chicken stock
- 1 yellow onion, peeled and diced
- 2 tablespoons butter
- 2 tablespoons flour
- ¾ cup whole milk
- 4 tablespoons fresh parsley, chopped
- 1 egg yolk
- ¼ cup heavy cream
- Salt and ground white pepper, to taste

Directions:

Put the stock and onion into the Instant Pot, set the Instant Pot on Manual mode, and bring to a boil. Heat up a pan with the butter over medium heat, add the flour and stir well to combine. Combine this mixture and whole milk with the stock and stir well. Bring to a boil, add the parsley, stir, cover, and cook on the Manual setting for 2 minutes. Release the pressure, uncover the Instant Pot, and set it back on Manual mode. In a bowl, mix the cream with egg yolk and some of the sauce from the Instant Pot. Stir this well, mix with the sauce, and whisk. Add the salt and pepper, stir again, cook for a couple of minutes until it thickens, and serve with chicken and rice.

Nutrition:

- Calories: 70
- Fat: 2.5
- Fiber: 0.5
- Carbs: 7.3
- Protein: 2.5

Cilantro Sauce

Preparation time: 5 minutes
Cooking time: 6 minutes
Servings: 6

Ingredients:

- 3 garlic cloves, peeled and minced
- 1 tablespoon olive oil
- 2 red chilies, minced
- 3 shallots, peeled and minced
- 3 scallions, chopped
- 3 tomatoes, cored and chopped
- Salt and ground black pepper, to taste
- 2 tablespoons fresh cilantro, chopped
- ¼ cup water

Directions:

Set the Instant Pot on Sauté mode, add oil and heat it up. Add garlic, shallots and chilies, stir and cook for 3 minutes. Add scallions, tomatoes, water, salt, pepper and cilantro, stir, cover and cook on High for 3 minutes. Release the pressure, uncover the Instant Pot, blend using an immersion blender, and serve.

Nutrition:

- Calories: 67
- Fat: 1
- Fiber: 0.4
- Carbs: 1
- Protein: 0.5

Chestnut Sauce

Preparation time: 10 minutes
Cooking time: 20 minutes
Servings: 6

Ingredients:
- 11 ounces sugar
- 11 ounces water
- 1½ pounds chestnuts, cut into halves and peeled
- ⅛ cup rum liquor

Directions:
In the Instant Pot, mix the sugar with the water, rum, and chestnuts. Stir, cover, and cook on the Manual setting for 20 minutes. Release the pressure for 10 minutes, uncover the Instant Pot, and blend everything with an immersion blender. Serve when needed.

Nutrition:
- Calories: 50
- Fat: 0
- Fiber: 0
- Carbs: 10
- Protein: 0
- Sugar: 12

Quince Sauce

Preparation time: 10 minutes
Cooking time: 15 minutes
Servings: 6

Ingredients:
- 2 pounds grated quince
- Juice of 1 lemon
- 10 cloves
- 2 pounds sugar
- ¼ cup water

Directions:
In the Instant Pot, mix the quince with the sugar and stir well. Add the water and stir again. Tie the cloves in cheesecloth and add to the Instant Pot. Cover and cook on the Manual setting for 10 minutes. Release the pressure for 10 minutes, uncover the Instant Pot, stir the sauce again, and transfer to jars .Serve on top of sweet pastries.

Nutrition:
- Calories: 60
- Fat: 0
- Fiber: 1
- Carbs: 16
- Sugar: 9
- Protein: 1

Rhubarb Sauce

Preparation time: 10 minutes
Cooking time: 13 minutes
Servings: 6

Ingredients:

- 8 ounces rhubarb, trimmed and chopped
- 1 tablespoon cider vinegar
- 1 small onion, peeled and chopped
- Ground cardamom
- 1 garlic clove, peeled and minced
- 2 jalapeño peppers, chopped
- ⅓ cup honey
- ¼ cup raisins
- ¼ cup water

Directions:

In the Instant Pot, mix the rhubarb with the vinegar, onion, cardamom, garlic, jalapeños, honey, water, and raisins, stir, cover, and cook on the Manual setting for 7 minutes. Release the pressure, uncover the Instant Pot, set it on Manual mode and cook for 3 minutes. Serve when needed.

Nutrition:

- Calories: 90
- Fat: 0
- Fiber: 1
- Carbs: 23
- Protein: 1

Corn Sauce

Preparation time: 10 minutes
Cooking time: 6 minutes
Servings: 4

Ingredients:

- 1 yellow onion, peeled and chopped
- 1 tablespoon olive oil
- 1 teaspoon white flour
- 1¾ cups chicken stock
- ¼ cup white wine
- 1 thyme sprig
- 2 cups corn kernels
- Salt and ground black pepper, to taste
- 2 teaspoons butter
- 1 teaspoon thyme, diced

Directions:

Set the Instant Pot on Sauté mode, add the oil and heat it up. Add the onion, stir, and cook for 3 minutes. Add the flour, stir well, and cook for 1 minute. Add the wine, stir, and cook for 1 minute. Add the thyme sprig, stock, and corn, stir, cover, and cook on the Manual setting for 1 minute. Release the pressure, uncover the Instant Pot, discard the thyme sprig, transfer the sauce to a blender, add salt, pepper, butter, and chopped thyme, and blend well. Return to pot set it on Sauté mode again and cook 1-2 minutes. Serve when needed.

Nutrition:

- Calories: 100
- Fat: 4.5
- Fiber: 2
- Carbs: 13
- Protein: 3

Instant Pot Dessert Recipes

Pumpkin Chocolate Cake

Preparation time: 10 minutes
Cooking time: 45 minutes
Servings: 12

Ingredients:

- ¾ cup white flour
- ¾ cup whole wheat flour
- Salt
- 1 teaspoon baking soda
- ¾ teaspoon pumpkin pie spice
- ¾ cup sugar
- 1 banana, mashed
- ½ teaspoon baking powder
- 2 tablespoons canola oil
- ½ cup Greek yogurt
- 8 ounces canned pumpkin puree
- Vegetable oil cooking spray
- 1 quart water
- 1 egg
- ½ teaspoon vanilla extract
- ⅔ cup chocolate chips

Directions:

In a bowl, mix the flours, salt, baking soda, baking powder, and pumpkin spice, and stir. In another bowl, mix the sugar with the oil, banana, yogurt, pumpkin puree, vanilla, and egg, and stir using a mixer. Combine the 2 mixtures, add the chocolate chips and mix well. Pour into a greased Bundt pan, cover the pan with paper towels and aluminum foil, and place in the steamer basket of the Instant Pot. Add the quart water to the Instant Pot, cover, and cook on the Manual setting for 35 minutes. Release the pressure for 10 minutes, uncover the Instant Pot, leave the cake to cool down before cutting and serving it.

Nutrition:

- Calories: 270
- Fat: 9
- Fiber: 1
- Carbs: 45
- Protein: 3

Chocolate Cheesecake

Preparation time: 60 minutes
Cooking time: 50 minutes
Servings: 12

Ingredients:

For the crust:
- 4 tablespoons melted butter
- 1½ cups chocolate cookie crumbs

For the filling:
- 24 ounces cream cheese, softened
- 2 tablespoons cornstarch
- 1 cup sugar
- 3 eggs
- 1 tablespoon vanilla extract
- Vegetable oil cooking spray
- 1 cup water
- ½ cup Greek yogurt
- 4 ounces white chocolate
- 4 ounces milk chocolate
- 4 ounces bittersweet chocolate

Directions:

In a bowl, mix the cookie crumbs with the butter and stir well. Spray a springform pan with some cooking oil, line with parchment paper, press the crumbs and butter mixture on the bottom and keep in the freezer. In a bowl, mix the cream cheese with cornstarch and sugar and stir using a mixer. Add the eggs, yogurt, and vanilla, stir to combine everything and divide into 3 bowls. Put the milk chocolate in a heatproof bowl and heat up in the microwave for 30 seconds. Add this to one of the bowls with the batter you made earlier and stir well. Put dark and white chocolate in separate heatproof bowls and heat them up in the microwave for 30 seconds each. Add these to the other 2 bowls with cheesecake batter, stir, and place them all in the refrigerator for 30 minutes. Take the bowls out of the refrigerator and layer your cheesecake. Pour the dark chocolate batter in the center of the crust. Add white chocolate batter on top and spread evenly and end with milk chocolate batter. Put the pan in the steamer basket of the Instant Pot, add 1 cup water to the Instant Pot, cover, and cook on the Manual setting for 45 minutes. Release the pressure for 10 minutes, take the cheesecake out of the Instant Pot , set aside to cool down, and serve.

Nutrition:
- Calories: 470
- Fat: 31
- Fiber: 2
- Carbs: 45
- Protein: 8

Apple Bread

Preparation time: 10 minutes
Cooking time: 1 hour and 10 minutes
Servings: 6
Ingredients:

- 3 cups apples, cored and cubed
- 1 cup sugar
- 1 tablespoon vanilla extract
- 2 eggs
- 1 tablespoon apple pie spice
- 2 cups white flour
- 1 tablespoon baking powder
- ½ cup butter
- 1 cup water

Directions:

In a bowl, mix the egg with the butter, apple pie spice, and sugar and stir using a mixer. Add the apples and stir again well. In another bowl, mix the baking powder with flour and stir. Combine the 2 mixtures, stir, and pour into a springform pan. Place in the steamer basket of the Instant Pot, add the water to the Instant Pot, cover, and cook on the Manual setting for 1 hour and 10 minutes. Release the pressure, fast, leave the bread to cool down, cut, and serve.

Nutrition:

- Calories: 89
- Fat: 3
- Fiber: 1
- Carbs: 17
- Protein: 0

Banana Bread

Preparation time: 10 minutes
Cooking time: 30 minutes
Servings: 6

Ingredients:

- ¾ cup coconut sugar
- ⅓ cup butter, softened
- 1 teaspoon vanilla extract
- 1 egg
- 2 bananas, mashed
- 1 teaspoon baking powder
- 1½ cups flour
- Salt
- ½ teaspoons baking soda
- ⅓ cup cashew milk
- 1½ teaspoons cream of tartar
- 2 cups water
- Vegetable oil cooking spray

Directions:

In a bowl, mix the milk with the cream of tartar and stir well. Add the sugar, butter, egg, vanilla, and bananas and stir everything. In another bowl, mix the flour with salt, baking powder, and soda. Combine the 2 mixtures, stir well, pour into a cake pan which you've greased with some cooking spray and arrange pan in the steamer basket of the Instant Pot. Add the water to the Instant Pot, cover and cook on the Manual setting for 30 minutes. Release the pressure, uncover the Instant Pot, take the bread out, set aside to cool down, slice, and serve it.

Nutrition:

- Calories: 325
- Fat: 2
- Fiber: 1.1
- Carbs: 44
- Protein: 4.5

Chocolate Lava Cake

Preparation time: 10 minutes
Cooking time: 6 minutes
Servings: 3

Ingredients:

- 1 egg
- 4 tablespoons sugar
- 2 tablespoons olive oil
- 4 tablespoons milk
- 4 tablespoons flour
- Salt
- 1 tablespoon cocoa powder
- ½ teaspoon baking powder
- ½ teaspoon orange zest
- 1 cup water

Directions:

In a bowl, mix the egg with the sugar, oil, milk, flour, salt, cocoa powder, baking powder, and orange zest and stir well. Pour into greased ramekins and place them into the steamer basket of the Instant Pot. Add the water to the Instant Pot, cover, and cook on the Manual setting for 6 minutes. Release the pressure, uncover the Instant Pot, take the lava cakes out, and serve them after they cool down.

Nutrition:

- Calories: 200
- Fat: 5
- Fiber: 1
- Carbs: 24
- Protein: 2

Apple Crisp

Preparation time: 10 minutes
Cooking time: 8 minutes
Servings: 4

Ingredients:

- 2 teaspoons ground cinnamon
- 5 apples, cored and cut into chunks
- ½ teaspoon nutmeg
- 1 tablespoon maple syrup
- ½ cup water
- 4 tablespoons butter
- ¼ cup flour
- ¾ cup old fashioned rolled oats
- ¼ cup brown sugar
- Salt

Directions:

Put the apples into the Instant Pot. Add the cinnamon, nutmeg, maple syrup, and water. In a bowl, mix the butter with the oats, sugar, salt, and flour and stir well. Drop spoonfuls of the oat mixture on top of apples, cover the Instant Pot and cook on the Manual setting for 8 minutes. Release the pressure, and serve warm.

Nutrition:

- Calories: 180
- Fat: 7
- Fiber: 2.5
- Carbs: 30
- Protein: 1.4
- Sugar: 14

Candied Lemon Peel

Preparation time: 20 minutes
Cooking time: 20 minutes
Servings: 80 pieces

Ingredients:
- 5 lemons
- 2¼ cups white sugar
- 5 cups water

Directions:

Wash the lemons, slice them in half, reserve the juice for another use, slice each half into quarters, remove the pulp and cut the peel into thin strips. Put the strips into the Instant Pot, add 4 cups of water, cover, and cook on the Manual setting for 3 minutes. Release the pressure, uncover the Instant Pot, discard the peel, rinse, and put in a bowl. Clean the Instant Pot and add 2 cups of the sugar and the remaining water to it. Add the lemon strips, stir, set the Instant Pot on Manual mode, and cook for 5 minutes. Cover the Instant Pot, cook on the Manual setting for 10 minutes, and release pressure naturally for 20 minutes. Strain the peels, spread them on a cutting board and set aside to cool for 10 minutes. Keep them in jars until you are ready to serve them.

Nutrition:
- Calories: 7
- Fat: 0
- Fiber: 0.2
- Carbs: 2
- Protein: 0

Baked Apples

Preparation time: 10 minutes
Cooking time: 10 minutes
Servings: 6

Ingredients:
- 6 apples, cored
- 1 cup red wine
- ¼ cup raisins
- 1 teaspoon ground cinnamon
- ½ cup raw sugar

Directions:

Put the apples into the Instant Pot. Add the wine, raisins, sugar, and cinnamon, cover the Instant Pot and cook on the Manual setting for 10 minutes. Release the pressure naturally, uncover the Instant Pot, transfer the apples and cooking liquid to plates, and serve.

Nutrition:
- Calories: 188
- Fat: 0.4
- Fiber: 3.5
- Carbs: 34
- Protein: 0.5

Chocolate Fondue

Preparation time: 10 minutes
Cooking time: 2 minutes
Servings: 4

Ingredients:
- 3.5 ounces crème fraiche
- 3.5 ounces dark chocolate, cut into chunks
- 1 teaspoon liquor
- 1 teaspoon sugar
- 2 cups water

Directions:

In a heat-proof container, mix the chocolate chunks with the sugar, crème fraiche, and liquor. Put the water into the Instant Pot, add the container in the steamer basket, cover the Instant Pot, and cook on the Manual setting for 2 minutes. Release the pressure naturally, uncover the Instant Pot, take the container out, stir well, and serve it right away with some fresh fruits.

Nutrition:
- Calories: 210
- Fat: 20
- Fiber: 3
- Carbs: 6.5
- Protein: 2

Holiday Pudding

Preparation time: 10 minutes
Cooking time: 40 minutes
Servings: 4

Ingredients:
- 4 ounces dried cranberries, soaked in hot water for 30 minutes, drained, and chopped
- Olive oil
- 2 cups water
- 4 ounces dried apricots, chopped
- 1 cup white flour
- 3 teaspoons baking powder
- 1 cup raw sugar
- 1 teaspoon ginger
- Ground cinnamon
- Salt
- 15 tablespoons butter
- 3 tablespoons maple syrup
- 4 eggs
- 1 carrot, peeled and grated

Directions:

Grease a heatproof pudding mold with a drizzle of oil and set the dish aside. In a blender, mix the flour with the baking powder, sugar, cinnamon, salt, and ginger and pulse a few times. Add the butter and pulse again. Add the maple syrup and eggs and pulse again. Add the dried fruits and carrot and fold into the batter. Spread this mix into the pudding mold, place in the steamer basket of the Instant Pot and add the water to the Instant Pot as well. Set the Instant Pot on Sauté mode and steam your pudding for 10 minutes. Cover the Instant Pot, cook the pudding at Manual for 30 minutes. Release the pressure naturally for 10 minutes, leave pot aside for another 10 minutes, uncover the Instant Pot, take the pudding out and set it aside to cool down before serving it.

Nutrition:
- Calories: 310
- Fat: 15
- Fiber: 2
- Carbs: 27.9
- Protein: 3.6

Pumpkin Pie

Preparation time: 10 minutes
Cooking time: 20 minutes
Serving: 8

Ingredients:

- 2 pounds butternut squash, peeled and chopped
- 2 eggs
- 2 cups water
- 1 cup whole milk
- ¾ cup maple syrup
- 1 teaspoon ground cinnamon
- ½ teaspoon ginger
- ¼ teaspoon ground cloves
- Salt
- 1 tablespoon cornstarch
- Whipped cream, for serving
- Chopped pecans, for serving

Directions:

Put squash cubes in the steamer basket of the Instant Pot, add 1 cup water, cover the Instant Pot, cook on the Manual setting for 4 minutes, release pressure, take squash and transfer to a strainer, cool it down and mash it a bit in a bowl. Add maple syrup, milk, eggs, cinnamon, ginger, cloves, salt and cloves and stir very well. Pour this into ramekins, place them in the steamer basket of the Instant Pot, add the remaining water to the Instant Pot, cover, and cook on the Manual setting for 10 minutes. Release the pressure, uncover the Instant Pot, take the ramekins out, garnish with whipped cream and chopped pecans, and serve.

Nutrition:

- Calories: 143
- Fat: 3
- Fiber: 2.1
- Carbs: 19
- Protein: 3.3

Tapioca Pudding

Preparation time: 10 minutes
Cooking time: 8 minutes
Servings: 6

Ingredients:

- 1¼ cups milk
- ⅓ cup tapioca pearls, rinsed
- ½ cup water
- ½ cup sugar
- Zest from ½ lemon
- 1 cup water

Directions:

In a heat-proof bowl, mix the tapioca with the milk, sugar, ½ cup water, and lemon zest and stir well. Put this in the steamer basket of the Instant Pot, add the 1 cup water to the Instant Pot, cover and cook on the Manual setting for 8 minutes. Release the pressure, set it aside for 5 minutes, uncover the Instant Pot, take the pudding out, and serve it warm.

Nutrition:

- Calories: 180
- Fat: 2.5
- Fiber: 0.1
- Carbs: 90
- Protein: 2.5

Upside-down Apple Cake

Preparation time: 10 minutes
Cooking time: 20 minutes
Servings: 8
Ingredients:

- 1 apple, sliced
- 1 apple, chopped
- 2 cup water
- 1 cup ricotta cheese
- ¼ cup raw sugar
- 1 tablespoon lemon juice
- 1 egg
- 1 teaspoon vanilla extract
- 3 tablespoons olive oil
- 1 cup white flour
- 2 teaspoons baking powder
- ⅛ teaspoon ground cinnamon
- 1 teaspoon baking soda

Directions:

Put the apples in a bowl, add the lemon juice, toss to coat and set the dish aside. Line a heatproof dish with some parchment paper, grease with some oil, and dust with some flour. Sprinkle some sugar on the bottom and arrange the sliced apple on top. In a bowl, mix the egg with cheese, sugar, vanilla extract, and oil and stir well. Add the flour, baking powder, baking soda, cinnamon, and stir again. Add the chopped apple, toss to coat, and pour everything into the pan. Place the pan in the steamer basket of the Instant Pot, add the water to the Instant Pot, cover and cook on the Manual setting for 20 minutes. Release the pressure, uncover the Instant Pot, turn cake onto a plate, and serve warm.

Nutrition:

- Calories: 241
- Fat: 10
- Fiber: 2
- Carbs: 20
- Protein: 5.8

Brownie Cake

Preparation time: 10 minutes
Cooking time: 50 minutes
Servings: 6

Ingredients:

- 1 cup pinto beans, soaked for 8 hours and drained
- 4 cups water

For the cake:

- 1/8 teaspoon almond extract
- ½ cup cocoa powder
- ½ cup raw sugar
- 3 tablespoons extra virgin olive oil
- Salt
- 2 eggs
- 2 teaspoons baking powder
- ¼ cup almonds, sliced

Directions:

Put the beans and water into the Instant Pot, cover, cook on the Bean/Chili setting for 12 minutes, release the pressure, uncover the Instant Pot, strain the beans, transfer them to a blender and puree them. Discard the water from the Instant Pot, keeping 1 cup's worth. Grease a heatproof bowl with some olive oil and set it aside for now. Add the cocoa powder, almond extract, honey, salt, eggs, and oil to a blender with the beans and puree everything for 1 minute. Transfer mixture to a greased bowl, spread, place the bowl in the steamer basket of the Instant Pot, add the reserved water from cooking the beans, cover, and cook on the Manual setting for 20 minutes. Release the pressure, take the cake out of the Instant Pot , set it aside for 15 minutes, transfer to a plate, sprinkle almonds on top, slice, and serve.

Nutrition:

- Calories: 164
- Fat: 7.8
- Fiber: 4
- Carbs: 24
- Protein: 4.4

Dulce De Leche

Preparation time: 10 minutes
Cooking time: 25 minutes
Servings: 6

Ingredients:
- 16 ounces canned sweet condensed milk
- Water to cover

Directions:
Put the condensed milk can in the steamer basket of the Instant Pot, add water to the Instant Pot to cover, and cook on the Manual setting for 20 minutes. Release the pressure naturally, uncover the Instant Pot, take the can out of the Instant Pot and set it aside to cool down. Serve alone or with pastries.

Nutrition:
- Calories: 300
- Fat: 10
- Fiber: 5
- Carbs: 24
- Protein: 10

Pears with Wine Sauce

Preparation time: 10 minutes
Cooking time: 10 minutes
Servings: 6

Ingredients:
- 6 green pears
- 1 vanilla pod
- 1 cloves
- Ground cinnamon
- 7 ounces sugar
- 1 glass red wine

Directions:
In the Instant Pot, mix wine with sugar, vanilla and cinnamon. Add pears and clove, cover the Instant Pot and cook on the Manual setting for 10 minutes. Release pressure, uncover the Instant Pot and leaves pears to cool down for 10 minutes. Transfer them to serving plates along with the wine sauce, and serve.

Nutrition:
- Calories: 151
- Fat: 7.7
- Fiber: 3
- Carbs: 14
- Protein: 1.1

Crème Brûlée

Preparation time: 1 hour
Cooking time: 15 minutes
Servings: 6

Ingredients:
- 2 cups fresh cream
- 1 teaspoon ground cinnamon
- 6 egg yolks
- 5 tablespoons white sugar
- Zest from 1 orange
- Nutmeg, for serving
- 4 tablespoons raw sugar
- 2 cups water

Directions:

In a pan, mix the cream with the cinnamon and orange zest, stir, and bring to a boil over medium-high heat. Take the pan off heat and set it aside for 30 minutes. In a bowl, mix the egg yolks with white sugar and whisk well. Add this to cooled cream and whisk again. Strain this mixture and then divide it into ramekins. Cover with aluminum foil, place them in the steamer basket of the Instant Pot, add the water to the Instant Pot, cover, and cook on Manual for 10 minutes. Release the pressure naturally, uncover the Instant Pot, take the ramekins out and set them aside for 30 minutes. Sprinkle with nutmeg and raw sugar on top of each, melt this with a culinary torch, and serve.

Nutrition:
- Calories: 210
- Fat: 10
- Fiber: 3
- Carbs: 18
- Protein: 13

Bread Pudding

Preparation time: 5 minutes
Cooking time: 25 minutes
Servings: 4

Ingredients:
- 4 egg yolks
- 3 cups brioche, cubed
- 2 cups half and half
- ½ teaspoon vanilla extract
- 1 cup sugar
- 2 tablespoons butter, softened
- 1 cup cranberries
- 2 cups warm water
- ½ cup raisins
- Zest from 1 lime

Directions:

Grease a baking dish with some butter and set the dish aside. In a bowl, mix the egg yolks with the half and half, cubed brioche, vanilla extract, sugar, cranberries, raisins, and lime zest and stir well. Pour this into greased dish, cover with some aluminum foil and set aside for 10 minutes. Put the dish in the steamer basket of the Instant Pot, add the warm water to the Instant Pot, cover, and cook on the Manual setting for 20 minutes. Release the pressure naturally, uncover the Instant Pot, take the bread pudding out, set it aside to cool down, slice, and serve it.

Nutrition:
- Calories: 300
- Fat: 7
- Fiber: 2
- Carbs: 46
- Protein: 11

Ruby Pears

Preparation time: 10 minutes
Cooking time: 10 minutes
Servings: 4

Ingredients:

- 4 pears
- Juice and zest of 1 lemon
- 26 ounces grape juice
- 11 ounces currant jelly
- 4 garlic cloves, peeled
- ½ vanilla bean
- 4 peppercorns
- 2 rosemary sprigs

Directions:

Pour the jelly and grape juice into the Instant Pot and mix with lemon zest and lemon juice. Dip each pear in this mix, wrap them in aluminum foil and arrange them in the steamer basket of the Instant Pot. Add the garlic cloves, peppercorns, rosemary, and vanilla bean to the juice mixture, cover the Instant Pot and cook on the Manual setting for 10 minutes. Release the pressure, uncover the Instant Pot, take the pears out, unwrap them, arrange them on plates, and serve cold with cooking juice poured on top.

Nutrition:

- Calories: 145
- Fat: 5.6
- Fiber: 6
- Carbs: 12
- Protein: 12

Rice Pudding

Preparation time: 5 minutes
Cooking time: 15 minutes
Servings: 6

Ingredients:

- 1 tablespoon butter
- 7 ounces long grain rice
- 4 ounces water
- 16 ounces milk
- 3 ounces sugar
- Salt
- 1 egg
- 1 tablespoon cream
- 1 teaspoon vanilla extract
- Ground cinnamon

Directions:

Put the butter into the Instant Pot, set it on Sauté mode, melt it, add the rice, and stir. Add the water and milk and stir again. Add the salt and sugar, stir again, cover the Instant Pot and cook on the Rice setting for 8 minutes. In a bowl, mix the cream with the vanilla and eggs and stir well. Release the pressure from the Instant Pot, uncover it, and pour some of the liquid from the Instant Pot over the egg mixture and stir well. Pour this into the Instant Pot and whisk well. Cover the Instant Pot, cook on the Manual setting for 10 minutes, release the pressure, uncover the Instant Pot, pour the pudding into bowls, sprinkle cinnamon on top, and serve.

Nutrition:

- Calories: 112
- Fat: 1.2
- Fiber: 0.4
- Carbs: 21
- Protein: 3.3

Ricotta Cake

Preparation time: 30 minutes
Cooking time: 30 minutes
Servings: 6

Ingredients:
- 1 pound ricotta
- 6 ounces dates, soaked for 15 minutes and drained
- 2 ounces honey
- 4 eggs
- 2 ounces sugar
- Vanilla extract
- 17 ounces water
- Orange juice and zest from ½ orange

Directions:

In a bowl, whisk the ricotta until it softens. In another bowl, whisk the eggs well. Combine the 2 mixtures and stir very well. Add the honey, vanilla, dates, orange zest, and juice to the ricotta mixture and stir again. Pour the batter into a heatproof dish and cover with aluminum foil. Place dish in the steamer basket of the Instant Pot, add the water to the Instant Pot, cover, and cook on the Manual setting for 20 minutes. Release the pressure, uncover the Instant Pot, allow the cake to cool down, transfer to a platter, slice, and serve.

Nutrition:
- Calories: 211
- Fat: 8.6
- Fiber: 0.5
- Carbs: 21
- Protein: 12

Pumpkin Rice Pudding

Preparation time: 30 minutes
Cooking time: 35 minutes
Servings: 6

Ingredients:
- 1 cup brown rice
- ½ cup boiling water
- 3 cups cashew milk
- ½ cup dates, chopped
- Salt
- 1 cinnamon stick
- 1 cup pumpkin puree
- ½ cup maple syrup
- 1 teaspoon pumpkin spice mix
- 1 teaspoon vanilla extract

Directions:

Put the rice into the Instant Pot, add boiling water to cover, set aside for 10 minutes and drain. Put the water in milk into the Instant Pot, add the rice, cinnamon stick, dates and salt, stir, cover and cook on the Rice setting for 20 minutes. Release pressure, uncover the Instant Pot, add the maple syrup, pumpkin pie spice, and pumpkin puree, stir, set the Instant Pot on Manual mode and cook for 5 minutes. Discard the cinnamon stick, add the vanilla, stir, transfer the pudding to bowls, set aside for 30 minutes to cool down, and serve.

Nutrition:
- Calories: 100
- Fat: 1
- Fiber: 4
- Carbs: 21
- Protein: 4.1

Lemon Marmalade

Preparation time: 10 minutes
Cooking time: 15 minutes
Servings: 8

Ingredients:

- 2 pounds lemons, washed, sliced, and cut into quarters
- 4 pounds sugar
- 2 cups water

Directions:

Put the lemon pieces into the Instant Pot, add the water, cover, and cook on the Manual setting for 10 minutes. Release the pressure naturally, uncover the Instant Pot, add the sugar, stir, set the Instant Pot on Manual mode, and cook for 6 minutes, stirring all the time. Divide into jars, and serve when needed.

Nutrition:

- Calories: 100
- Fat: 2
- Fiber: 2
- Carbs: 4
- Protein: 8

Orange Marmalade

Preparation time: 10 minutes
Cooking time: 25 minutes
Servings: 8

Ingredients:
- Juice from 2 lemons
- 3 pounds sugar
- 1 pound oranges, cut into halves
- 1-pint water

Directions:

Squeeze the juice from the oranges and cut the peel into pieces. Put the peel in a bowl, cover with water and set aside overnight. In the Instant Pot, mix the lemon juice with the orange juice, water, and peel. Cover the Instant Pot, cook on the Manual setting for 15 minutes, release the pressure, uncover, add the sugar and set the Instant Pot on Manual mode. Cook until sugar dissolves, divide into jars, and serve when needed.

Nutrition:
- Calories: 50
- Fat: 0
- Fiber: 0.1
- Carbs: 12
- Protein: 0.1

Berry Jam

Preparation time: 60 minutes
Cooking time: 20 minutes
Servings: 12

Ingredients:
- 1 pound cranberries
- 1 pound strawberries
- ½ pound blueberries
- 3.5 ounces black currant
- 2 pounds sugar
- Zest from 1 lemon
- Salt
- 2 tablespoon water

Directions:

In the Instant Pot, mix the strawberries with the cranberries, blueberries, currants, lemon zest, and sugar. Stir and set aside for 1 hour. Add the salt and water, set the Instant Pot on Manual mode, and bring to a boil. Cover the Instant Pot, cook on Manual for 10 minutes, and release pressure for 10 minutes. Uncover the Instant Pot, set it on Manual mode again, bring to a boil, and simmer for 4 minutes. Divide into jars and keep in the refrigerator until you need it.

Nutrition:
- Calories: 60
- Fat: 0
- Fiber: 0
- Carbs: 12
- Sugar: 12
- Protein: 0

Tomato Jam

Preparation time: 10 minutes
Cooking time: 30 minutes
Servings: 12

Ingredients:
- 1½ pounds tomatoes, cored and chopped
- 2 tablespoons lime juice
- 1 cup white sugar
- 1 tablespoon ginger, grated
- 1 teaspoon ground cinnamon
- 1 teaspoon cumin
- ⅛ teaspoon ground cloves
- Salt
- 1 jalapeño pepper, minced

Directions:
In the Instant Pot mix the tomatoes with sugar, lime juice, ginger, cumin, cinnamon, cloves, salt, and jalapeño pepper, stir, cover, and cook on the Manual setting for 30 minutes. Release the pressure, uncover the Instant Pot, divide the jam into jars, and serve when needed.

Nutrition:
- Calories: 239
- Fat: 0
- Fiber: 2
- Carbs: 59
- Sugar: 55
- Protein: 0

Pear Jam

Preparation time: 10 minutes
Cooking time: 4 minutes
Servings: 12

Ingredients:
- 8 pears, cored and cut into quarters
- 2 apples, peeled, cored, and cut into quarters
- ¼ cup apple juice
- 1 teaspoon cinnamon, ground

Directions:
In the Instant Pot, mix the pears with apples, cinnamon, and apple juice, stir, cover, and cook on the Manual setting for 4 minutes. Release the pressure naturally, uncover the Instant Pot, blend using an immersion blender, divide the jam into jars, and keep in a cold place until you serve it.

Nutrition:
- Calories: 90
- Fat: 0
- Fiber: 1
- Carbs: 20
- Sugar: 20
- Protein: 0

Peach Jam

Preparation time: 10 minutes
Cooking time: 5 minutes
Servings: 6

Ingredients:
- 4½ cups peaches, peeled and cubed
- 6 cups sugar
- ¼ cup crystallized ginger, chopped
- 1 box fruit pectin

Directions:
Set the Instant Pot on Manual mode, add the peaches, ginger, and pectin, stir and bring to a boil. Add the sugar, stir, cover and cook on the Manual setting for 5 minutes. Release the pressure, uncover the Instant Pot, divide the jam into jars, and serve.

Nutrition:
- Calories: 50
- Fat: 0
- Fiber: 1
- Carbs: 3
- Protein: 0
- Sugar: 12

Raspberry Curd

Preparation time: 10 minutes
Cooking time: 5 minutes
Servings: 4

Ingredients:
- 1 cup sugar
- 12 ounces raspberries
- 2 egg yolks
- 2 tablespoons lemon juice
- 2 tablespoons butter

Directions:
Put the raspberries into the Instant Pot. Add the sugar and lemon juice, stir, cover, and cook on the Manual setting for 2 minutes. Release the pressure for 5 minutes, uncover the Instant Pot, strain the raspberries and discard the seeds. In a bowl, mix the egg yolks with raspberries and stir well. Return this to the Instant Pot, set it on Sauté mode, simmer for 2 minutes, add the butter, stir, and transfer to a container. Serve cold.

Nutrition:
- Calories: 110
- Fat: 4
- Fiber: 0
- Carbs: 16
- Protein: 1

Berry Compote

Preparation time: 10 minutes
Cooking time: 5 minutes
Servings: 8

Ingredients:
- 1 cup blueberries
- 2 cups strawberries, sliced
- 2 tablespoons lemon juice
- ¾ cup sugar
- 1 tablespoon cornstarch
- 1 tablespoon water

Directions:
In the Instant Pot, mix the blueberries with lemon juice and sugar, stir, cover, and cook on the Manual setting for 3 minutes. Release the pressure naturally for 10 minutes and uncover the Instant Pot. In a bowl, mix the cornstarch with water, stir well, and add to the Instant Pot. Stir, set the Instant Pot on Sauté mode, and cook compote for 2 minutes. Divide into jars and keep in the refrigerator until you serve it.

Nutrition:
- Calories: 260
- Fat: 13
- Fiber: 3
- Carbs: 23
- Protein: 3

Key Lime Pie

Preparation time: 10 minutes
Cooking time: 15 minutes
Servings: 6

Ingredients:
For the crust:
- 1 tablespoon sugar
- 3 tablespoons butter, melted
- 5 graham crackers, crumbled

For the filling:
- 4 egg yolks
- 14 ounces canned condensed milk
- ½ cup key lime juice
- ⅓ cup sour cream
- Vegetable oil cooking spray
- 1 cup water
- 2 tablespoons key lime zest, grated

Directions:
In a bowl, whisk the egg yolks well. Add the milk gradually and stir again. Add the lime juice, sour cream, and lime zest and stir again. In another bowl, whisk the butter with the graham crackers and sugar, stir well, and spread on the bottom of a springform greased with some cooking spray. Cover the pan with some aluminum foil and place it in the steamer basket of the Instant Pot. Add the water to the Instant Pot, cover and cook on the Manual setting for 15 minutes. Release the pressure for 10 minutes, uncover the Instant Pot, take the pie out, set aside to cool down and keep in the refrigerator for 4 hours before slicing and serving it.

Nutrition:
- Calories: 400
- Fat: 21
- Fiber: 0.5
- Carbs: 34
- Protein: 7

Stuffed Peaches

Preparation time: 10 minutes
Cooking time: 4 minutes
Servings: 6

Ingredients:

- 6 peaches, pits and flesh removed
- Salt
- ¼ cup coconut flour
- ¼ cup maple syrup
- 2 tablespoons coconut butter
- ½ teaspoon ground cinnamon
- 1 teaspoon almond extract
- 1 cup water

Directions:

In a bowl, mix the flour with the salt, syrup, butter, cinnamon, and half of the almond extract and stir well. Fill the peaches with this mix, place them in the steamer basket of the Instant Pot, add the water and the rest of the almond extract to the Instant Pot, cover and cook on the Steam setting for 4 minutes. Release the pressure naturally, divide the stuffed peaches on serving plates, and serve warm.

Nutrition:

- Calories: 160
- Fat: 6.7
- Carbs: 12
- Fiber: 3
- Sugar: 11
- Protein: 4

Peach Compote

Preparation time: 10 minutes
Cooking time: 3 minutes
Servings: 6

Ingredients:

- 8 peaches, pitted and chopped
- 6 tablespoons sugar
- 1 teaspoon ground cinnamon
- 1 teaspoon vanilla extract
- 1 vanilla bean, scraped
- 2 tablespoons Grape Nuts cereal

Directions:

Put the peaches into the Instant Pot and mix with the sugar, cinnamon, vanilla bean, and vanilla extract. Stir well, cover the Instant Pot and cook on the Manual setting for 3 minutes. Release the pressure for 10 minutes, add the cereal, stir well, transfer the compote to bowls, and serve.

Nutrition:

- Calories: 100
- Fat: 2
- Carbs: 11
- Fiber: 1
- Sugar: 10
- Protein: 1

Fruit Cobbler

Preparation time: 10 minutes
Cooking time: 12 minutes
Servings: 4

Ingredients:

- 3 apples, cored and cut into chunks
- 2 pears, cored and cut into chunks
- 1½ cup hot water
- ¼ cup honey
- 1 cup steel-cut oats
- 1 teaspoon ground cinnamon
- ice cream, for serving

Directions:

Put the apples and pears into the Instant Pot and mix with hot water, honey, oats, and cinnamon. Stir, cover, and cook on the Manual setting for 12 minutes. Release the pressure naturally, transfer the cobbler to bowls, and serve it with ice cream on top.

Nutrition:

- Calories: 170
- Fat: 4
- Carbs: 10
- Fiber: 2.4
- Protein: 3
- Sugar: 7

Simple Carrot Cake

Servings: 6
Preparation time: 10 minutes
Cooking time: 30 minutes

Ingredients:

- 5 ounces flour
- Salt
- ¾ teaspoon baking powder
- ½ teaspoon baking soda
- ½ teaspoon ground cinnamon
- ¼ teaspoon nutmeg
- ½ teaspoon allspice
- 1 egg
- 3 tablespoons yogurt
- ½ cup sugar
- ¼ cup pineapple juice
- 4 tablespoons coconut oil, melted
- ⅓ cup carrots, peeled and grated
- ⅓ cup pecans, toasted and chopped
- ⅓ cup coconut flakes
- Vegetable oil cooking spray
- 2 cups water

Directions:

In a bowl, mix the flour with baking soda, baking powder, salt, allspice, cinnamon, and nutmeg and stir. In another bowl, mix the egg with yogurt, sugar, pineapple juice, oil, carrots, pecans, and coconut flakes and stir well. Combine the two mixtures and stir everything well. Pour this into a springform greased with some cooking spray, add the water to the Instant Pot, and place the pan into the steamer basket. Cover the Instant Pot and cook on the Manual setting for 32 minutes. Release the pressure for 10 minutes, remove the cake from the Instant Pot, let it cool briefly, then cut, and serve it.

Nutrition:

- Calories: 140
- Fat: 3.5
- Carbs: 23.4
- Fiber: 4.1
- Sugar: 5.2
- Protein: 4.3

Zucchini Nut Bread

Preparation time: 10 minutes
Cooking time: 25 minutes
Servings: 6

Ingredients:

- 1 cup applesauce
- 3 eggs, whisked
- 1 tablespoon vanilla extract
- 2 cups sugar
- 2 cups zucchini, grated
- 1 teaspoon salt
- 2½ cups white flour
- ½ cup baking cocoa
- 1 teaspoon baking soda
- ¼ teaspoon baking powder
- 1 teaspoon cinnamon
- ½ cup walnuts, chopped
- ½ cup chocolate chips
- 1½ cups water

Directions:

In a bowl, mix the zucchini with sugar, vanilla, eggs, and applesauce and stir well. In another bowl, mix the flour with salt, cocoa, baking soda, baking powder, cinnamon, chocolate chips, and walnuts and stir. Combine the 2 mixtures, stir, pour into a Bundt pan, place the pan in the steamer basket of the Instant Pot, add the water to the Instant Pot, cover and cook on the Manual setting for 25 minutes. Release the pressure naturally, uncover the Instant Pot, transfer bread to a plate, cut, and serve it.

Nutrition:

- Calories: 217
- Fat: 8
- Fiber: 2
- Carbs: 35
- Sugar: 22
- Protein: 3

Samoa Cheesecake

Preparation time: 15 minutes
Cooking time: 1 hour
Servings: 6

Ingredients:

For the crust:
- 2 tablespoons butter, melted
- ½ cup chocolate graham crackers, crumbled

For the filling:
- ¼ cup heavy cream
- ½ cup sugar
- 12 ounces cream cheese, softened
- 1½ teaspoon vanilla extract
- ¼ cup sour cream
- 1 tablespoon flour

- 1 egg yolk
- 2 eggs
- Vegetable oil cooking spray
- 1 cup water

For the topping:
- 3 tablespoons heavy cream
- 12 caramels
- 1½ cups coconut, sweet and shredded
- ¼ cup semi-sweet chocolate, chopped

Directions:

Grease a springform pan with some cooking spray and set it aside. In a bowl, mix the crackers with the butter, stir, spread in the bottom of the pan, and place in the freezer for 10 minutes. In another bowl, mix the cheese with the sugar, heavy cream, vanilla, flour, sour cream, and eggs and stir well using a mixer. Pour this into the pan on top of crust, cover, with aluminum foil and place in the steamer basket of the Instant Pot. Add 1 cup water to the Instant Pot, cover and cook on the Steam setting for 35 minutes. Release the pressure for 10 minutes, uncover, take the pan, remove aluminum foil, and let the cheesecake cool down in the refrigerator for 4 hours. Spread the coconut on a lined baking sheet, place it in the oven at 300° F, and bake for 20 minutes, stirring often. Put caramels in a heatproof bowl, place in the microwave for 2 minutes, stir every 20 seconds, and mix with toasted coconut. Spread this on the cheesecake and set the dish aside. Put the chocolate in another heatproof bowl, place into the microwave for a few seconds until it melts, and drizzle this over the cheesecake, and serve.

Nutrition:
- Calories: 310
- Fat: 8
- Fiber: 2
- Carbs: 20
- Protein: 10

Pina Colada Pudding

Preparation time: 10 minutes
Cooking time: 5 minutes
Servings: 8

Ingredients:

- 1 tablespoon coconut oil
- Salt
- 1½ cups water
- 1 cup Arborio rice
- 14 ounces canned coconut milk
- 2 eggs
- ½ cup milk
- ½ cup sugar
- ½ teaspoon vanilla extract
- 8 ounces canned pineapple chunks, drained and halved

Directions:

In the Instant Pot, mix the oil, water, rice, and salt, stir, cover and cook on the Manual setting for 3 minutes. Release the pressure for 10 minutes, uncover the Instant Pot, add the sugar and coconut milk and stir well. In a bowl, mix the eggs with milk and vanilla, stir, and pour over rice. Stir, set the Instant Pot on Sauté mode and bring to a boil. Add the pineapple, stir, divide into dessert bowls, and serve.

Nutrition:

- Calories: 113
- Fat: 3.2
- Fiber: 0.2
- Carbs: 15
- Protein: 4.2

Quick Flan

Preparation time: 10 minutes
Cooking time: 15 minutes
Servings: 6

Ingredients:

For the caramel:
- ¼ cup water
- ¾ cup sugar

For the custard:
- 2 egg yolks
- 3 eggs
- 1½ cups water
- Salt
- 2 cups milk
- ⅓ cup sugar
- ½ cup whipping cream
- 2 tablespoons hazelnut syrup
- 1 teaspoon vanilla extract

Directions:

Heat up a pot over medium heat, add ¼ cup water¾ cup sugar, stir, cover, bring to a boil, boil for 2 minutes, uncover, and boil for a few minutes. Pour this into custard cups and coat evenly their bottoms. In a bowl, mix the eggs with the yolks, a pinch of salt ⅓ cup sugar, and stir using your mixer. Put the milk in a pan and heat up over medium heat. Add this to the egg mixture and stir well. Add the hazelnut syrup, vanilla, and cream, stir, and strain the mixture. Pour this into custard cups, place them in the steamer basket of the Instant Pot, add the remaining water to the Instant Pot, cover and cook on the Steam setting for 6 minutes. Release the pressure, uncover the Instant Pot, remove the custard cups and set aside to cool. Keep in the refrigerator for 4 hours before you serve them.

Nutrition:

- Calories: 145
- Fat: 4
- Fiber: 0
- Carbs: 23
- Sugar: 20
- Protein: 4.5

Chocolate Pudding

Preparation time: 10 minutes
Cooking time: 20 minutes
Servings: 4

Ingredients:
- 6 ounces bittersweet chocolate, chopped
- ½ cup milk
- 1½ cups heavy cream
- 5 egg yolks
- ⅓ cup brown sugar
- 2 teaspoons vanilla extract
- 1½ cups water
- ¼ teaspoon cardamom
- Salt
- Crème fraîche, for serving
- Chocolate shavings, for serving

Directions:
Put the cream and milk in a pot, bring to a simmer over medium heat, take off the heat, add the chocolate and whisk well. In a bowl, mix the egg yolks with the vanilla, sugar, cardamom, and a pinch of salt, stir, strain, and mix with chocolate mixture. Pour this into a soufflé dish, cover with aluminum foil, place in the steamer basket of the Instant Pot, add water to the Instant Pot, cover, cook on Manual for 18 minutes, release the pressure naturally. Take the pudding out of the Instant Pot, set aside to cool down and keep it in the refrigerator for 3 hours before serving with crème fraîche and chocolate shavings on top.

Nutrition:
- Calories: 200
- Fat: 3
- Fiber: 1
- Carbs: 20
- Protein: 14

Sticky Pudding

Preparation time: 15 minutes
Cooking time: 20 minutes
Servings: 8
Ingredients:
- 2 cups water
- 1¼ cups dates, chopped
- ¼ cup blackstrap molasses
- ¾ cup hot water
- 1 teaspoon baking powder
- 1¼ cups white flour
- Salt
- ¾ cup brown sugar
- ⅓ cup butter, softened
- 1 teaspoon vanilla extract
- 1 egg

For the caramel sauce:
- ⅓ cup whipping cream
- ⅔ cup brown sugar
- ¼ cup butter
- 1 teaspoon vanilla extract

Directions:
In a bowl, mix the dates with the hot water and molasses, stir and set the dish aside. In another bowl, mix the baking powder with the flour and salt. In a third bowl, mix the sugar with the butter, egg, and 1 teaspoon vanilla extract and stir using a hand mixer. Add the flour and dates mixtures to this bowl and stir well. Divide this mixture into 8 ramekins that greased with some butter, cover, with aluminum foil, place them in the steamer basket of the Instant Pot. Add 2 cups water to the Instant Pot, cover, and cook on Manual for 20 minutes. Heat up a pan with the butter for the caramel sauce over medium high heat. Add the cream, vanilla extract, and brown sugar, stir, and bring to a boil. Reduce the temperature to medium-low and simmer for 5 minutes, stirring often. Release the pressure from the Instant Pot, uncover it, take the ramekins out, remove the foil, drizzle sauce over pudding, and serve them warm.

Nutrition:
- Calories: 260
- Fat: 14
- Fiber: 1
- Carbs: 33
- Protein: 2
- Sugar: 21

Rhubarb Compote

Preparation time: 10 minutes
Cooking time: 30 minutes
Servings: 8

Ingredients:

- ⅓ cup water
- 2 pounds rhubarb, chopped
- 3 tablespoon honey
- Fresh mint, torn
- 1 pound strawberries, chopped

Directions:

Put the rhubarb and water into the Instant Pot, cover, cook on the Manual setting for 10 minutes, release the pressure and uncover the Instant Pot. Add the strawberries and honey, stir, set the Instant Pot on Manual mode and cook the compote for 20 minutes. Add the mint, stir, divide into bowls, and serve.

Nutrition:

- Calories: 71
- Fat: 0.1
- Fiber: 1
- Carbs: 18
- Protein: 0.5
- Sugar: 16

Simple Chocolate Cake

Preparation time: 10 minutes
Cooking time: 40 minutes
Servings: 6

Ingredients:

- ¾ cup cocoa powder
- ¾ cup white flour
- ½ cup butter
- 1 cup water
- 1½ cups white sugar
- ½ teaspoon baking powder
- 3 eggs, whites and yolks separated
- 1 teaspoon vanilla extract

Directions:

In a bowl, beat the egg whites with a mixer until soft peaks form. In another bowl, beat the egg yolks until foamy. In a third bowl, mix the flour with the baking powder, sugar, and cocoa powder. Add the egg white, the egg yolks, and vanilla extract and combine gently. Grease a springform pan with butter, line with parchment paper, pour the cake batter, arrange the pan in the steamer basket of the Instant Pot, add 1 cup water to the Instant Pot, cover and cook on Manual mode for 40 minutes. Release the pressure, uncover the Instant Pot, take the pan out, let cake to cool, transfer to a platter, cut, and serve.

Nutrition:

- Calories: 379
- Fat: 5
- Fiber: 2
- Carbs: 53
- Protein: 5

Simple Carrot Pudding

Preparation time: 10 minutes
Cooking time: 1 hour
Servings: 8

Ingredients:
- 1½ cups water
- Vegetable oil cooking spray
- ½ cup brown sugar
- 2 eggs
- ¼ cup molasses
- ½ cup flour
- ½ teaspoon allspice
- ½ teaspoon ground cinnamon
- Salt
- Nutmeg
- ½ teaspoon baking soda
- ⅔ cup shortening, frozen, grated
- ½ cup pecans, chopped
- ½ cup carrots, peeled and grated
- ½ cup raisins
- 1 cup bread crumbs

For the sauce:
- 4 tablespoons butter
- ½ cup brown sugar
- ¼ cup heavy cream
- 2 tablespoons rum
- ¼ teaspoon ground cinnamon

Directions:
In a bowl, mix the molasses with eggs½ cup sugar and stir. Add the flour, shortening, carrots, nuts, raisins, bread crumbs, salt, ½ teaspoon cinnamon, allspice, nutmeg, and baking soda and stir everything. Pour this into a Bundt pan that you've greased with some cooking spray, cover with aluminum foil, place in the steamer basket of the Instant Pot, add the water to the Instant Pot, cover and cook on the Manual setting for 1 hour. Release the pressure, uncover the Instant Pot, take the pudding out and set it aside to cool down. Heat up a pan with the butter for the sauce over medium heat. Add ½ cup brown sugar, stir, and cook for 2 minutes. Add the cream, rum, ½ teaspoon cinnamon, stir, and simmer for 2 minutes. Serve the pudding with the rum sauce.

Nutrition:
- Calories: 316
- Fat: 16
- Fiber: 5
- Carbs: 44
- Protein: 7
- Sugar: 7

Eggnog Cheesecake

Preparation time: 15 minutes
Cooking time: 20 minutes
Servings: 6

Ingredients:

- 2 cups water
- 2 teaspoons butter, melted
- ½ cup ginger cookies, crumbled
- 16 ounces cream cheese, softened
- 2 eggs
- ½ cup sugar
- 1 teaspoon rum
- ½ teaspoon vanilla extract
- ½ teaspoon nutmeg

Directions:

Grease a pan with the butter, add the cookie crumbs, and spread them evenly. In a bowl, beat the cream cheese with a mixer. Add the nutmeg, vanilla, rum, and eggs and stir well. Pour this in the steamer basket of the Instant Pot, add the water to the Instant Pot, cover, and cook on the Manual setting for 15 minutes. Release the pressure, uncover the Instant Pot, take the cheesecake out, set aside to cool down, and keep in the refrigerator for 4 hours before slicing and serving it.

Nutrition:

- Calories: 400
- Fat: 25
- Fiber: 0
- Carbs: 30
- Protein: 6
- Sugar: 19

Poached Figs

Preparation time: 10 minutes
Cooking time: 7 minutes
Servings: 4

Ingredients:

- 1 cup red wine
- 1 pound figs
- ½ cup pine nuts, toasted
- ½ cup sugar

For the yogurt crème:
- 2 pounds plain yogurt

Directions:

Put the yogurt in a strainer, press well, transfer to a container, and keep in the refrigerator overnight. Put the wine into the Instant Pot, place the figs in the steamer basket, cover, and cook on Steam mode for 4 minutes. Release the pressure, uncover the Instant Pot, take the figs out, and arrange them on plates. Set the Instant Pot on Manual mode, add the sugar and stir. Cook until sugar melts and then drizzle this sauce over the figs. Add the yogurt mixture on top or the side, and serve.

Nutrition:

- Calories: 100
- Fat: 0
- Fiber: 1
- Carbs: 13
- Sugar: 0.6
- Protein: 0

Lemon Crème Pots

Preparation time: 30 minutes
Cooking time: 5 minutes
Servings: 4

Ingredients:

- 1 cup whole milk
- Zest from 1 lemon
- 6 egg yolks
- 1 cup fresh cream
- 1 cup water
- ⅔ cup sugar
- Blackberry syrup, for serving
- ½ cup fresh blackberries

Directions:

Heat up a pan over medium heat, add the milk, lemon zest, and cream, stir, bring to a boil, take off heat and set aside for 30 minutes. In a bowl, mix the egg yolks with the sugar and cold cream mixture and stir well. Pour this into ramekins, cover them with aluminum foil, place them in the steamer basket of the Instant Pot, add the water to the Instant Pot, cover, and cook on the Manual setting for 5 minutes. Release the pressure for 10 minutes, uncover the Instant Pot, take the ramekins out, let them cool down, and serve with blackberries and blackberry syrup on top.

Nutrition:

- Calories: 145
- Fat: 4
- Fiber: 3
- Carbs: 10
- Protein: 1

Super Sweet Carrots

Preparation time: 10 minutes
Cooking time: 16 minutes
Servings: 4

Ingredients:

- 1 tablespoon brown sugar
- 2 cups baby carrots
- Salt
- ½ cup water
- ½ tablespoon butter

Directions:

Set the Instant Pot on Sauté mode, add the butter and melt it. Add the sugar, water, and salt, stir, and cook for 1 minute. Add the carrots, toss to coat, cover the Instant Pot, and cook on the Manual setting for 15 minutes. Release the pressure, uncover the Instant Pot, transfer the carrots to plates, and serve.

Nutrition:

- Calories: 80
- Fat: 1
- Fiber: 1
- Carbs: 3
- Protein: 4

Pineapple and Ginger Risotto Dessert

Preparation time: 10 minutes
Cooking time: 12 minutes
Servings: 4

Ingredients:

- ¼ cup candied ginger, chopped
- 20 ounces canned pineapple chunks
- ½ cup coconut , shredded
- 1¾ cups Arborio rice
- 4 cups milk

Directions:

In the Instant Pot, mix the milk with the rice, coconut, pineapple, and ginger, stir, cover the Instant Pot, and cook on the Rice setting for 12 minutes. Release the pressure naturally, uncover the Instant Pot, and serve.

Nutrition:

- Calories: 100
- Fat: 2
- Fiber: 3
- Carbs: 3
- Protein: 2

Corn Pudding

Preparation time: 10 minutes
Cooking time: 30 minutes
Servings: 4

Ingredients:

- 11 ounces canned creamed corn
- 2 cups water
- 2 cups milk
- 3 tablespoons sugar
- 2 eggs, whisked
- 2 tablespoons flour
- Salt
- 1 tablespoon butter
- Vegetable oil cooking spray

Directions:

Put the water into the Instant Pot, set on Manual mode, and bring to a boil. In a bowl, mix the corn with the eggs, milk, butter, flour, sugar, and a pinch of salt and stir well. Grease a baking dish with some cooking spray, pour the corn mixture into the pan, cover with aluminum foil and arrange in the steamer basket of the Instant Pot. Cover and cook on the Steam mode for 20 minutes. Release the pressure, uncover the Instant Pot, take the pudding out, set it aside to cool down, and serve.

Nutrition:

- Calories: 200
- Fat: 5
- Fiber: 2
- Carbs: 12
- Protein: 9

Conclusion

We know you want to become a master chef in the kitchen. We know you want to impress your guests, friends, and loved ones with your cooking skills. With the Instant Pot and this recipe book, now you can. This magnificent cookbook provides you the tools you may have seeking for so long. You now know how to make the best dishes in the world in the easiest way possible: using an Instant Pot.

If you don't have such a wonderful machine yet, it's time to go and purchase one. Then, get your hands on this recipe book and start making some of the tastiest, unique, rich, and flavorful dishes ever.

You are sure to get admiring looks from now on when you bring your dishes to the table. Everyone will adore your food. Your success in the kitchen is guaranteed with just two simple tools: this great cookbook and an Instant Pot.

Have fun!

Recipe Index

A

Ancho Chili Sauce, 236
Apple Bread, 261
Apple Cider Pork, 113
Apple Crisp, 262
Applesauce, 235
Apricot Sauce, 248
Artichoke Hearts, 155
Artichoke Soup, 189
Artichokes, 62
Artichokes and Spinach Dip, 156
Artichokes with Lemon Sauce, 155
Asian Short Ribs, 120
Asparagus and Shrimp, 157

B

Babaganoush, 172
Baked Apples, 263
Baked Beans, 226
Banana Bread, 261
Barbecue Sauce, 237
Barbecue Tofu, 42
Barley and Mushroom Risotto, 207
Barley Salad, 208
Barley with Vegetables, 207
Beef and Barley Soup, 198
Beef and Broccoli, 104
Beef and Cabbage, 105
Beef and Pasta Casserole, 103
Beef and Rice Soup, 183
Beef and Root Vegetables Stew, 205
Beef and Vegetables, 101
Beef Bourguignon, 98
Beef Chili, 100
Beef Curry, 99
Beef Meatloaf, 127
Beef Pot Roast, 101
Beef Stew, 198
Beef Stroganoff, 99
Beet and Orange Salad, 159
Beet and Tomato Salad, 159
Beet Salad, 158
Beet Soup, 190
Beets and Garlic, 65
Beets with Blue Cheese, 158
Berry Compote, 275
Berry Jam, 272
Black Beans, 55
Black Beans, 224
Black Beans and Chorizo, 223
Black Beans in Sauce, 224
Blackberry Jam, 35
Black-eyed Pea Curry, 229

Braised Duck and Potatoes, 74
Braised Endive, 169
Braised Fennel, 173
Braised Kale, 174
Braised Pork, 116
Braised Quail, 80
Braised Squid, 154
Braised Turkey Wings, 80
Bread Pudding, 268
Bread Sauce, 246
Breakfast Banana Cake, 20
Breakfast Bread Pudding, 29
Breakfast Burritos, 32
Breakfast Chia Pudding, 31
Breakfast Cobbler, 21
Breakfast Hash, 31
Breakfast Jam, 34
Breakfast Millet Pilaf, 30
Breakfast Potatoes, 40
Breakfast Pudding, 30
Breakfast Quiche, 25
Breakfast Quinoa Salad, 28
Breakfast Rice Bowl, 27
Breakfast Risotto, 26
Breakfast Salad, 40
Breakfast Sandwiches, 33
Breakfast Sausages and Peppers, 33
Breakfast Tacos, 34
Broccoli and Bacon Soup, 196
Broccoli and Garlic, 161
Broccoli Sauce, 250
Brownie Cake, 266
Brussels Sprouts and Bacon, 162
Brussels Sprouts and Potatoes, 163
Brussels Sprouts with Parmesan Cheese, 162
Brussels Sprouts with Pomegranate, 161
Buckwheat Porridge, 211
Buffalo Chicken, 87
Bulgur Pilaf, 210
Bulgur Salad, 210
Butter Beans with Bacon, 231
Butternut and Apple Mash, 59
Butternut Squash Soup, 181

C

Cabbage and Sausages, 164
Cabbage Soup, 188
Cabbage Stew, 202
Cabbage with Bacon, 164
Cacciatore Chicken, 70
Calamari and Tomatoes, 64
Candied Lemon Peel, 263
Carrot Oatmeal, 25

Carrot Sauce, 250
Carrot Soup, 187
Carrots with Molasses, 166
Cauliflower and Barley Risotto, 49
Cauliflower Mash, 57
Cauliflower Sauce, 240
Cauliflower Soup, 192
Cauliflower with Pasta, 167
Cauliflower, Broccoli, and Citrus, 64
Celery Soup, 191
Cheese Sauce, 239
Cheesy Grits, 36
Cheesy Tuna, 137
Cherry Farro, 47
Cherry Sauce, 251
Chestnut Sauce, 257
Chestnut Soup, 191
Chicken and Broccoli, 96
Chicken and Cabbage, 97
Chicken and Chickpea Masala, 90
Chicken and Dumplings, 91
Chicken and Lentils, 88
Chicken and Noodles, 92
Chicken and Pomegranate, 93
Chicken and Potatoes, 69
Chicken and Rice, 78
Chicken and Shrimp, 94
Chicken and Wild Rice Soup, 184
Chicken Chili Soup, 195
Chicken Curry, 85
Chicken Curry with Eggplant and Squash, 89
Chicken Delight, 82
Chicken Enchilada Soup, 197
Chicken Gumbo, 83
Chicken in Tomatillo Sauce, 73
Chicken Liver Spread, 37
Chicken Meatball Soup, 194
Chicken Noodle Soup, 183
Chicken Romano, 72
Chicken Sandwiches, 69
Chicken Soup, 180
Chicken Stew, 199
Chicken with Corn, 97
Chicken with Duck Sauce, 91
Chickpeas and Dumplings, 219
Chickpeas and Garlic, 220
Chickpeas and Pesto, 220
Chickpeas Curry, 219
Chickpeas Spread, 37
Chili Con Carne, 100
Chili Jam, 246
Chili Lime Black Beans, 225
Chinese Barbecue Pork, 116
Chocolate Cheesecake, 260

Chocolate Fondue, 264
Chocolate Lava Cake, 262
Chocolate Pudding, 281
Chorizo, Chicken, and Kale Soup, 196
Cilantro Sauce, 256
Cinnamon Steel-cut Oats, 20
Cioppino, 141
Clams and Chorizo, 142
Classic Collard Greens, 168
Clementine Sauce, 245
Coca-Cola Chicken, 84
Cod and Peas, 131
Collard Greens and Bacon, 167
Colombian Chicken, 88
Coq au Vin, 85
Corn Pudding, 286
Corn Sauce, 258
Corn Soup, 180
Corned Beef, 98
Country-style Ribs, 118
Couscous with Chicken and Vegetables, 211
Cracked Wheat and Vegetables, 209
Cracked Wheat Surprise, 209
Cranberry Bean Chili, 216
Cranberry Beans and Pasta, 215
Cranberry Beans Mixture, 215
Cranberry Sauce, 235
Cream of Asparagus, 189
Cream of Broccoli, 190
Creamy Chicken, 87
Creamy Fish Stew, 135
Creamy Millet, 213
Creamy Pork Chops, 114
Creamy Tomato Soup, 184
Creamy White Beans, 227
Crème Brûlée, 268
Crispy Chicken, 79
Crispy Potatoes, 177
Crispy Salmon Fillet, 132

D
Date Sauce, 251
Delicious Pear Oatmeal, 19
Drunken Lamb Stew, 204
Drunken Peas, 62
Duck and Vegetables, 74
Duck Chili, 84
Dulce De Leche, 267

E
Easy Refried Beans, 54
Egg Muffins, 26
Eggnog Cheesecake, 284
Eggplant, 63
Eggplant Marinara, 171
Eggplant Ratatouille, 171

Eggplant Sauce, 249
Eggplant Surprise, 172
Elderberry Sauce, 252
Endive Risotto, 170
Endive Soup, 197
Endive with Ham, 169

F

Fast Bean Stew, 200
Fava Bean Dip, 229
Fava Bean Puree, 230
Fava Bean Sauté, 65
Fennel Risotto, 173
Fennel Sauce, 252
Fennel Soup, 192
Filipino Chicken, 73
Fish and Shrimp, 149
Fish Curry, 130
Fish Pudding, 136
Flavored Mashed Sweet Potatoes, 46
French Fries, 53
Fruit Cobbler, 277
Full Mudammas, 230

G

Garlic and Parmesan Asparagus, 61
Garlicky Potatoes, 49
German Stew, 205
Glazed Carrots, 59
Goat and Potatoes, 113
Goat with Roasted Tomatoes, 112
Goose with Chili Sauce, 94
Goose with Cream, 93
Grape Sauce, 247
Gravy, 237
Greek Octopus, 152
Green Beans, 66
Green Beans and Mushrooms, 53
Green Tomato Sauce, 243
Guava Sauce, 253

H

Ham and White Bean Soup, 187
Harvest Vegetables, 63
Herbed Polenta, 48
Holiday Pudding, 264
Honey Barbecue Chicken Wings, 71
Hot Sauce, 241

I

Indian Butter Chicken, 95
Indian Lentils, 218
Indian-style Mung Beans, 228
Israeli Couscous, 67
Israeli Couscous, 212
Italian Chicken, 86
Italian Lentils, 217

Italian Sausage Stew, 206

J

Jambalaya, 136

K

Kale and Bacon, 175
Kale with Garlic and Lemon, 174
Kalua Pork, 125
Key Lime Pie, 275
Kidney Bean Curry, 222
Kidney Beans and Ham, 223
Kidney Beans Étouffée, 221
King Crab Legs, 143
Korean Beef, 103

L

Lamb and Barley Dish, 110
Lamb and White Beans, 111
Lamb Chops, 108
Lamb Curry, 107
Lamb Ragout, 110
Lamb Ribs, 106
Lamb Shanks, 105
Lamb Stew, 204
Leek Sauce, 255
Lemon Crème Pots, 285
Lemon Marmalade, 35
Lemon Marmalade, 271
Lemon Parmesan and Peas Risotto, 50
Lemongrass Chicken, 68
Lemony Broccoli, 60
Lentil Soup, 188
Lentil Tacos, 216
Lentils and Tomato Sauce, 217
Lentils Salad, 218

M

Mackerel with Lemon, 139
Mango Sauce, 240
Maple-glazed Carrots, 166
Marinara Sauce, 234
Marrow Beans with Lemon, 225
Mashed Squash, 52
Mashed Turnips, 58
Meatball Delight, 128
Meatballs and Tomato Sauce, 128
Meatloaf, 127
Mediterranean Fish, 130
Mediterranean Lamb, 106
Melon Sauce, 254
Mexican Cranberry Beans, 214
Mexican Rice, 48
Mexican-style Lamb, 111
Millet Pudding, 29
Millet with Vegetables, 212
Minestrone Soup, 185

Miso Mackerel, 138
Moroccan Chicken, 70
Moroccan Lamb, 109
Mung Beans, 227
Mushroom and Beef Stew, 203
Mushroom Oatmeal, 19
Mushroom Pate, 38
Mushroom Risotto, 45
Mushroom Sauce, 239
Mussels and Spicy Sauce, 140
Mussels with Sausage, 141
Mustard Sauce, 249

N

Navy Beans and Cabbage, 228

O

Oats and Vegetables, 213
Octopus and Potatoes, 150
Octopus Stew, 152
Okra and Corn, 176
Okra Pilaf, 175
Okra Stew, 206
Onion Sauce, 244
Orange and Ginger Sauce, 236
Orange Marmalade, 272
Orange Sauce, 245
Oxtail Stew, 203

P

Parmesan Clams, 142
Parsley Sauce, 256
Parsnips and Onions, 57
Party Chicken Wings, 81
Pea and Pineapple Curry, 233
Peach and Whiskey Sauce, 255
Peach Compote, 276
Peach Jam, 274
Peach Sauce, 254
Pear Jam, 273
Pear Sauce, 253
Pears with Wine Sauce, 267
Pecan Sweet Potatoes, 39
Pina Colada Pudding, 280
Pineapple and Cauliflower Rice, 55
Pineapple and Ginger Risotto Dessert, 286
Pineapple Sauce, 244
Pink Rice, 44
Plum Sauce, 243
Poached Eggs, 23
Poached Fennel, 61
Poached Figs, 284
Poached Salmon, 131
Pomegranate Porridge, 21
Pomegranate Sauce, 248
Pork Carnitas, 121

Pork Chops and Brown Rice, 117
Pork Chops and Onion, 114
Pork Chops and Smashed Potatoes, 117
Pork Roast with Fennel, 115
Pork Sausages and Mashed Potatoes, 126
Pork Stew, 199
Pork Tamales, 123
Pork Tostadas, 124
Pork with Hominy, 125
Pork with Orange and Honey, 122
Potato and Cheese Soup, 182
Potato Casserole, 52
Potato Hash, 32
Potatoes and Tofu Breakfast, 42
Potatoes Au Gratin, 51
Pulled Pork, 115
Pumpkin Butter, 39
Pumpkin Chocolate Cake, 259
Pumpkin Oats Granola, 22
Pumpkin Pie, 265
Pumpkin Rice Pudding, 270
Pumpkin Risotto, 45

Q

Quick Flan, 280
Quince Sauce, 257
Quinoa and Vegetables, 214
Quinoa Pilaf, 43
Quinoa with Almonds, 44

R

Raspberry Curd, 274
Red Beans and Rice, 56
Red Cabbage, 67
Rhubarb Compote, 282
Rhubarb Sauce, 258
Ribs and Coleslaw, 119
Rice and Artichokes, 51
Rice Pudding, 269
Ricotta Cake, 270
Ricotta Cheese Spread, 38
Roasted Chicken, 81
Roasted Mackerel, 138
Roasted Potatoes, 177
Ruby Pears, 269

S

Salmon and Raspberry Sauce, 135
Salmon and Rice, 132
Salmon and Vegetables, 133
Salmon Burger, 134
Salmon with Tomatoes, 134
Salsa Chicken, 68
Samoa Cheesecake, 279
Sausage and Red Beans, 126
Sautéed Endive, 170

Savory Artichoke Dip, 156
Savory Bok Choy, 66
Savory Collard Greens, 168
Savory Stuffing, 56
Savoy Cabbage and Cream, 163
Scotch Eggs, 23
Seafood Gumbo, 151
Sesame Chicken, 90
Short Ribs and Beer, 120
Shrimp and Dill Sauce, 146
Shrimp and Potatoes, 146
Shrimp Boil, 144
Shrimp Creole, 147
Shrimp Curry, 145
Shrimp Paella, 144
Shrimp Scampi, 148
Shrimp Teriyaki, 147
Shrimp with Risotto and Herbs, 149
Simple Carrot Cake, 277
Simple Carrot Pudding, 283
Simple Chicken Salad, 77
Simple Chocolate Cake, 282
Simple Fish Chowder, 200
Simple Spaghetti Sauce, 234
Simple Turkey Stew, 202
Special Eggs Breakfast, 24
Special French Toast, 18
Special Rice Pudding, 27
Spicy Mussels, 140
Spicy Salmon, 133
Spicy Shrimp and Rice, 148
Spicy Shrimp Curry, 145
Spicy Shrimp Delight, 143
Spicy Turnips, 179
Spinach and Goat Cheese Risotto, 50
Spinach Stew, 201
Split Pea and Squash Curry, 232
Split Pea Curry, 231
Split Pea Soup, 182
Squid Masala, 153
Squid Roast, 154
Sriracha Sauce, 247
Steamed Eggs, 24
Steamed Fish, 129
Steamed Leeks, 176
Steamed Mussels, 139
Sticky Pudding, 281
Strawberry Sauce, 241
Stuffed Bell Peppers, 160
Stuffed Chicken Breasts, 77
Stuffed Peaches, 276

Stuffed Squid, 153
Stuffed Tomatoes, 179
Super Sweet Carrots, 285
Sweet and Spicy Cabbage, 165
Sweet and Tangy Chicken, 71
Sweet Brussels Sprouts, 60
Sweet Carrot Puree, 58
Sweet Carrots, 165
Sweet Potato Stew, 201

T
Tapioca Pudding, 265
Tasty Breakfast, 36
Tasty Saffron Risotto, 47
Teriyaki Chicken, 86
Three Bean Medley, 54
Tofu Breakfast, 41
Tofu Scramble, 41
Tomato and Spinach Breakfast, 22
Tomato Chutney, 242
Tomato Jam, 273
Tomato Sauce, 242
Tomato Soup, 186
Tuna and Noodle Casserole, 137
Turkey and Sweet Potato Soup, 193
Turkey Chili, 72
Turkey Meatballs, 75
Turkey Mix and Mashed Potatoes, 76
Turkey-stuffed Bell Peppers, 160
Turnips and Carrots, 178

U
Upside-down Apple Cake, 266

V
Vanilla Steel-cut Oats, 18
Veal with Mushrooms, 102
Vegetable Soup, 195
Vegetables and Rice, 46
Vegetarian Sauce, 238

W
Wheat Berry Salad, 208
White Beans and Shrimp, 226
White Fish with Orange Sauce, 129
Wild Rice and Farro Pilaf, 43
Wrapped Asparagus Spears, 157

Z
Zucchini Nut Bread, 278
Zucchini Pesto, 238
Zucchinis and Tomatoes, 178
Zuppa Toscana, 185

Made in the USA
Lexington, KY
08 December 2017